Corporate Culture

The corporation – an immortal collective bound to act for the common good – was developed in the seventeenth century, but comparatively little attention has been paid to its literary ramifications. This work combines corporate history with literary analysis to demonstrate how corporations, and the literature they engendered, shaped ideas of the public sphere, trust, the morality of trade and exchange, national identity and salvation.

Drawing on a wide range of genres – including corporate publications, letters and minute books; dramatic works; epic poetry and sermons – this study shows how widely corporate rhetoric spread, and how embedded it was in the early modern social imagination.

Liam D. Haydon is a postdoctoral fellow in the Centre for the Political Economies of International Commerce at the University of Kent.

Routledge Studies in Renaissance and Early Modern Worlds of Knowledge
Series Editor: Harald E. Braun

This series explores Renaissance and Early Modern worlds of knowledge (c.1400–c.1700) in Europe, the Americas, Asia and Africa. The volumes published in this series study the individuals, communities and networks involved in making and communicating knowledge during the first age of globalisation. Authors investigate the perceptions, practices and modes of behaviour which shaped Renaissance and Early Modern intellectual endeavours and examine the ways in which they reverberated in the political, cultural, social and economic spheres.

The series is interdisciplinary, comparative and global in its outlook. We welcome submissions from new as well as existing fields of Renaissance Studies, including the history of literature (including neo-Latin, European and non-European languages), science and medicine, religion, architecture, environmental and economic history, the history of the book, art history, intellectual history and the history of music. We are particularly interested in proposals that straddle disciplines and are innovative in terms of approach and methodology.

The series includes monographs, shorter works and edited collections of essays. The Society for Renaissance Studies (www.rensoc.org.uk) provides an expert editorial board, mentoring, extensive editing and support for contributors to the series, ensuring high standards of peer-reviewed scholarship. We welcome proposals from early career researchers as well as more established colleagues.

Political Representation in the Ancien Régime
Edited by Joaquim Albareda and Manuel Herrero Sánchez

Corporate Culture
National and Transnational Corporations in Seventeenth-Century Literature
Liam D. Haydon

For a full list of titles in this series, please visit www.routledge.com

Corporate Culture

National and Transnational Corporations in Seventeenth-Century Literature

Liam D. Haydon

Routledge
Taylor & Francis Group
LONDON AND NEW YORK

First published 2019
by Routledge
2 Park Square, Milton Park, Abingdon, Oxon OX14 4RN

and by Routledge
605 Third Avenue, New York, NY 10017

First issued in paperback 2021

Routledge is an imprint of the Taylor & Francis Group, an informa business

Publisher's Note
The publisher has gone to great lengths to ensure the quality of this reprint but points out that some imperfections in the original copies may be apparent.

British Library Cataloguing-in-Publication Data
A catalogue record for this book is available from the British Library

Library of Congress Cataloging-in-Publication Data
Names: Haydon, Liam D., author.
Title: Corporate culture : national and transnational corporations in seventeenth century literature / by Liam D. Haydon.
Description: 1st Edition. | New York : Routledge, [2018] | Series: Routledge studies in renaissance and early modern worlds of knowledge ; 4 | Includes bibliographical references and index. |
Identifiers: LCCN 2018021263 (print) | LCCN 2018021813 (ebook) | ISBN 9781315531052 () | ISBN 9781138693241
Subjects: LCSH: Corporate culture—History—17th century. | Commerce—Social aspects—History—17th century. | Foreign exchange—History—17th century.
Classification: LCC HD58.7 (ebook) | LCC HD58.7. H4169 2018 (print) | DDC 338.709/032—dc23
LC record available at https://lccn.loc.gov/2018021263

ISBN 13: 978-1-03-209499-1 (pbk)
ISBN 13: 978-1-138-69324-1 (hbk)

Typeset in Sabon
by Apex CoVantage, LLC

For Nichi, who gives both life and sense

Contents

Figure

Acknowledgements

This research was carried out as part of the Leverhulme-funded project 'Global Determinants of the English Constitution', and I gratefully acknowledge their support. Parts of the initial research for the book was done in my fellowship at the Brotherton Library in Leeds, and although this wasn't quite the expected outcome of that grant, it put me on the right path, for which I am thankful.

It has been a pleasure to develop this work as part of a research team, and I owe thanks to the Principal Investigator of my project, Will Pettigrew, as well as fellow travellers Aske Brock, Misha Ewan, Peter Good, Emily Mann, Edmond Smith, Haig Smith, Tristan Stein and David Veevers. Although they were not all present for all of the book, everyone I have worked with has read some of it, and I am enormously grateful for their time, the thoroughness of their reading and their helpful suggestions. In particular, I'd like to thank Aske and Edmond for their generosity in sharing archival finds; some of those made it in to the book, others did an excellent job of cheering me up during the writing. My colleagues at Kent, in particular my fellow early modernists Amy Blakeway and Stuart Palmer, provided encouragement, plenty of good cheer, and coffee.

This book is not my thesis, but I nonetheless owe thanks to my supervisor, Jerome de Groot, who has continued to support my work, as have, in various and generous ways, Hilary Hinds, Liz Oakley-Brown, Jennifer Richards and Rachel Willie.

Additional thanks are due to Joe Sterrett and Julia Lupton, organisers and hosts of the Trust and Risk workshop at the University of California, Irvine. This was an especially stimulating conference as I finished the book, and I thank the participants for their perceptive questions and their encouraging response; in particular, I'd like to thank Alison Findlay for her support and company in California.

The staff of the British Library, the Brotherton at Leeds, the Goldsmiths archive, Nottinghamshire Record Office, the TNA, the LMA and the Huntington were all enormously helpful in their own ways, whether pointing me to useful material, answering queries or simply making archive visits more pleasurable.

I gave versions (sometimes very early versions) of work in the book at departmental seminars in Birmingham and Bangor, at the British Milton Seminar and at the Northern Renaissance Seminar, and I am thankful for the conversations that emerged from those papers, as well as the support of the RHS in funding my travels. Phil Withington and Tom Leng at Sheffield were particularly helpful in their guidance, and extra thanks are owed to Tom for a reference to the Merchant Adventurers that came very late in the day.

Some of the work in Chapter 1, on early modern pamphlets and Amboyna, shares its underlying data and argument with an article forthcoming in *JEMCS* (Liam D. Haydon and William A. Pettigrew, "Blanching the Corporate Blush: Corporate Language in the Seventeenth Century Public Sphere"), and I am grateful for their permission to reprint.

Finally, my greatest debt is to Nichola Haydon; not only was she a wonderful interlocutor as I developed and honed the project, but also she is the best editor I could hope for and a constant support. Jasper entertained and soothed us in equal measure. And last to Beatrice, who was blissfully unaware of the book that was growing at the same time as she was.

Note on sources

In manuscript transcription I have aimed to retain the spelling and punctuation of sources, while adapting the rest of their conventions for print. Common contractions such as 'ct' for 'court' and 'comp' for 'company' have been silently expanded. Where the contraction is a plural or possessive (such as 'comps' for 'companies/company's') I have selected the appropriate expansion. Likewise, common substitutions such as 'ye' for 'the', 'j' for 'i', 'v' for 'u', as well as the long 's', have been silently made. Where there are marks to indicate double or missing letters, these letters have been inserted and the marks removed. Line breaks from the original are not retained. Names of places, goods and people are not corrected, except to ensure consistency within a source.

Printed material is left as it appeared in print, including modern editions of early modern works.

Dates are given as they appear on the text, with the start of the year silently corrected to 1st January.

Abbreviations

Bible citations are taken from Rev C. I. Scofield, ed. *Holy Bible: Authorized King James Version* (Oxford: Oxford University Press, 1945)
BL British Library, London
Bod Bodleian Library, Oxford
CSPD Calendar of State Papers Domestic
EIC East India Company
FQ Edmund Spenser, *The Faerie Queene*, ed. by A. C. Hamilton, rev. ed. (Longman, 2007)
Huntington Huntington Library, Los Angeles
IOR India Office Records, Asia, Pacific and Africa Collections, British Library, London
OED Oxford English Dictionary
PL John Milton, *Paradise Lost*, ed. by Alastair Fowler (Harlow: Longman, 2007)
PR John Milton, *Paradise Regained* in *The Complete Shorter Poems*, ed. by John Carey, 2nd edn (Longman, 2007)
RAC Royal Africa Company
ROLLCO Records of London's Livery Companies Online
TNA The National Archives, Kew
VOC Dutch East India Company (Vereenigde Oost-Indische Compagnie)

Introduction

We might view the seventeenth century as one of profound economic shock – not just in the technical sense of an interruption in economic growth, although there were plenty of those – but in the broader, almost traumatic sense, of a fundamental change in understanding, or shift in worldview. It was in the seventeenth century that the move from land to trade as the key source of wealth was solidified, and when forms of exchange such as financial instruments or institutional debt were developed and consolidated in the public imagination.

Crucial to this change was the development of organisation and aggregation of capital: the joint-stock corporation. What exactly a corporation, especially the joint-stock corporation, was has animated much recent historical work, and I do not intend here, or in this work generally, to propose a new way of understanding the early modern corporate form; rather, I am interested in its cultural and intellectual importance. I take as a working definition that the corporation was a community, founded and bounded by a charter, which was at least in theory perpetual and indivisible, and which engaged in a certain primary activity (trading, urban, colonial or guild governance, charitable work, construction and so on) and took on a range of secondary activities as they were required and permitted. The international joint stock is an interesting and unusual variety of this form because from its inception it combined the interests of private citizens (capital, stock investment and trade), the 'public' (exploration, material distribution and printing) and the state (territorial governance and diplomatic missions). Consequently, it was innovative about its own form, and in its business and governmental practices, in a way that other domestic corporations were not, so that they "took the lead, and altered the practice of trade," both in the forms of overseas trading, and in the networks of individuals which were created under the framework of the companies.[1]

Generally, early modern corporations had a social purpose, as well as economic or governmental functions, and even the most fiscally oriented corporation took care to present itself in public in terms of common good, not private profit. Trading companies portrayed themselves as guardians of the national interest, both as a mercantilist bulwark against other nations and in the provision of shipping, fortifications and a coherent trading policy:

> In all confused traffique it must necessarily happen, that while every single person pursues his own particular interest, the publique is deserted by all, and consequently must fall to ruine. For which reason, the crown hath erected and established fraternities or companies of merchants.[2]

For this anonymous author, only merchant companies can provide the stability and common purpose to support the trade to Africa to serve the public, rather than simply private, good. Moreover, the company is elided with the older term 'fraternity', usually used in connection with the livery companies, suggesting a social and regulatory element to the Royal African Company's activities as well.

Indeed, it would be difficult to separate economic, social, regulatory and moral concerns in early modern writing, for these concepts (and more) intertwined in ways which they now rarely, if ever, do. There was no concept of an 'economy' or 'political economy' distinct from societal concerns: Questions of good government and proper behaviour animated discussion on a range of issues, including, but hardly limited to, trade and the corporation. Consequently, no separate language of economic thought developed over the seventeenth century; in fact, "innovations in the period's scientific and moral discourse deeply inspired, influenced, and informed political economic thinking."[3]

In the early modern period the corporation functioned in several overlapping spheres of trade, government, religion, law and charity, among others. It had implications for how people understood social action, trust, risk, fairness, the common good and even national identity. Understanding the ways in which the ideas of and about the corporation (while never being entirely fixed or certain) became deeply embedded in public consciousness lets us see the way that corporations were used to solve some of the most pressing questions – of morality, of political economy, of social organisation – in the early modern world. Moreover, the integration of economic, moral and social terminology (and ideology) has continued from the seventeenth century to the present day.

The hybrid nature of the early modern corporate form, and the flexibility in purpose and organisation which it allowed, goes some way to explaining why seventeenth-century thinkers and jurists did not definitively establish the nature of the corporate person. A corporation, however examined, is essentially an elusive form: an abstraction which nonetheless has a direct and measurable effect on the society in which it acts; a state-licensed body which by its very nature functions across multiple territories and jurisdictions; and a community of individuals which purports to act as a singular entity. It is, in short, neither a solely practical thing, nor entirely an ideology, and it is the interaction between those two states of corporate being with which this book is concerned.

This work is therefore interested in the way in which the fictions, metaphors and ideas of the corporation were developed and circulated in early modern England. Such an analysis has much to tell us about how and why concepts like legal personhood, so central to both the past and the present, were developed, but also offers a valuable lens through which to read the society which was generating and deploying these concepts in ways that extended beyond the corporation itself. Just as the concept of fictional personhood had great bearing on state power in the concept of the king's two bodies, corporate ideas on jurisdiction, privacy, social unification and collective benefits reverberated through the political and cultural events of the early modern period.[4] These ideas circulated between literature and the political-economic texts generated by corporations themselves, and this book offers a thematic overview of the broad conceptual areas (the public sphere, nationhood, religion, exchanges) in which corporate ideas and discourse were developed.

Beyond a very few authors specifically marked as 'corporate' – such as Daniel Defoe and Charles Davenant, and economic writers such as Thomas Mun and Gerard Malynes – literary critics have not much engaged with the idea of the corporation.[5] When they have, the tendency has been simply to follow the overlaps between an author and a corporation (Shakespeare's investment in a theatre company, for example[6]). Tracey Hill has detailed the complex interactions among public display, civic governance and the livery companies in London, although her focus is more on the display than the corporation as a form.[7] Yet the past 30 years of early modern criticism has retained a keen interest in political organisation and resistance at a broader level. To do so without including the idea of the corporation is to overlook a fundamental structuring aspect of early modern political thought.

In many ways, all trade in the early modern period was corporate, to one degree or another, and the ideas and discourses generated by and through corporate activities permeated multiple spheres of early modern thought, social organisation and belief. It is for this reason that this book takes the 'corporation', or more precisely the *idea* of the corporation, as its unit of analysis. How did the early moderns use the changing form and functions of the corporation to make sense of the world around them? What could the development of corporate ideas tell them (and us) about conceptions of the society in which they lived and worked? How did they develop corporate ideas and ideals to think about bigger questions, such as the 'public', the 'state' or even the nature of heaven and salvation? The key shift which enabled this thinking was the concept of collectivity. Early modern corporations increasingly drew, partly as a consequence of the joint-stock model, on the idea that they were collective enterprises which served the commonality more than individuals.

The joint stock

The collective nature of a corporation, and the necessity of a 'body corporate' acting on behalf of its members, had already been partly established by livery and urban corporations. These companies, though, were largely regulatory, more concerned with providing a framework within which individuals could work, whether as traders in England or abroad, or for local government (passing laws, electing officials and so forth). Their establishment as a 'body corporate' was a convenience to allow the holding of property, land or titles in perpetuity.

The idea of collaborative or collective activity was the innovation of the joint-stock model. This was a crucial development in early modern economic thinking in England: Investors bought shares in an enterprise or company, and the money spent on those shares provided a capital 'stock' which the company itself would use to fund its activities (sending ships, supporting administration and providing infrastructure, as well as trading on its own account). The profit from those activities would pay a dividend to shareholders, and they might also enjoy other privileges, such as preferential access to company goods or information, as well as the ability to choose the governing body of the company (the Governor and Court of Assistants).[8] The advantage of a joint stock over individual merchants or small partnerships is that it allows longer-term, larger-scale investing, two attributes crucial for early modern long-distance trading. The idea probably arose in medieval Italy, and spread across Europe; in England, both the Merchant Adventurers and Muscovy Companies were established on at least partially joint-stock lines, having shareholders and company assets.[9] The East India Company was initially established as a collective enterprise where shares were bought in each voyage, and then redeemed completely once the ships returned to London. After 1613, this changed to a semi-permanent joint stock, with shares in the company being traded among different investors, and the company itself holding assets over the longer term; this arrangement was formalised in 1657 with the establishment of the permanent joint stock, although in practice the idea of a joint stock had been part of the internal and public understanding of the workings of the EIC long before then.[10]

Through the joint-stock company, in theory, if not always in practice, markets could be created and defended, trade organised for long-term returns (and shares, essentially a prediction of future gain, could be traded too), information gathered and shared more effectively, capital (cash, shares or goods) acquired and deployed with lower transaction costs, and the inefficiencies of the existing marketplace felt by individuals gradually eroded by belonging to a company. Critics of the corporation often argued that, in effect, they had removed these 'inefficiencies' not by superior organisation or information-sharing (as the companies pretended), but by illegally restricting the right to trade. In Chapter 22 of

Leviathan, Hobbes discusses the nature of trading corporations, and the (monopolist) reasons for their establishment:

> In a Bodie Politique, for the well ordering of forraigne Traffique, the most commodious Representative is an Assembly of all the members; that is to say, such a one, as every one that adventureth his mony, may be present at all the Deliberations, and Resolutions of the Body, if they will themselves. For proof whereof, we are to consider the end, for which men that are Merchants, and may buy and sell, export, and import their Merchandise, according to their own discretions, doe neverthelesse bind themselves up in one Corporation. It is true, there be few Merchants, that with the Merchandise they buy at home, can fraight a Ship· to export it; or with that they buy abroad, to bring it home; and have therefore need to joyn together in one Society; where every man may either participate of the gaine; according to the proportion of his adventure; or take his own, and sell what he transports, or imports, at such prices as he thinks fit. But this is no Body Politique, there being no Common Representative to oblige them to any other Law, than that which is common to all other subjects. The End of their Incorporating, is to make their gaine the greater; which is done two wayes; by sole buying, and sole selling, both at home, and abroad. So that to grant to a Company of Merchants to be a Corporation, or Body Politique, is to grant them a double Monopoly, whereof one is to be sole buyers; another to be sole sellers.[11]

Hobbes acknowledges that there are reasons for common enterprise – the difficulty of raising capital and the need to share resources such as ships. Crucially, though, he argues that there is no need for this to be a chartered corporation: a single joint stock (to be wound up with dividends in proportion to investment) or a regulated society allowing individual trade would suffice to allow the practice of trade to continue unhindered by geographical or practical difficulties. In fact, he argues that the reason to seek incorporation is to enforce a 'law' on the members of a corporation, in effect allowing the company to profit by price control for both purchase and sale. Hobbes takes the same information and understanding available to proponents of the company (the benefits of aggregation), but deploys it for the opposite rhetorical effect; supporters and opponents of the company spent much of the century engaged in similar rhetorical practices, and by drawing on the same, publicly available information, their printed debates went some way to shaping the incipient public sphere.

In any case, the companies were never as monopolistic as either their charter or their opponents claimed. In practice, they could not shut out either foreign trade or 'interlopers' (private citizens, often in combines, engaging in the 'monopoly' trade), however much they tried. Many companies were open to investment from anyone who could afford a share – and frequently made that point in public, citing the 'widows and orphans' among their shareholders as a great public benefit. Companies also allowed a certain amount of private trade, either in goods that the company "deal not in," or because they suffered it as a necessary evil to ensure the good behaviour of factors and governors once stationed overseas.[12] Indeed, as Emily Erikson has recently argued, the East India Company benefited significantly from "the combination of its hierarchical corporate form and what was often perceived as a challenge to the monopoly privileges of the firm: private trade."[13] Not least, the decentralising impulse of private trade allowances for factors overseas encouraged the construction of personal networks for information-sharing, and better integration into local markets, both of which ultimately benefited the company. Moreover, the trade of the joint stock produced secondary effects within the domestic economy, on both the supply- and demand-side. Not least of these was the development of movable, even ephemeral forms of wealth (luxurious goods such as silks or carpets, and foodstuffs, whether currants from the Mediterranean, tobacco from the Americas or spices from the East Indies). Although many investors had stakes in these businesses as well, they remained outside of the remit of the trading companies which imported the materials, even if they often still came under the remit of livery or urban corporations.

Not all trade was organised on the joint-stock model, and the development of joint-stock companies is not, by itself, sufficient to explain the development of economies in early modern Europe (such a story would have to include changes in modes of production, technological advances and alterations to property rights and obligations, as well as the influence of non-European civilisations, among many others). But corporations, whether joint-stock, regulated, urban or charitable, were nevertheless crucial components not just of economic development but (perhaps even more importantly) in the development of economic ideologies.

Despite the clear overlaps between state and corporate activity, this book does not subscribe to the view that the influence of mercantile corporations on the development of economic policy and ideology was limited to a direct lobbying operation. Rather, it takes the broader view that corporations were involved in creating the public sphere, although this was not as malleable or manipulable as they had hoped (as Chapters 1 and 2 demonstrate), and that as their ideas spread to the public sphere they were themselves transformed by the process. Recent work has shown how such a process worked in natural science and other forms of knowledge, and I wish to extend those findings to the more abstract field of textual culture.[14]

I thus consider the way in which the corporation existed as an idea, a conceptual space onto which could be mapped all kinds of associations, prejudices or political imaginings. The 'corporation' is, after all, an idea, an imaginary person which incorporates a diverse group of people unified by the very fiction of their unification. The second half of the book deals particularly with this question. Chapters 3 and 4 consider the questions of exchange and the way in which the morality of exchange became encoded in literary texts and public discourse. Chapter 5 shows how the idea of the corporation transmuted into questions of good governance in church and state alike. By viewing the corporation in this rather abstract way, we can better understand how it developed in, or more precisely was developed by, the literary and cultural forces at play in early modern England. Understanding the corporation as an idea, or an ideology, thus helps us to see how it engages with the public sphere, print culture, literary productions, religion, or even apparently basic and neutral concepts such as 'exchange', 'value', 'debt' and 'worth'.

The impact of the corporation on the development of the state or state functions (such as the judiciary) was as much second-hand as it was a direct consequence of their involvement in those areas (or in their setting up of parallel state functions). That is not to deny that there were sometimes direct effects, but rather to move our focus away from those specific events or bodies and towards a more generalised history of corporate ideas and functions which played a long-term, cultural-social role in the development of the state and national ideology.[15] In particular, I wish to consider the 'feedback loop' which played out in the early modern public sphere, in which ideas generated within or about the corporation were diffused (either approvingly or as challenges) into literary and discursive productions, and then re-appropriated by the companies or by those writing about them. How, in short, did ideas of corporate-ness enter literature, and how did public writing in turn affect the business, actions and, most importantly, the self-conception of the corporations?

I address this question by considering the role of the corporation in the development of early modern social and political ideologies in Britain. I split this into two separate, but linked, areas of corporate activity. The first is direct activity: sponsored pamphlets, statements of political economy, interventions in crises. The second is indirect activity: ideas either generated or developed by corporations filtering back into cultural and political discourse. A corollary here is the use of corporations, or the imagined ideals of incorporation and the corporation, to allow writers and thinkers to work through alternative models of social organisation. The book thus moves from the corporations themselves, to the effects they had on the public sphere at large, and finally to the way society picked up and used the ideas of the corporation in new and imaginative ways.

This work has as its starting point the deep and fundamental connections between text, political culture and event, and has as a fundamental principle the idea that the prevailing political economy is manifested and challenged in literary culture. By 'culture', I primarily mean literary or print culture, and it is from textual production (whether printed or manuscript) that this work draws most of its evidence – although I would tentatively suggest that many of the processes of representing corporate ideals which I discuss had their parallels in other forms of culture, such as art or music; such developments remain outside the scope of this volume. But I also use the term as something akin to the Foucauldian *episteme*, as a way of ordering and understanding the world; my use of the phrase aims to encapsulate the ideas and ideals which animated a range of social groups: the corporation (as a single body); the merchants, investors and administrators who made up the corporation; and the writers and political thinkers who borrowed, rejected or otherwise engaged with those ideas and ideals.

A key part of this understanding of 'corporate culture' is the recent work of corporate historians, who have presented some of the shapes – state, community, legal fiction, geographers, explorers – into which this protean organisation might contort itself. This work has demonstrated how deeply embedded in, and indeed constructive of, the corporation was of the early modern political economy, and the ways in which its activities undulated out into society as a whole.

That overseas activities had an effect on the early modern political economy, and the writing which engaged with it, is not an especially new observation. Robert Markley has demonstrated the effects of encounters with the East, especially China, arguing that the realisation that Asian powers were in fact significantly more advanced than their European counterparts caused consternation for writers which inflected a whole range of writing.[16] Markley, though, tends to focus on precisely those canonical writers (Milton, Dryden, Swift and Defoe) where a direct link to Asian trade can be made, and does not consider the form of the corporation as such, focusing instead on the practices of the East India Company. More recently, scholars have attempted to expand Markley's insights into other trading spheres or to other corporations. Christina Lee's edited collection builds on Markley's work as it demonstrates the impact of the Iberian nations on European understandings of the East, with particular emphasis on activity which might be described as 'corporate' (missionary or diplomatic engagements), although the idea of corporations is not really addressed.[17]

Similarly, numerous scholars of literary history have noted the overlap between *poesis* and economic writing. Blair Hoxby's study of the 'commercial revolution' on Milton and his contemporaries notes that "new lines of inquiry in one cultural field would be informed by those in others and would, in turn, make themselves felt in contemporary verse and prose."[18] For Hoxby, the languages of trade and poetry are linked in the questions they ask of systems of language, symbolism and abstraction. Mary Poovey makes a similar observation, arguing that economic and 'literary' writing has a special relationship, because "What economic and Literary writing share, both historically and theoretically, is an engagement with the problematic of representation."[19] Poovey is interested in the moment at which representation becomes problematic, because it becomes visible (as in the South Sea Bubble, or the issuing of paper money without gold reserves to back it). Jonathan Gil Harris's study, *Sick Economies*, brilliantly demonstrates the power of one specific type of representation, pathology, which encompassed literary, social and mercantile activity. Gil Harris outlines the interplay between the healthy 'inside' and virulent 'outside' in economic discourse, drama and questions of national identity: "It is in the fertile soil of pathological discourse that the mercantilist drama of national economy first takes root. And conversely, it is in that drama that the language of disease is reformulated and reenergized."[20]

Under the broad banner of the 'New Economic Criticism' scholars have recognised the potency of economic thought in early modern literature – not only as a field of reference, or source of language, but as an integral part of the functioning of literature, and especially, drama. Developing from the ways in which historicist and cultural studies of the 1980s engaged with disciplines outside of literature, this school of thought analyses "the historical and philosophical parallels – usually termed homologies – between economic and linguistic systems."[21] One crucial development of the New Economic Criticism has been an apolitical critical method: "Freed from the dialectics that underpinned previous modes of economic criticism, these works instead seem to assume that the economic was an intrinsic part of early modern life."[22] This is where the present study is most closely aligned to that critical tradition: By eschewing value judgements on the activities of the early modern corporation, and following instead its embeddedness in early modern literature, we can open up a new avenue of investigation for the development of both corporate ideology and literary culture in the seventeenth century.

As well as rich cultural studies, New Economic Criticism has explored the ways in which the material conditions of authorship (patronage, copyright, the market economy in which books exist and circulate) affect the work under production. Much attention has been paid to the twin developments of the novel and 'professionalised' economics (in the disciplinary sense in which we might recognise the term) during the eighteenth and nineteenth centuries; however, the early modern period, where capitalism is developed through venture capital, credit, debt, insurance and consumerism, has also proved to be fertile ground indeed for economically minded investigation.[23]

Douglas Bruster has argued that the New Economic Criticism has generally split into two critical tendencies he describes (while deliberately eschewing a moral judgement) as the 'rash' and the 'reckoned'. The 'reckoned' school focuses on the rational decisions of *homo economicus*, presuming that "people have done what they have done after carefully reckoning the odds (financial or otherwise)" and that the same process of calculation exists in the 'real' and 'literary' economies.[24] Consequently, understanding the price of goods, or inflation, on the early modern economy is crucial to understand the exchanges, ideas of value and the 'economy' presented in literature. Alternatively, the 'rash' school aims at the metaphorical. Although few studies correspond entirely to one or other of these positions, Bruster identifies a disciplinary divide running broadly along this axis, with the theoretical and general against the economic and specific.

It is perhaps too early to talk of a 'corporate turn' in this scholarly tradition, although there have recently been attempts to return to these questions of economy and representation via a corporate lens. John O'Brien's *Literature Incorporated* has as its aim the exploration of points of intersection between literary texts and other kinds of writing – economic, political, polemical, legal – that respond to the emergence of the business corporation in Anglo-American culture; "he tends to see the literary aspects of his text simply as static mirrors of the dynamic corporate world."[25] The texts he selects are those which reveal or deploy the metaphors used in economic writing as if they were 'real' (such as Smith's famous 'invisible hand'), or otherwise exemplify some part of a fairly standard corporate narrative. Locke's *Essay Concerning Human Understanding*, for example, is used as an example of Locke's unconscious 'homology between the economy of *Ideas* and the economy of money," but most of the chapter is spent on the historical background to the text (Locke's corporate activities), with no real consideration of the way in which Locke's literary activities might have influenced his corporate or governmental practices.[26]

Most recently, Henry Turner has argued for a literary reading of corporate-inflected texts through something akin to Erikson's understanding of the corporation as a 'compositional' form, a "network of words, images, and objects of all kinds that put into circulation an *idea* of unity."[27] For Turner, the corporation, as a *persona ficta*, moves between reality and fiction (that is, imagination or the abstraction of an idea); indeed, corporations "are real *because* they are fictional," as they transform ideas of fellowship, commonwealth, nation or belief into reality as an enduring and institutional form.

Turner's excellent work is primarily concerned with political theory, especially the relationship between the corporation and the state (or commonwealth). Turner reads his period (from *Utopia* in 1518 to *Leviathan* in 1651) as one in which there is a gradual shift in the allegiance of the citizenry from local institutions to the nation state, yet, paradoxically, also one in which corporations (in all their associational forms) create a pluralistic environment of political allegiance and understanding. I share Turner's interest in the political possibilities of the associational structures of corporations; his work, however, focuses more on the qualities of the person (real or fictional) that the corporation enables and dissolves. Consequently, his analysis tends to come back to which "assemblages the corporate person conceals and the compositional procedures it employs to create new ones."[28] His excellent and necessary work thus teases out the philosophical problems of corporate-ness as it related to the self or the state. Although I consider the political questions raised by commonality, especially in Chapters 4 and 5, I am more interested in demonstrating the way in which the model of the corporation circulated, and was re-imagined, in literary forms. Like Turner, I suggest that it is by understanding the origins of the corporation, and the variety of its forms – many of which are forgotten, abandoned or normalised now – that we can understand how corporate ideas continue to shape our understanding of society and the economy.

Turner's literary analysis is situated in the context of politics and psychoanalysis, since it centres (particularly for Shakespeare) on the problems of personhood and the tragic dissolution of corporate forms; by contrast, I am interested in the way the corporation was reconstituted, often in surprising and positive ways, by authors such as Denham or Milton, who saw in the corporate form opportunities for a glorious sublimation to the greater good. That is, this monograph attempts to place the 'reckoned' historicised understanding of the discrete institutional structure of the corporation alongside the thematic, ideological and imaginary understandings of the corporation and a corporate society which developed in the seventeenth century. That is, it goes some way to answering Bruster's call for an expansion of "the language and ideas we use to account for this diversity of economic experience."[29] The corporation sits on both the reckoned and the rash axis, and was used in precisely that way by the early modern authors studied here, who were able to mediate imaginatively between the corporation as an economic force, a social organisation, a legal fiction and a political actor.

The embedded nature of the corporate form in the early modern imagination allowed writers to engage with questions of sociability, collectivity and cooperation, even when they did not mention the corporation directly. Imagery and metaphor associated with the corporation or the corporate body was developed throughout the early modern period, most obviously the fictional 'body' itself. Consequently, I argue that to fully understand the interactions between literature and politics in the early modern period we must be more alive to the functions and manifestations of the corporation, and corporate ideology more generally, within the early modern public sphere. This is not to suggest that the ideas discussed here came solely or even directly from the corporation into literature (and/or vice versa). Rather, it is to add nuance to our awareness of the workings of the early modern literary and political economies, and to see in a different light the ways in which texts call attention to the dominant ideologies at the time of their production. Literary scholars ought to be more aware of the ways in which the ideas of the corporation existed within texts, even (or especially) those which do not make an explicit claim to 'corporate-ness'. Conversely, historians of the corporation might benefit from a clearer picture of how the ideas and systems they describe in the corporation circulated among early modern society more generally. This book aims to bring those two disciplinary strands into conversation, and in so doing deepen our understanding of the workings of the early modern world. My work thus integrates the literary tradition of historically oriented textual criticism, which reads the world as a series of connected texts, and a historical praxis which observes the changing and developing nature of institutions as more or less 'real' things. The corporation is the ideal mediator between these two states, since it is both clearly a 'thing', a developing institution, and yet at the same time precisely not, since it is also a legal fiction and ideological construct.

The urban corporation was perhaps the most significant way in which early moderns, especially those outside of London and the ports, encountered corporate activity and governance. As Philip Withington has shown, the number of incorporated towns in England rose from 38 in 1500 to 181 by 1640, reflecting a general population growth and urbanisation, but also a mode of local governance which allowed for commercial development checked by local structures and oversight.[30] Urban corporations were frequently re-incorporated, too, demonstrating the flexibility (for both crown and town) inherent in the chartered corporate form. New charters might reflect growing economic or social importance, codify or ratify local powers and grants or, more frequently, were used as a way of 'purging' opponents of whichever faction had taken control of the corporation. They could even serve as a reward, as in the case of Newark during the Civil Wars, which was promised a new charter by Charles I:

> And for that corporation itself which did so early and hath so constantly given such eminent testimony of their affection and loyalty to us [. . .] you shall let our mayor, aldermen and inhabitants of that our good town know that we will give them some such signal of our extraordinary acceptance and value of their duty as may be an evidence to the whole kingdom, thereof, in the mean time, we would have them send us a copy of their charter that we may upon viewing thereof make such additions of grace, favour and advantage to them as may be most convenient for them, and in the preamble of the same leave a monument to posterity of their faithful and loyal demeanor.[31]

Newark's existing charter had been granted only as recently as 1626, and so there was little 'convenient' for them to have added; in any case, Charles was hardly in a position to make significant additional grants. Consequently, it took until 1677 for a new charter to be issued, which confirmed Newark's existing rights and conferred on them the status of a Parliamentary borough (one of the last boroughs to be created in this way). Nonetheless, the incident is suggestive of the relationship between the crown and the corporation: the pattern of good actions being rewarded with expanded rights and privileges (or, more frequently, the converse wherein the desire for new privileges prompted behaviour favourable to the crown) was a familiar one during the seventeenth century.

Alongside the growth in urban corporations was a boom in trading and exploration companies: Commercial missions to Russia (Muscovy Company, 1553), the Levant and Eastern Mediterranean (Turkey Company, 1581; Venice Company, 1583; Levant Company, 1591), East Indies (East India Company [EIC], 1600) and North America (Virginia Company, 1606) all had as their rationale the discovery of new sea routes and trades, with the ultimate goal of boosting the English economy by entering into markets outside of the traditional bases of the Merchant Adventurers in the Low Countries. In actual fact, many of these markets were predominantly import and re-export markets, especially in Asia, where European and American bullion was required, instead of broadcloth; the prosperity these companies brought was in re-export markets, as well as strengthening domestic consumption, not an expansion in the wool trade.

However, the growing need to export gold and silver created problems of economic theory which the companies had to address. Critics of the new trades argued that exporting bullion weakened the English economy; simultaneously, the sharp growth in customs revenue and fear of 'losing' the new trades to other European rivals (especially the Dutch) helps to explain their staunch defenders, and reveals something of the zero-sum way in which international trade was generally imagined. With these guiding impulses, economic thought at the turn of the century is still largely classed as 'mercantilist', despite the fact that term barely sums up the range of positions taken regarding the import and export of bullion, international competition and warfare, and the opening of new trades.[32] Corporations, or their paid writers, responded to these charges partly on their own terms ('proving' they brought in more wealth than they exported'), but also by stressing other kinds of wealth creation such as productivity or navigational advances.

Classic studies of the trading corporations tend to see them as more or less monolithic entities – taking particular political positions, pursuing specific commercial and colonial ambitions – which the fiction of the 'body corporate' encourages. K.N. Chaudhuri, despite noting that the East India Company of the 1620s and '30s was dominated by a "difference in attitude and interest of its two principal groups of investors," nonetheless tends to view this as an internal conflict which emerged from time to time and was then resolved without disrupting the process of formulating a single, 'corporate', policy, especially in regard to its possessions in Asia.[33] Robert Brenner's study of early modern corporate commerce, despite its focus on mercantile networks, nonetheless took for granted that the corporation ought to be considered as an institution, with fixed ideas and motives, personnel and possessions. This is clearest in his political analysis of corporate engagement in the Civil Wars, which he draws as a divide between "the merchant elite derived to a large degree from the Levant-East India trades" who supported the King, and the 'new merchants' who were trading to the Americas outside of the framework of companies and supported Parliament.[34]

Later historians of the corporation emphasised instead the diffuse nature of its organisation and business practice, especially those which operated overseas. Emily Erikson's work marked a shift in thinking about the corporation, turning away from institutional practices and instead conceiving of the corporation as a carapace or framework in which individuals could operate. Nuala Zahediah, while focusing largely on free trade in the Atlantic world, has nonetheless shown how corporate activities encouraged "interested parties to vie for control of the institutions which could be used to manage economic activity, secure access to the most profitable opportunities and reduce risk."[35] Such institutions, as well as major regulatory and trading bodies, also include small trading combines, which were found all over the globe during the seventeenth century, both in- and outside of corporations. Consequently, the idea of a centralised corporation had to fall by the wayside in favour of a flexible and often rapidly changing network of competing interests held together under the auspices of a centralised body of directors.

For this reason, understanding the corporation through networks and network analysis is a growing trend in the studies of international corporations in particular. Julia Adams has shown the ways in which the links between "a merchant capitalist class, an estatist state, and the elite patriarchal families" were crucial components of the "spectacular ascent" of the Dutch state and VOC during the seventeenth century.[36] Other studies have shown the ways in which individuals or privileged groups interacted around the globe.[37] The family is an important part of such studies, and continues to be an important unit of analysis in the case of the East India Company. For example, Margot Finn's work on the intersections between company, state and family in British India, demonstrates the way in which "kin-based financial mechanisms [. . .] underpinned British and European economic and political expansion on the subcontinent."[38] Linked to these works are attempts to consider the networks of companies as a whole, rather than through particular groups, and in particular the relationships between companies as defined by those who participated in multiple companies, as merchants, shareholders or directors ('assistants' to the Governor).[39] Thinking about the corporation in this way helps us understand the form of a corporation as an accretion of competing/complementary interests, not the single voice of a *societas* as found in its classical definition.

Questions over the precise form and nature of the corporation are as old as the corporation itself, and were generated by those engaged in establishing corporations, or taking part in their activities, as well as, perhaps more frequently, those who opposed the corporation. Was the corporation open and inclusive, or a monopolistic enterprise? Was it a useful mode of local governance, or a dangerous interloper in the business of state? Could it speak or act as a single person, or was it dominated by one or few individuals? Such disputes often ended in the courts, especially as reactions to what was seen as corporate overreach, and so it is that core definitions of the corporate form have tended to be established by jurists such as Coke, Blackstone and Maitland.[40]

These ontological questions have been revisited as part of what might be termed the 'corporate turn' in constitutional history (and/or a constitutional turn in corporate historiography). Historians have increasingly discussed corporations not just as economic or social entities, but as constitutional actors in their own rights, embedded in a system of government which is not a monolithic nation state but rather overlapping networks of power and sovereignty, some of which were embodied in corporations of various forms. The early modern system in England, then, is best understood as something akin to the Weberian idea of patrimonialism; the delegation of power and privilege from the crown to its dependent factions and citizens created a political economy which was mutually constitutive, where the King and the urban corporation "needed the other because each was made of the other."[41] This was, as Halliday demonstrates, not without its fault lines and tensions, but it was also a productive and surprisingly stable relationship.

In particular, the advent of the large, multinational trading corporations in the late sixteenth and early seventeenth centuries marked a shift in the constitutional activities of the corporation: No longer linked to a specific place, group of citizens or single legal framework, corporations began to take on a number of administrative and governmental forms which sat within and echoed the incipient nation state. The corporations "achieved these feats with the aid of often contentious constitutional privileges provided by the English state at a time when the English constitution was the subject of intense and sometimes violent disagreement."[42] As with so much of their activity during the century, corporations did not go unopposed. Thomas Hobbes famously listed among the things which weaken the commonwealth "the great number of Corporations; which are as it were many lesser Common-wealths in the bowels of a greater, like wormes in the entrayles of a naturall man."[43] He was not alone in this (now much quoted) critique; Thomas Johnson, a merchant and strident critic of the companies, argued that corporate oath-taking revealed the powers of corporations as small power bases within the state:

> What high, illegall and transcendent power they assume to themselves to make Statutes, which is *proper and peculiar only to*

> *Parliaments:* Moreover, they stile themselves a Commonwealth, in so much that though they cannot be termed *Regnum in Regno*, they may be well termed *Dominium in Dominio*.[44]

Although this attack was aimed at the Merchant Adventurers – perhaps a strange target, considering how much their power and influence waned over the seventeenth century, although they did continue to insist on patrimony or service as part of the requirement for membership – it covered the activities of a range of trading companies. For both Johnson and Hobbes, the slippage between corporation and commonwealth is significant: "If the corporation is but a lesser commonwealth, then the commonwealth must be but a greater corporation."[45] For both writers, the devolution or duplication of governmental functions by corporations challenges the unity of the state, and suggests the ways in which corporations, however they might be legally formed, tend to accrete powers and status to themselves by aping constitutional functions. As Vicky Hsueh has shown, the legal and constitutional framework of both the state or of chartered enterprises was relatively unstable, tending to exist not as a single grant or document but rather an "accretion of legal and political instruments" which allowed both corporations and the state to "cobble together constitutions out of the available resources."[46] Hobbes and Johnson alike fear this accretion, which might ultimately form associations – either entirely new, or significantly altered from their first conception – to challenge the power of the state or sovereign.

Although these shifts in function could, and did, take place at home, it was abroad that charters came under greatest strain. Corporations began governing overseas, either by accident or design, and so were obliged to create a functioning polity when the wholesale importation of English governance systems was impossible or undesirable; indeed, their charters gave them the power to make "all manner of laws direction instructions forms and ceremonies of government and magistracy."[47] Occasionally this failed outright, as in the 1624 revocation of the Virginia Company's charter resulting from bankruptcy brought on by poor trade and the failure to establish a government which could co-exist with the Native Americans.[48] More frequent were printed rejoinders or legal challenges to corporations which had overstepped the mark and made laws or taken actions "contrary and repugnant" to those in England, such as the seizure of ships and goods.[49] This might even extend as far as the use of martial law to punish its own citizens, or, as one contemporary commentator put it, "the passing Sentence of Death, and executing Men, by the Governor at St. *Helena*, in a Method not wholly agreeable to the Laws of *England*."[50] The fact that the East India Company had actually secured a grant from James II for the execution of those planters on St Helena found guilty of treason did not spare them from this charge, demonstrating the way in which this hybrid constitutionalism was not simply a matter of law but also public opinion: Not only was the company roundly criticised for its actions once reports reached England, the fact it sought additional protection from the crown beforehand revealed both its uncertainty over its chartered position and its awareness of the controversy the trials and executions would likely cause.[51]

The first two chapters of the book examine these issues of corporate representation and self-representation (what we might now call public relations). Chapter 1 examines the ways in which corporations manipulated public and governmental opinion through print in order to secure new rights and charters. To do so, I develop the concept of the 'corporate public sphere', a set of texts printed for the public which explicitly engaged with the ideas and strategies of the trading companies. These have never previously been considered as a 'genre', but I suggest that, when taken together, they are an important strand in our understanding of the development of the print marketplace. The ability to speak as an anonymous collective was a key privilege of the companies, and this had ramifications for the ways in which information and argumentation was presented in print more generally. The chapter considers these questions in light of the printed response of corporations to moments of crisis such as the Amboyna massacre of 1623. Similarly, the form of corporate lobbying, particularly of Parliament, also affected the public sphere, as corporate pamphlets shifted from broad economic treatises, with a relatively explicit agenda, to anonymous, apparently objective texts taking the form of letters to MPs or newsbooks for public consumption. Through a study of the debate surrounding the necessity of overseas fortifications, and the nature of the fortifications which did exist, the chapter closes by demonstrating the ways in which corporate discourse became embedded in models of representation and textuality beyond the purely economic.

Chapter 2 continues to use printed material relating to the corporation to consider the corporation as an agent for managing risk. It details the way in which both the corporation as a whole, and its individual members, attempted to build trust networks, in particular through and for the use of credit. These questions of trust were more than simply practical considerations; they spoke to broader questions about the ontology of the corporation itself, as well as an anxiety over new forms of credit and moral authority which the corporations established. The chapter also details the difficulties companies had with their office holders and servants overseas, in record keeping, communication networks and fraud; these, too, contributed to the general public discourse about the risks associated with the international trading corporation. The chapter closes with a study of the phenomenon of stock-jobbing, artificially inflating the price of stock to make a quick sale. Here, too, there are anxieties over new types of markets, and the fear that capital was becoming unproductive. But such anxieties were not limited to the stock exchange itself, but rather intersected with broader moral concerns over circulation, social capital and even religion.

The final three chapters develop some of the key intellectual ideas from this work on the corporation's relationship with the commonwealth and the public sphere. Each chapter takes a key theme from corporate discourse – exchanges and circulation, national identity, religion – and demonstrates the way corporate ideology was disseminated through society, and the ways in which popular discourse interacted with that ideology, sometimes adopting it wholesale, sometimes appropriating it to new ends, and occasionally challenging it outright.

The third chapter, 'The world's exchange', explores the shifts in economic thinking engendered by corporations and their related financial instruments, beginning with the idea of 'exchange' itself. The term was developed in the seventeenth century directly from commercial activity, especially Bills of Exchange, financial instruments allowing the transfer of money or, increasingly, credit. But 'exchange' was primarily used culturally in the sense of a place of exchange, at first the Royal Exchange and then, synecdochically, London itself. Descriptions of London, an increasingly corporate city, as 'the World's Exchange' were common throughout the century, and I track the movement of the phrase from a confident assertion of trading power to a nostalgic attempt to create a national mythology and glorious past based on trade. Alongside these issues, the chapter details the ways in which the economic and cultural meanings of 'exchange' discussed in early modern political and economic writing transferred into translations and other literary texts. In particular, I focus on those texts which, explicitly or implicitly, consider the morality of exchanges. Milton's *Masque Presented at Ludlow Castle [Comus]* contains a lengthy discourse between the Lady and the titular enchanter, which centres on the morality of use-value and exchange-value in the individual body, read by those characters as a symbol of the economy as a whole, in much the same way as the corporate body and body politic were interlinked. The debates in these texts draw on corporate arguments which stress both the value of their international exchanges to the commonwealth as a whole, and its moral virtue in bringing nations closer together.

Chapter 4, 'Epic, nationalism and the corporation' takes as its starting point the idea that epic is a reflection on, and idealisation of, national character. It therefore re-examines the presence of economic and corporate activity in epic poetry such as Camões's *Os Lusiados*, Sylvester's translation of the *Divine Weeks and Works*, Davenant's *Gondibert* and Milton's *Paradise Lost*. These national epics offer a glimpse into the way that corporate ideas were being used to reshape or reimagine public life more generally. They also demonstrate the way in which corporate ideology became fused with intellectual tradition during the seventeenth century.

The final chapter, 'The corporation of heaven', examines the similarities between the language of corporate and religious activity. Preachers throughout the century, but especially during the Civil Wars, deployed corporate imagery to explain the City of God, and appeal to their audience's loyalty. Using this material, I argue that the corporation became a key mechanism for imagining and analysing collective activity during the seventeenth century, allowing writers and thinkers a means to consider the ideal forms of community and society.

Notes

1 Alison Games, *The Web of Empire: English Cosmopolitans in an Age of Expansion 1560–1660* (Oxford: Oxford University Press, 2008), 83.
2 Anon, *Certain Considerations Relating to the Royal African Company of England* (London?: s.n., 1680), 1.
3 Philip J. Stern and Carl Wennerlind, "Introduction," in *Mercantilism Reimagined: Political Economy in Early Modern Britain and Its Empire*, ed. Philip J. Stern and Carl Wennerlind (Oxford: Oxford University Press, 2013), 7.
4 See David Norbrook, "The Emperor's New Body? Richard II, Ernst Kantorowicz, and the Politics of Shakespeare Criticism," *Textual Practice* 10, no. 2 (1996).
5 On those authors, see, for example, Christopher Borsing, *Daniel Defoe and the Representation of Personal Identity* (Abingdon: Routledge, 2016), 28, 91–9; Stephen H. Gregg, *Defoe's Writings and Manliness: Contrary Men* (Farnham: Ashgate, 2009), 153–5; Philip J. Stern, "Corporate Virtue: The Languages of Empire in Early Modern British Asia," *Renaissance Studies* 26, no. 4 (2012); Andrea Finkelstein, *Harmony and the Balance: An Intellectual History of Seventeenth-Century English Economic Thought* (Ann Arbor: University of Michigan Press, 2000), 219–46.
6 See Tiffany Stern, "The Theatre of Shakespeare's London," in *The New Cambridge Companion to Shakespeare*, ed. Margreta De Grazia and Stanley W. Wells (Cambridge: Cambridge University Press, 2010).
7 Tracey Hill, *Pageantry and Power: A Cultural History of the Early Modern Lord Mayor's Show, 1585–1639* (Manchester: Manchester University Press, 2010).
8 The nomenclature for these governing bodies shifted slightly over time and between different companies; for convenience, I generally use the terms 'court' or 'directors' to mean this governing group.
9 On the Italian origins of the joint-stock concept, see M. Schmitthoff, "The Origin of the Joint-Stock Company," *The University of Toronto Law Journal* 3, no. 1 (1939).
10 On the development of joint-stock companies generally, see the introduction to William Robert Scott, *The Constitution and Finance of English, Scottish and Irish Joint-Stock Companies to 1720*, 2 vols. (New York: Peter Smith, 1951). For an overview of the East India Company's joint-stock model, see Philip Lawson, *The East India Company: A History* (London: Longman, 1993).
11 Thomas Hobbes, *Leviathan* (London: Andrew Crooke, 1651), 119.
12 BL IOR B/12, 3rd March 1628
13 Emily Erikson, *Between Monopoly and Free Trade: The English East India Company, 1600–1757* (Princeton, NJ: Princeton University Pres, 2014), 3.

14 See, for example, Anna Winterbottom, *Hybrid Knowledge in the Early East India Company World* (Basingstoke: Palgrave Macmillan, 2016).

15 See David Harris Sacks, "Metropolis and Revolution," in *The Culture of Capital: Property, Cities, and Knowledge in Early Modern England*, ed. Henry S. Turner (New York; London: Routledge, 2002).

16 Robert Markley, *The Far East and the English Imagination, 1600–1730* (Cambridge: Cambridge University Press, 2006).

17 Christina Hyo Jung Lee, ed. *Western Visions of the Far East in a Transpacific Age, 1522–1657* (Farnham: Ashgate, 2012).

18 Blair Hoxby, *Mammon's Music: Literature and Economics in the Age of Milton* (New Haven, CT: Yale University Press, 2002), 5.

19 Mary Poovey, *Genres of the Credit Economy: Mediating Value in Eighteenth- and Nineteenth-Century Britain* (Chicago, IL: University of Chicago Press, 2008), 6.

20 Jonathan Gil Harris, *Sick Economies: Drama, Mercantilism, and Disease in Shakespeare's England* (Philadelphia: University of Pennsylvania Press, 2004), 185.

21 Martha Woodmansee and Mark Osteen, "Taking Account of the New Economic Criticism: An Historical Introduction," in *The New Economic Criticism: Studies at the Intersection of Literature and Economics*, ed. Martha Woodmansee and Mark Osteen (London: Routledge, 1999), 14.

22 Peter F. Grav, "Taking Stock of Shakespeare and the New Economic Criticism," *Shakespeare* 8, no. 1 (2012): 133.

23 As well as the studies discussed here, see Lars Engle, *Shakespearean Pragmatism: Market of His Time* (Chicago: University of Chicago Press, 1993); Theodore B. Leinwand, *Theatre, Finance, and Society in Early Modern England* (Cambridge: Cambridge University Press, 1999); Craig Muldrew, *The Economy of Obligation: The Culture of Credit and Social Relations in Early Modern England* (Basingstoke: Palgrave Macmillan, 1998).

24 Douglas Bruster, "On a Certain Tendency in Economic Criticism of Shakespeare," in *Money and the Age of Shakespeare: Essays in New Economic Criticism*, ed. Linda Woodbridge (Basingstoke: Palgrave Macmillan, 2003), 73.

25 John O'Brien, *Literature Incorporated: The Cultural Unconscious of the Business Corporation, 1650–1850* (Chicago: University of Chicago Press, 2016), 1.

26 *Literature Incorporated*, 33.

27 Henry S. Turner, *The Corporate Commonwealth: Pluralism and Political Fictions in England 1516–1651* (Chicago: University of Chicago Press, 2016), 28.

28 *Corporate Commonwealth*, 114.

29 Bruster, "On a Certain Tendency," 76.

30 Phil Withington, *The Politics of Commonwealth: Citizens and Freemen in Early Modern England* (Cambridge: Cambridge University Press, 2005), 18.

31 Nottinghamshire Record Office, Corporation of Newark Minute Book, DC/NW/3/1/1, Charles I to Sir Richard Byron, Governor of Newark, 26th March 1644.

32 See Istvan Hont, *Jealousy of Trade: International Competition and the Nation State in Historical Perspective* (London: Belknap, 2005), 185–8.

33 K. N. Chaudhuri, *The English East India Company: The Study of an Early Joint-Stock Company 1600–1640* (London: Routledge, 1999), 60.

34 Robert Brenner, *Merchants and Revolution: Commercial Change, Political Conflict, and London's Overseas Traders, 1550–1653* (London: Verso, 2003), 317.

35 Nuala Zahedieh, *The Capital and the Colonies : London and the Atlantic Economy, 1660–1700* (Cambridge: Cambridge University Press, 2010), 44.

36 Julia Adams, *The Familial State: Ruling Families and Merchant Capitalism in Early Modern Europe* (Ithaca, NY: Cornell University Press, 2005), 77.

37 Emma Rothschild, *The Inner Life of Empires: An Eighteenth-Century History* (Princeton, NJ: Princeton University Press, 2011); David Hancock, *Citizens of the World: London Merchants and the Integration of the British Atlantic Community, 1735–1785* (Cambridge: Cambridge University Press, 1995).

38 Margot Finn, "Family Formations: Anglo India and the Familial Proto-State," in *Structures and Transformations in Modern British History*, ed. David Feldman and Jon Lawrence (Cambridge: Cambridge University Press, 2011), 102. See also David Veevers, "'Inhabitants of the Universe': Global Families, Kinship Networks, and the Formation of the Early Modern Colonial State in Asia," *Journal of Global History* 10, no. 1 (2015).

39 See Natasha Glaisyer, *The Culture of Commerce in England, 1660–1720* (Woodbridge: Boydell, 2006); Perry Gauci, *The Politics of Trade: The Overseas Merchant in State and Society, 1660–1720* (Oxford: Oxford University Press, 2001); Richard Grassby, *Kinship and Capitalism: Marriage, Family, and Business in the English Speaking World, 1580–1740* (Cambridge: Cambridge University Press, 2000); Edmond J. Smith, "The Global Interests of London's Commercial Community, 1599–1625: Investment in the East India Company," *Economic History Review* Early Access (2018).

40 See Philip J. Stern, "'Bundles of Hyphens': Corporations as Legal Communities in the Early Modern British Empire," in *Legal Pluralism and Empires, 1500–1850* (New York: New York University Press, 2013), 22–3; F. W. Maitland, "The Corporation Sole (1900)," in *Maitland: State, Trust and Corporation*, ed. D. Runciman and M. Ryan (Cambridge: Cambridge University Press, 2003).

41 Paul D. Halliday, *Dismembering the Body Politic : Partisan Politics in England's Towns, 1650–1730* (Cambridge: Cambridge University Press, 1998), xi.

42 William A. Pettigrew, "Corporate Constitutionalism and the Dialogue between the Global and Local in Seventeenth-Century English History," *Itinerario* 39, no. 3 (2015): 488.

43 Hobbes, *Leviathan*, 174.

44 Thomas Johnson, *A Discourse Consisting of Motives for the Enlargement and Freedome of Trade* (London: Richard Bishop for Stephen Bowtell, 1646), 14.

45 David Runciman, *Pluralism and the Personality of the State* (Cambridge: Cambridge University Press, 1997), 25.

46 Vicki Hsueh, *Hybrid Constitutions: Challenging Legacies of Law, Privilege and Culture in Colonial America* (Durham, NC: Duke University Press, 2010), 3.

47 Charter of the Newfoundland Company, 1610 in Cecil Thomas Carr, ed. *Select Charters of Trading Companies, 1530–1707* (London: Selden Society, 1913), 56.

48 On the revocation, see Wesley F. Craven, *Dissolution of the Virginia Company: The Failure of a Colonial Experiment* (Oxford: Oxford University Press, 1932).

49 Charter of the Levant Company, 1600 in Carr, *Select Charters of Trading Companies, 1530–1707*, 34.

50 William Atwood, *An Apology for the East India Company* (London: For the Author, 1690), 4.

51 John M. Collins, *Martial Law and English Laws, C.1500–C.1700* (Cambridge: Cambridge University Press, 2016), 224.

Works cited

Manuscript

BL IOR B/12

Nottinghamshire Record Office, Corporation of Newark Minute Book, DC/NW/3/1/1

Print

Adams, Julia. *The Familial State: Ruling Families and Merchant Capitalism in Early Modern Europe*. Ithaca, NY: Cornell University Press, 2005.

Anon. *Certain Considerations Relating to the Royal African Company of England*. London?: s.n., 1680.

Atwood, William. *An Apology for the East India Company*. London: For the Author, 1690.

Borsing, Christopher. *Daniel Defoe and the Representation of Personal Identity*. Abingdon: Routledge, 2016.

Brenner, Robert. *Merchants and Revolution: Commercial Change, Political Conflict, and London's Overseas Traders, 1550–1653*. London: Verso, 2003. 1993.

Bruster, Douglas. "On a Certain Tendency in Economic Criticism of Shakespeare." In *Money and the Age of Shakespeare: Essays in New Economic Criticism*, edited by Linda Woodbridge, 67–77. Basingstoke: Palgrave Macmillan, 2003.

Carr, Cecil Thomas, ed. *Select Charters of Trading Companies, 1530–1707*. London: Selden Society, 1913.

Chaudhuri, K. N. *The English East India Company: The Study of an Early Joint-Stock Company 1600–1640*. London: Routledge, 1999. 1965.

Collins, John M. *Martial Law and English Laws, C.1500–C.1700*. Cambridge: Cambridge University Press, 2016.

Craven, Wesley F. *Dissolution of the Virginia Company: The Failure of a Colonial Experiment*. Oxford: Oxford University Press, 1932.

Engle, Lars. *Shakespearean Pragmatism: Market of His Time*. Chicago: University of Chicago Press, 1993.

Erikson, Emily. *Between Monopoly and Free Trade : The English East India Company, 1600–1757*. Princeton, NJ: Princeton University Pres, 2014.

Finkelstein, Andrea. *Harmony and the Balance: An Intellectual History of Seventeenth-Century English Economic Thought*. Ann Arbor: University of Michigan Press, 2000.

Finn, Margot. "Family Formations: Anglo India and the Familial Proto-State." In *Structures and Transformations in Modern British History*, edited by David Feldman and Jon Lawrence, 100–17. Cambridge: Cambridge University Press, 2011.

Games, Alison. *The Web of Empire: English Cosmopolitans in an Age of Expansion 1560–1660*. Oxford: Oxford University Press, 2008.

Gauci, Perry. *The Politics of Trade: The Overseas Merchant in State and Society, 1660–1720*. Oxford: Oxford University Press, 2001.

Gil Harris, Jonathan. *Sick Economies: Drama, Mercantilism, and Disease in Shakespeare's England*. Philadelphia: University of Pennsylvania Press, 2004.

Glaisyer, Natasha. *The Culture of Commerce in England, 1660–1720*. Woodbridge: Boydell, 2006.

Grassby, Richard. *Kinship and Capitalism: Marriage, Family, and Business in the English Speaking World, 1580–1740*. Cambridge: Cambridge University Press, 2000.

Grav, Peter F. "Taking Stock of Shakespeare and the New Economic Criticism." *Shakespeare* 8, no. 1 (2012): 111–36.

Gregg, Stephen H. *Defoe's Writings and Manliness: Contrary Men*. Farnham: Ashgate, 2009.

Halliday, Paul D. *Dismembering the Body Politic : Partisan Politics in England's Towns, 1650–1730*. Cambridge: Cambridge University Press, 1998.

Hancock, David. *Citizens of the World: London Merchants and the Integration of the British Atlantic Community, 1735–1785*. Cambridge: Cambridge University Press, 1995.

Hill, Tracey. *Pageantry and Power: A Cultural History of the Early Modern Lord Mayor's Show, 1585–1639*. Manchester: Manchester University Press, 2010.

Hobbes, Thomas. *Leviathan*. London: Andrew Crooke, 1651.

Hont, Istvan. *Jealousy of Trade: International Competition and the Nation State in Historical Perspective*. London: Belknap, 2005.

Hoxby, Blair. *Mammon's Music: Literature and Economics in the Age of Milton*. New Haven, CT: Yale University Press, 2002.

Hsueh, Vicki. *Hybrid Constitutions: Challenging Legacies of Law, Privilege and Culture in Colonial America*. Durham, NC: Duke University Press, 2010.

Johnson, Thomas. *A Discourse Consisting of Motives for the Enlargement and Freedome of Trade*. London: Richard Bishop for Stephen Bowtell, 1646.

Lawson, Philip. *The East India Company: A History*. London: Longman, 1993.

Lee, Christina Hyo Jung, ed. *Western Visions of the Far East in a Transpacific Age, 1522–1657*. Farnham: Ashgate, 2012.

Leinwand, Theodore B. *Theatre, Finance, and Society in Early Modern England*. Cambridge: Cambridge University Press, 1999.

Maitland, F. W. "The Corporation Sole (1900)." In *Maitland: State, Trust and Corporation*, edited by D. Runciman and M. Ryan, 9–31. Cambridge: Cambridge University Press, 2003.

Markley, Robert. *The Far East and the English Imagination, 1600–1730*. Cambridge: Cambridge University Press, 2006.

Muldrew, Craig. *The Economy of Obligation: The Culture of Credit and Social Relations in Early Modern England*. Basingstoke: Palgrave Macmillan, 1998.

Norbrook, David. "The Emperor's New Body? Richard II, Ernst Kantorowicz, and the Politics of Shakespeare Criticism." *Textual Practice* 10, no. 2 (1996): 329–57.

O'Brien, John. *Literature Incorporated: The Cultural Unconscious of the Business Corporation, 1650–1850*. Chicago: University of Chicago Press, 2016.

Pettigrew, William A. "Corporate Constitutionalism and the Dialogue between the Global and Local in Seventeenth-Century English History." *Itinerario* 39, no. 3 (2015): 487–501.

Poovey, Mary. *Genres of the Credit Economy: Mediating Value in Eighteenth- and Nineteenth-Century Britain*. Chicago: University of Chicago Press, 2008.

Rothschild, Emma. *The Inner Life of Empires: An Eighteenth-Century History*. Princeton, NJ: Princeton University Press, 2011.

Runciman, David. *Pluralism and the Personality of the State*. Cambridge: Cambridge University Press, 1997.

Sacks, David Harris. "Metropolis and Revolution." In *The Culture of Capital: Property, Cities, and Knowledge in Early Modern England*, edited by Henry S. Turner, 139–62. New York, London: Routledge, 2002.

Schmitthoff, M. "The Origin of the Joint-Stock Company." *The University of Toronto Law Journal* 3, no. 1 (1939): 74–96.

Scott, William Robert. *The Constitution and Finance of English, Scottish and Irish Joint-Stock Companies to 1720.* 2 vols. New York: Peter Smith, 1951.

Smith, Edmond J. "The Global Interests of London's Commercial Community, 1599–1625: Investment in the East India Company." *Economic History Review* early access (2018): 1–29.

Stern, Philip J. "Corporate Virtue: The Languages of Empire in Early Modern British Asia." *Renaissance Studies* 26, no. 4 (2012): 510–30.

———. " 'Bundles of Hyphens': Corporations as Legal Communities in the Early Modern British Empire." In *Legal Pluralism and Empires, 1500–1850*, 21–48. New York: New York University Press, 2013.

Stern, Philip J., and Carl Wennerlind. "Introduction." In *Mercantilism Reimagined: Political Economy in Early Modern Britain and Its Empire*, edited by Philip J. Stern and Carl Wennerlind, 3–24. Oxford: Oxford University Press, 2013.

Stern, Tiffany. "The Theatre of Shakespeare's London." In *The New Cambridge Companion to Shakespeare*, edited by Margreta De Grazia and Stanley W. Wells, 45–60. Cambridge: Cambridge University Press, 2010.

Turner, Henry S. *The Corporate Commonwealth: Pluralism and Political Fictions in England 1516–1651.* Chicago: University of Chicago Press, 2016.

Veevers, David. " 'Inhabitants of the Universe': Global Families, Kinship Networks, and the Formation of the Early Modern Colonial State in Asia." *Journal of Global History* 10, no. 1 (2015): 99–121.

Winterbottom, Anna. *Hybrid Knowledge in the Early East India Company World.* Basingstoke: Palgrave Macmillan, 2016.

Withington, Phil. *The Politics of Commonwealth: Citizens and Freemen in Early Modern England.* Cambridge: Cambridge University Press, 2005.

Woodmansee, Martha, and Mark Osteen. "Taking Account of the New Economic Criticism: An Historical Introduction." In *The New Economic Criticism: Studies at the Intersection of Literature and Economics*, edited by Martha Woodmansee and Mark Osteen, 3–50. London: Routledge, 1999.

Zahedieh, Nuala. *The Capital and the Colonies : London and the Atlantic Economy, 1660–1700.* Cambridge: Cambridge University Press, 2010.

1 The corporate-public sphere

This chapter examines the range of corporate engagement with the incipient public sphere in early modern England. Using some moments of crisis, in particular the massacre at Amboyna, it details how corporations took the decision to enter print, and what forms of public speaking this encompassed. It also considers the interplay between pro- and anti-corporate writing, as well as the roles of those writers (anonymous or otherwise) who took it upon themselves to speak for the corporation. Finally, it demonstrates the ways in which the self-interest of corporate printing had broader effects on the political imagination in early modern England, taking as a case study the debate over the establishment of forts overseas.

In 1651, William Ball produced a document, declaring itself to be a petition presented to Parliament, calling for printing to once again become regulated. Little is known about Ball, although other pamphlets under the same name (William Ball, Esq.) from the preceding decade had argued for the King's cause, and had family ties to the Maryland plantations. Ball argued that, like coinage, printing ought to be a monopoly privilege at the grant of the sovereign power within a state, since the people might as easily be taken in by false or seditious printing as by counterfeit coin. This debate, of course, was nothing new in 1651; questions of censorship and the dangers of the press had been prominent for at least a decade before Ball published, with a series of Acts of Parliament required at regular intervals to attempt to curtail the explosion in unlicensed printing after 1641. Indeed, Ball's intervention was particularly timely, as it chimed with the Cromwellian state's attempts to shift control over press regulation away from Parliament and towards the Council of State. As Jason Peacey has shown, "by the early 1650s, intelligence and press censorship were being linked administratively," especially in the figures of the MP Thomas Scot, and first Walter Frost, then John Thurloe as secretaries to the Council of State.[1] The attacks which Ball makes on the printers as being unable to self-regulate pre-empt those which would be made later against the Stationers' Company itself:

> There would be none found, who might subordinately regulate, and reforme such abuses, and disorders which those innovating, and meane undertakers may in all probability from time to time commit.[2]

However, Ball's pamphlet differs in its suggested remedy; rather than state control, Ball recommends stronger corporate oversight of their members' activities, whether the stationers or other corporations whose members seek to go into print. Consequently, the pamphlet thinks deeply about the implications and necessities of a ban on unlicensed printing, and in particular the corporate activities and privileges involved in such a ban.

Ball's general statement of his ban deliberately includes corporate entities as a subsection of the commonwealth which he wishes to protect from unruly print:

> That no person or persons whatsoever Print, or cause to be Printed any offensive Bookes, Pamphlets, Papers, or Ballads to the Derogation of this present Government, or seditious disturbance of this Common-wealth, or of any Dominion, Member, or Corporation thereof.[3]

Ball evidently sees the Corporation as an entity which can be libelled, or otherwise disturbed by 'offensive' printing. His remedy, alongside limiting who can print, is to allow experts from the corporation (as well as state bodies such as the Councils of State or War) to licence books pertaining to their discipline or function; he demands, for example, that "all Books touching Phisicke [ought] to be Licenced by three of the Colledge of Phisitians appointed for that purpose," and the Herald at Arms and Chancellors of Universities have similar vetoes.[4]

Ball goes on to consider the practical effects of a ban on corporate activity, in particular the skilled guilds such as ironmongers needed to manufacture presses, and the role of the Stationers' Company (and a putative Printers' Company, which he opposes as being unregulated) in policing the written word. The more abstract point that a corporation might be offended or offer offence just as a natural man – the member of the commonwealth – could, is taken for granted and not developed further.

Others, though, did consider what rights a corporation had to print. The year before Ball's treatise, an anonymous pamphlet defending a Levant Company consul against his imprisonment and dismissal by the Company claimed, albeit somewhat ironically, the corporation's right to print:

> Though Companies (especially this) are confident enough, and because they cannot blush, may say what they please, yet these have

> not hitherto taken the liberty to assert any such thing against Sir Sa. in any of their publike complaints, or petitions to the Parliament, but by private whispers and insinuations.[5]

For the anonymous author, the fact that the Levant Company has *not* gone into print, or otherwise on record, with its complaints against its own servant, preferring instead 'private whispers', is particularly noteworthy. Not only does the Levant Company have the right to enter print, in this case it is perceived to have a duty to do so, bringing its proceedings into the public domain for open discussion and consideration.

Before detailing the particular ways in which corporations engaged with the world of print, it is worth detailing the concept of the 'public sphere' which is used in this chapter. It is now well established that the rise of printing during the seventeenth century, especially periods in which it was more or less unregulated, created opportunities for more open and public debate. Consequently, scholars have moved the formation of the 'public sphere' significantly further back in time, so that it is now perceived to have begun closer to the Reformation than the Enlightenment.[6] Lake and Pincus see at least a version of the public sphere, or the incipient presence of one, in the reign of Elizabeth I, and the "opinion which was mobilized both in and outside Parliament" to "induce the Queen to take actions that she did not wish to do, or to prevent her from doing things she wanted to do."[7] However, as Lake and Pincus note, such pamphlets were more usually from alternative factions within the court rather than constitutive of an actually politically engaged populace. The printing culture at the turn of the sixteenth century, then, may not have been a public sphere in the strictly Habermasian sense: it is not clear, for example, that early modern printing had any serious effect on government policy, despite the frequent printing of petitions, appeals, dedications and 'speeches' to Parliament.

Scholars looking to locate the origins of the public sphere in the sixteenth and seventeenth centuries have broadened Habermas's criteria, stressing larger conceptual issues such as public/private, gender and space as forms of self-interest which are not purely economic. Martine van Elk, for example, has recently shown the ways in which "new ideas about privacy, the household, and domesticity" contributed to an emerging, if unstable and often contradictory, division of public and private over the seventeenth century, which was manipulated and deployed by female writers (in both print and manuscript).[8]

Although pamphlets relating to corporations (indeed, to political economy more generally) made up a relatively small section of printing undertaken in the seventeenth century, it is nonetheless an important section of the print market precisely because it demonstrates that even on his own terms Habermas's conception of the public sphere was in fact already under way as early as the 1610s and '20s. In the early years of the seventeenth century, the Virginia Company took to print to defend the economic value of its colonies, and the East India Company countered public narratives relating to Amboyna in both England and the Netherlands. These companies leveraged their peculiar constitutional forms to ensure good access to the print marketplace and consequently became one of the "forces endeavouring to influence the decisions of state authority" who "appealed to the critical public in order to legitimate [their] demands."[9] This process began, as we shall see, long before the Glorious Revolution which Habermas posits as the turning point, although the volume and virulence of pamphleteering did increase after 1688.

Consequently, these pamphlets demonstrate something more like the Habermasian public sphere specifically interested in private interests and public policy; corporate texts exist as a subsection of the print marketplace concerned with the economic consequences of corporate activity (increases or reductions in overall trade, or trade goods such as bullion), or the political consequences, most notably international relations. This reading of corporate discourse develops other studies of pamphlet culture more generally, which emphasise the public sphere not as a rational mediation between conflicting or competing claims on a general and neutral market economy, but rather the site of "a conflict of interests between those whom the market might satisfy or serve, and those who are excluded from its satisfactions or service."[10]

In another sense, corporate printing is a reification of the Habermasian transfer of cultural power from the 'burghers' to the 'bourgeois' clerks and professional writers who crafted their discourse, even as the pamphlets confidently advertised the power and prestige of the mercantile corporation.[11] This can be observed in the ossified nature of the debate – with a fairly fixed set of claims and counter-claims arounds forts/diplomacy, monopoly/private trade and self-interest/community provision (famously widows and orphans), all of which claimed to represent the public good. Pamphlets found new ways to articulate old themes, constructing competing languages of ideological concepts which could be applied to new crises or political developments.

The privilege of corporate speech

One of the privileges naturally arising from being chartered as a corporation was the ability to speak and act as one. Such a right was explicitly granted in later charters as it pertained to legal proceedings: corporations were deemed able to "possess enjoy and retain lands" and could "plead and be impleaded" in courts "in such manner as any other our liege people of this our realm of England being persons able and capable in law."[12] Here, the conceptual permeability of the body corporate and the body natural creates a legal fiction of an individual person, speaking on behalf of the company members as a whole; it was not an enormous leap to imagine that a corporation might be able to speak as one outside of the constraints of the courtroom as well.

Yet if the right to corporate speech was a necessary prerogative of the corporate form, companies were aware of the limitations to that prerogative, particularly where it impinged upon the actions of the state. In March 1628, for example, the East India Company's court of directors debated the form of a proclamation regarding private trading, which they had already decided to issue:

> Mr Mun presented to the court a declaration of orders conceived by him, whereby their commanders, factors and pursers &c might have liberty given them according to the restriction therein approved to use private trade, which being read was allowed and ordered to be printed, and to be affixed to the Kings proclamation.[13]

However, the decision to print soon came under question. Just a few days later, the court met again, and, having been

> Informed that the declaration formerly ordered to be printed cannot be done without his majesties hand first had thereunto, ordered that their secretary shall attend Mr Attorney General therewith, and desire his favour to procure the same that by his majesties allowance it may be therewith printed and sent abroad with his proclamation.[14]

The Company found, apparently to their surprise, that there were limits on their public speech after all. This particular publication still had to be authorised by the King, because they wanted it to coincide with another proclamation. Clearly, this was not always the case; in fact, very few corporate documents were printed in this fashion, in part because of the difficulties of such enmeshing of polities. While the EIC doubtless saw advantage for the maintenance of their royally sanctioned trade monopoly in printing the two together, the rebuke reminded them, at a time when they were in negotiations regarding the future of that monopoly and the company itself, that the king and company had very different privileges when it came to public speech.

One privilege they did have, though, was secrecy: the affairs of the companies remained, at least in theory, private to the corporations themselves. In fact, James I reminded Parliament in 1621 that "information on the Merchant Adventurers was privileged."[15] Most corporate writing (internal letters, court minutes and accounts) remained restricted to a select few with roles in corporate governance, unless the company themselves chose to divulge it.

Consequently, much corporate activity in writing (preparing petitions, lists of subscribers, internal letters and notes) was still done by hand, with fair copies being made for examination outside of the corporation where necessary. Nevertheless, from the 1620s onwards corporations were accustomed to printing, both to allow public examination of documents such as charters or accounts, and to engage with the marketplace of public opinion. This they did especially on key elements of their activities, such as the export of bullion or increase of shipping, as well as responding to current events or scandals.

Miles Ogborn has argued that, while being shaped by their own internal epistolary culture, the East India Company "was often a reluctant entrant to the world of print."[16] Ogborn suggests that the East India Company preferred suppression of critical materials to answering them in open debate. It is true that the Company was able to use political influence to prevent printed materials from reaching the public, but this was not always an advisable course of action. One court committee of February 1615, discussing the (anonymous) publication of Robert Kayll's *The Trade's Increase*, which argued that the East India Company's monopoly restricted the growth of trade, as did their use of shipping which could be put to better use, considered the idea of censorship:

> Concerning the book called the Trades Increase; opinion of the Archbishop of Canterbury that it should rather be suffered to die than be suppressed, which would cause many men to seek after it the more earnestly, but promising a warrant to that effect if the Governor desired it.[17]

Here, the Company is aware that while it might technically have the power to suppress a text, it did so at the risk of making a text much more popular than it might otherwise have been – the act of censorship might draw the public's attention to a particular text, or argument, when judiciously ignoring countervailing views would allow them to simply 'die' in the marketplace of ideas. Consequently, the EIC did engage in print from relatively early in its existence, seeking instead of censorship to actively counter critical materials, and to offer a positive narrative of its own activities. For this reason, they commissioned Dudley Digges to write a response, *The Defence of Trade*, which was registered with the Stationers' Company a month later, and featured the East India Company prominently on the title page.[18]

By the end of the century, this sort of corporate speech had become rather axiomatic. In a 1681 discourse, looking back over the past 20 years, one writer noted the apparent paradox of the rights of the (urban) corporation to speak:

> This is very mysterious, now and then, when you please, a *Westminster* Grand Jury shall be the voice of the Nation, but no heed given

> to any other; and the majority of a Corporation shall then speak the sense of the whole Town, but at other times shall scarce have leave given them to speak even for themselves.[19]

The assertion of the corporate (in this case, an urban corporation) right to speech comes with the caveat that gets to the ontological questions of corporate being: Is a corporation a single entity composed of, and speaking for all its members? Perhaps it is just a set of people, a majority or even governing minority of its members; or, conversely, corporations may even be able to speak for those outside of their remit but still affected by them (strangers and other non-citizens, in this example).

In the midst of a lengthy pamphlet debate with the Royal African Company, William Wilkinson – a separate trader whose brother had been driven to suicide by the Company, leading him to mount a "propaganda campaign" against it[20] – alluded to this question as he acknowledged the right of the Company to reply to accusations in print, although he was naturally dissatisfied with their answers: "It was not contrary to expectation, that the Royal African Company have endeavoured to answer the many Accusations laid against them by the generality of traders."[21] The significant rise in corporate pamphlets published over the last decade of the seventeenth century demonstrates the extent to which this sort of publishing had become 'expected'.

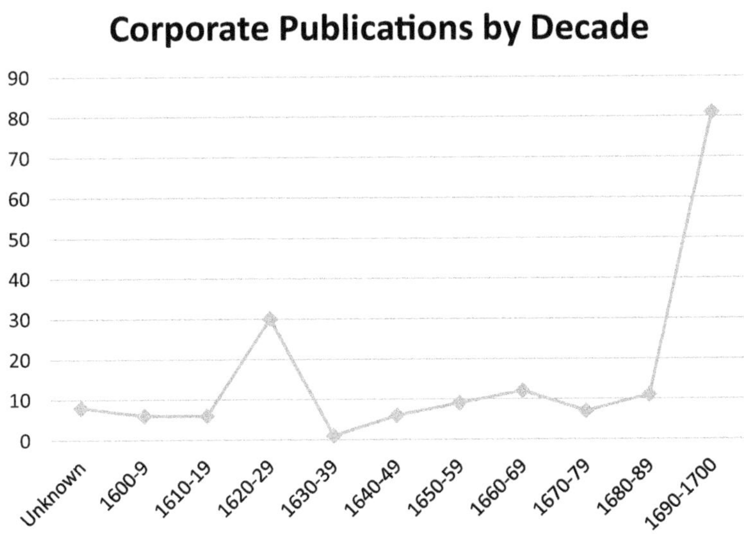

Figure 1.1 Corporate publications by decade, 1600–1700

By the 1680s, then, the idea of corporate speech, and corporate engagement in the public sphere, was well established. To analyse this phenomenon, I have constructed a database of the texts (pamphlets, broadsides, regulations, petitions and so on) published in the seventeenth century which can be described as directly corporate. The dataset includes publications issued under the name of specific companies, as well as texts written directly in opposition or defence of corporate activity, and those texts which deal with more general problems (lack of bullion, decline in shipping) but with a specifically corporate focus.

There were as many publications in the 1690s (81) as the rest of the century combined (81). Half of those (42) were primarily concerned with the activities of the East India Company; not only were their opponents more active, but they appeared more frequently in print directly, rather than relying on named persons as spokespeople for the company position. These pamphlets, rather than being ad hoc responses of company activity (as in the case of the Levant Company and 'Sir Sa'), were increasingly part of an ongoing public conversation about the rights and responsibilities of companies, especially the question of whether they impinged on a natural 'right to trade'. Authors on both sides of the corporate question increasingly made reference to other pamphlets on the topic, as was the case for the East India Company themselves when discussing its relationships with foreign rulers:

> The War with the *Great Mogul* was occasion'd by pure necessity, and that necessity did arise, from the breaking in of the *Interlopers* upon them, in their Trade, when by dividing the *English* Interest in *India*, the Natives there took advantage of the said division, to extort very great, and most unreasonable Sums of Money from the Company, contrary to their Phirmaunds given to them, as has been more at large demonstrated by the Company in Print.[22]

The EIC clearly expects its readers to either already be familiar with the material relating to these 'unreasonable' demands, or to be able to find it quickly, since they discuss that material without any particular reference or requoting. Other writers followed this tactic, clearly anticipating an informed readership already familiar with the issues at hand:

> And indeed, it more immediately concerns this Nation, than all the rest of *Europe*, because all of them put together consume not One fourth of those Commodities this Bill prohibits, that we do; and that the *East-India* Company themselves allow, in a Print of their own last Sessions, which I then answer'd.[23]

This anonymous writer acknowledges the fact of the company's printing, and refers the reader to his previous answer on the topic, but once more no specifics are given. These pamphlets constructed, or imagined they constructed, a community of readers, rather like the newsbooks did with their inside references, learnt allusions, and book advertisements, which

> Always emphasised the agency of their readers in the present, offering a fleeting imagining of their future as the enlightening potential of encounters with books and bookish people as yet unread, unmet or well acquainted.[24]

Moreover, the company can begin to make assumptions about this imagined community, helping it shape public opinion as well as providing implicit support for the company when it needed to conjure the image of popular support for its actions. For the rest of this chapter, I focus on three case studies, drawn from across the century, which demonstrate the ways corporations, their sponsors and detractors attempted to create and manipulate public opinion.

Amboyna

Nowhere is this better exemplified than in the East India Company's response to an incident which coloured overseas adventures and Anglo-Dutch relations for nearly half a century. In March 1623, Dutch troops massacred the garrison of an English trading post on Amboyna, in modern-day Indonesia. The attack became an infamous example of the 'perfidious Dutch', and coloured relationships between the two states, and their East India companies, for the rest of the century. News of the event did not reach the English East India Company for more than a year, the Company's governor reporting on the 31st May 1624 that he had informed the King of the business.

Within the Company, attention soon turned to the question of public perception. The court of June 1624 decried the "false friends the Dutch" and the growth of "common obloquy at home, where every one cries out against the Trade, and the Company suffers and is subject to common reproach."[25] News also reached the Company that month that the Dutch East India Company were putting forward their own version of events – that it was not a massacre, but a series of executions in response to a plot to overthrow the fort – in print in the Netherlands, copies of which had reached England.

The Company therefore decided to put forward their own version of events to the public. The Court of July 2nd noted that the company was preparing a text for publication:

> But he maketh no doubt but that God the avenger of all such bloody acts will in his due time bring the truth to light, and the company had not failed of their part to set down in writing to be published as far

> as may stand with these duties the unspeakable tyrannies done upon the unfortunate men.[26]

Startlingly, the corporation aligned themselves with the operation of divine justice, stressing the need for a 'truth' to be publicly available. The directors of the East India Company, at least, knew how important the print marketplace was as a means of disseminating their version of the truth of Amboyna, and of drumming up support – both public and state – for the campaign for restitution and reparations that would follow. The text was ready by October, and the Company considered how they might best publish it:

> The court was moved whether they will print the book concerning the cruelties of the Dutch towards the English at Amboyna & it was said that for £12 10S they may have 500 printed. The court considered that it will be fit to print 2000 in all, but to see that the press be broken, and all the books being brought to the Company, then that some few of them be given to some principal persons of the nobility, and if they be well taken then to adventure to put abroad the rest, which if they shall do, the benefit will pay for the printing.[27]

The primary focus of the Company remained on the nobility, no doubt in part to garner support for their claim to reparations at court and with the King himself. However, the minutes reveal that the Company is aware both of the need to control the message, and the power (and financial benefit) of printing. The instruction to break the press is remarkable, pointing perhaps to a fear that their words might be corrupted or twisted in future printings. It certainly illuminates how keen the Company were to keep a very tight control on the production and dissemination of their version of events. Equally, the substantial increase in the number of books ordered (to 2000 from a suggested 500), most of which were for public sale, shows the Company's serious engagement with the print marketplace. That the Company believes the sale of the non-gifted texts will recoup the costs of printing suggests a confidence that there is a public appetite for news of the massacre, even (or perhaps especially) if it is inflected by the corporation.

In fact, just two days later the Company upped the order again:

> The court took into consideration the printing of the relation of the business between the Dutch and the English at Amboyna. And it was agreed that there shall be 3000 books printed whereof 2000 in English to be spread here, and 1000 in Dutch to be sent over, and that it may not be taken for a libel, there shall be set upon the front of each book the armes of this Company in token that they own them to be true.[28]

The company was extending its operations from England to the Netherlands, confidently supposing that their authority gave sufficient weight to the 'truth' of their pamphlet even on foreign soil. They are also sufficiently engaged with the detail of the printing to be concerned about the text's presentation. As well as a guarantee of truth, perhaps the presentation of corporate arms on an anonymous text is as close as a corporation can get to speaking directly – the text becomes the deliberation and conclusion of an entire corporate body, instead of any single 'natural man'. The East India Company was thus forced into print as a response to crisis, but took the opportunity to establish themselves as a force in both the print marketplace and the marketplace of ideas as a guarantor of truth. The Company clearly see themselves, and seek to position themselves in print, as a separate, independent body politic attempting to bring truth to light for the benefit of both the public and the state.[29]

The ongoing ramifications of Amboyna, and the Dutch hegemony in the East India trade, continued to create problems for the East India Company. In July 1627, the Company had serious internal discussions about giving up its charter and leaving the trade entirely, prompted by what they saw as the VOC's "settled resolution" to "drive the English out of the Indies."[30] This resolution was confirmed not just by the VOC's actions, but in their writings, with the governor noting that

> Many letters have been received out of Holland (some whereof he caused now to be read) importing a resolution in the Bewinthebbers, nay in some of the state themselves to justify the Act of Amboyna, and to give satisfactory reasons for the sending away of Coen.[31]

The EIC were nervous of another round of public disputes over the Amboyna massacre, particularly since the previous attempts at manipulating court and public opinion had failed to produce any sort of reparations or support for the English company. The previous month the company had complained that their printer, Nicholas Bourne, had allowed copies of a pamphlet to be exposed too early to public view, including the Dutch ambassador, "whose inevitable complaint to the privy council led to the book's suppression."[32] 'Bewinthebbers' was an unusual choice of word for a group usually known as the 'Heren Zeventien' [seventeen gentlemen], or more simply as the Directors of the VOC; it is possible that the printing the EIC court had in mind was a reissue of the 1624 *Remonstrance of the Bewinthebbers or directors of the Netherlands East India Company*, with a new preface explaining that the English company's complaints against the governor of Amboyna, Herman van Speult, had been ignored, and "neither have the officers of the said Netherlands Company in all this respite of 18 months made any restitution or reparation to the English, as was promised and pretended."[33] That 18-month respite was concluded in January 1627; although the *Remonstrance* was not formally printed until 1632, which was, as far as I can tell, the first printed use of Bewinthebber, the reference to the time frame suggests some version of it was circulating earlier.

Although the Company had formally resolved to leave off the trade at the court of the 20th July, discussions over the precise nature of that withdrawal continued, not least the ramifications for the country as a whole, since, as they acknowledged, the East India trade "was undoubtedly more beneficial to the state than any other now on foot yet to the adventurers hath it proved by accident unprofitable."[34]

In September 1627, Sir John Wolstenholme communicated to the court (via Mr Styles) that he had spoken with the king about the "general decay of trade and particularly with the declining of the East India Company, and showed of what consequence that trade was for benefit of the kingdom if supported." According to Wolstenholme, "his majesty had seriously protested he would not lose the East India trade, and seemed to require the company to set down their demands what they would have him do for them."[35] The court resolved to prepare their demands, but were concerned about the best way to present them, some calling for a corporate publication, others suggesting it would be preferable

> If any particular man (as of himself without the company's direction) will employ his pains to advance the business by his private solicitation as opportunities shall favour, it will be far better than that the company should solicit the same.[36]

The idea that a 'particular man' (as opposed to the corporate *persona ficta*) should 'as of himself' put forward the company's agenda is probably written with a certain coyness, as the company was already willing to pay agents to write on its behalf, either before publication or in the form of a generous grant afterwards. In fact, although the Company had some disagreement on strategy, the idea that the public should be in some way motivated to take up the Company's cause seems to have had fairly solid support among the directors. No publication was explicitly agreed to at the meeting, nor do the minutes record any reaching out to any 'particular man'.

The Company nonetheless continued to hope for redress for Amboyna, noting on the 19th November that they required "the issue of the Dutch ships to be known before any consultations" on the future of the Company and a second stock.[37] In the meantime, the company carried on its activities, despite a turbulent general court in January 1628; the directors argued that the activities of the company needed to be wound down slowly rather than be brought to an immediate halt to preserve whatever value was left in the stock.

On 28th March 1628, the Company sent a committee to answer a complaint from Mr Warmer in Parliament, which would ultimately provide them the opportunity to put forward a justification in print. The Company charged Thomas Mun with drafting a petition "showing the honor and benefit accruing to his majesty and his kingdom by the East India trade, and aspersions that lie upon the company, by which aspersions the adventurers are much discouraged."[38] The court was pleased with Mun's work, and once more discussed the proper way to enter the material into the public realm:

> Some were of opinion that it were not fit for the company to exhibit the petition, but rather to be called into the Parliament by some accidental occasion and then to exhibit it, or at least to acquaint the King and Lords therewith, and have their approval before it be delivered, others to have it exhibited by the company considering it will wipe off those scandals and aspersions which lie upon the company, but the general opinion was that some other occasion were fitter then that the company should deliver it themselves.[39]

Once more, the court at least appears reluctant to enter print directly, and yet despite this apparent reluctance there were soon manoeuvrings to have the company called to Parliament after all. Mr Sherbourne acquainted the next court, on the 21st of April, that "according to their directions he had attended Sir John Coke with the company's petition," but that Coke advised him to wait, before he attended the Lord President "whose advice was upon altering 3 or 4 words according to his Lordship's directions the exhibiting thereof may be of good avail to the company."[40] A subsequent second consultation with Coke revealed that he "hath since bethought himself a little better," and he advised on a scheme to have Sir John Wolstenholme send down material relating to the East India Company from the Lords to the Commons, which "would be the way to have the company called thither."[41] At the same court, the deputy reported that he had "had some conference with Sir Dudley Digges about the same, who relished the motion very well," and the court "entreated Mr Deputy to take a copy of the petition to acquaint Sir Dudley Digges therewith."[42]

On the 25th April the court pressed Mun once more for a draft "to be made ready that a conference may be had thereupon before they be exhibited to the house."[43] The court records do not record either the specific changes requested by the Lord President, or any suggestions made by Dudley Digges, but the redrafting process suggests that Mun was taking some informal advice on the composition of the text. It was not until the 5th of May that Mun was able to bring his draft back to the company:

> At this court was read Mr Mun his reasons and proofs which he hath collected to make good the queries in the company's petition which is to be exhibited in Parliament; And howbeit some dispute upon the

> reading happened thereupon in diverse particular passages thereof, which was conceived by some ought to be well and fully argued, and fully explained before they be put to the press, yet generally the court well approved of them and acknowledged many thanks to Mr Mun for his great care and pains bestowed therein, nevertheless it was thought fit to have the same read a second time before it be printed which was appointed to be done next court.[44]

The existence of 'queries', too, hints at some private discussions over the wording of the text; nevertheless, the 'dispute' had in court over whether the diverse passages were sufficiently well argued and explained suggests the court saw itself as a final arbiter rather than meekly accepting and implementing the outside advice. It also reveals the extent to which this genuinely was a 'corporate' output – drafted by Mun, with advice from other writers who had written in support of the Corporation, and then amended by the board as whole, this text truly represented the thoughts of the company as an impersonal 'body politic'. The court records do not show a second reading of the petition, but it was evidently accepted since the matter is not mentioned again until the 30th May, with members of the court asking "to know what success the company's petition had in Parliament."[45]

The discussion over the viability of the trade, and what privileges would be required to maintain the East India Company (and, by extension, the East India trade itself), echoes the Levant Company's requests for a new patent in 1589–90. The Company attempted to restrict membership of the monopoly trade to just 40 merchants, and, in response to complaints from independent merchants, "nineteen of the most prominent Turkey and Venice company merchants haughtily laid down the conditions under which they would find it worthwhile to continue their trade."[46] If these conditions were not met, they threatened to withdraw from the trade entirely. Both companies used print to advance their agenda in the face of crises and shifts in public opinion, and did so from relatively early in their existence. As we shall see, corporations became especially engaged in the print marketplace towards the end of the seventeenth century, but they learnt their public relations strategies early, and were clearly conscious of 'the public' even if they were not yet active in shaping that opinion.

Thomas Violet, goldsmith

Attempts to manipulate the world of print were not limited to the multinational trading companies; livery companies, too, took to the press either directly or through agents. Where the large multinational companies framed their interventions in terms of the national good and international relations, livery companies focused on the detail of regulation. As suggested by William Ball's pamphlet which opened this chapter, the

Stationers' Company, of course, were heavily involved, and their engagement with the press is discussed in more detail in the following chapter on trust in regulation. So, too, were the Goldsmiths' Company, a group which was naturally concerned about its own reputation given its vital regulatory role over precious metals and currency.

In this section, I move from the broad debate over corporate speech to a specific case study, a printed argument between Thomas Violet and Peter Blondeau over models of regulating the Royal Mint, which ran from 1647 to 1653. These pamphlets demonstrate the ways in which the questions of social good through corporate activity were becoming widespread and normalised; moreover, the operations of corporate interests within the public sphere are thrown into sharp relief by the Civil War context in which these pamphlets operated.

Thomas Violet was one of the Goldsmiths' more controversial figures; he spent much of his career at the mint. He is now better known for his virulent anti-Semitic writings, although he was also an indefatigable pamphleteer and promoter of new schemes for the improvement of coining and coinage. Violet's early engagement with public writing did not go well; in 1644, he was imprisoned in the Tower for delivering a letter from Charles I to the City of London. In July 1647, a single-page broadside appeared in print, which contained the original letter from Charles, as well as an additional letter from Violet himself, to the Lord Mayor and Common Council, complaining of his "nine hundred twenty eight dayes" imprisonment.[47] Violet's letter asks for his release, and the return of his estate, but remarkably does so by recommending another printed work to the attention of the Council:

> I doe likewise send to you here inclosed, a booke printed by *Peter Cole*, in *Corne hill* neare the Royall Exchange the 16. of *Ianuary*, 1643. Wherein you may see the transaction of this Businesse concerning this his Majesties Letter, at large, printed by order of the two houses of Parliament, a booke worthy of your serious consideration.[48]

If Cole did print the 'business' concerning Parliament's response to this letter, it has been lost, although Cole was expanding from theological printing to political print, especially petitions, around the time that Violet claims he printed this book. These texts were not all aligned to the same cause. They included a petition from clothiers in Suffolk and Essex to Charles I complaining about the citizens "of *London*, in whom the breath of our Trade and livelyhood consisteth [who] have so blasted their hopes, that the Merchants forbeare exportation."[49] Conversely, the following year he printed a petition from the inhabitants of London, warning of "misery through decay of Trade," and proposing that the citizens be conscripted into a second army.[50] Cole also printed the confession of

Richard Challenor under order of Parliament in July 1643. Challenor, along with Tomkins and Edmund Waller, was part of a plot to seize the leaders of the Houses of Parliament, and open the gates of London to allow in the King's forces; after the plot was discovered, Challenor and Tomkins were prosecuted by court-martial and executed, while Waller, as a serving MP, successfully convinced the House that it should accept no other authority to try its members, and so went in exile to Paris. Challenor's confession on the scaffold appeared in print soon after, with the coda that "It is this day Ordered by the Committee of the House of Commons in Parliament concerning printing, that the Confession of Richard Challenor be printed by Peter Cole."[51]

It is quite possible, then, that the Council was already well aware of Cole's role as a printer of political works, and perhaps even the book Violet commended to them. In any case, Violet's decision to assign the authority in his case to a text printed some years earlier is surprising, and is suggestive of how highly he esteems the printed word. The fact he recommends it to the Council's 'serious consideration', too, points to a mode of active readership, in which careful reflection on the arguments put forward in print might lead to changed minds, and changed political outcomes in the world outside of the marketplace of ideas.

Violet continued to use print to answer print, and a few years later, having secured his release, was the author of a pamphlet on behalf of the 'company of moniers at the mint' in answer to what he claimed were libels printed under the authorship of Peter Blondeau. Blondeau alleged that it was too easy to 'clip' gold and silver from the edges of coins, and proposed a new model for coinage which involved standardised sizes ("the pieces will bee of an equal bigness and largeness"), as well as "marking the coyn not onely on both the flat sides, but also upon the thickness or the edges."[52] As well as his charges of poor craftsmanship against the mint workers, and the accusation that the moneirs overcharge the state for gold and embezzle the difference, Blondeau alleges poor corporate governance, explaining that after the Council of the Mint had asked the Goldsmiths to

> Present their Proposition for coyning of the monie marked upon the thickness or edge, as that of the said *Blondeau* is; But after the exspiration of the long time demanded by them, they brought such a Proposition, that the said Committee having read it over and over, could not understand it, nor the sens of it; and even those that brought it could not explain it; whereby it was apparent to the said Committee, that they were not able to make their Proposition good, much less to coyn the mony after that way.[53]

Violet's rejoinder to Blondeau is clear in its belief in the importance of print to the making and unmaking of public opinion:

> This day came unto my hands a false and scandalous Libell put in print, against the Moniers and Officers in the Mint; Truly, if you value your good names, and to bee esteemed honest men, these Pamphlets must have a Replie: I am privie to all the transaction of this businesse, and know there are more lies then lines in his Libells.[54]

For Violet, a speedy response is the only way in which these libels can be countered, and he seeks to offer a correction the very day he sees these scurrilous texts, which might "undeceive all the good People that have seen or read the said *Peter Blondeau*'s false and scandalous Libells."[55] Violet's determination to get the truth – or at least a rebuttal of a public position – into print demonstrates a conception of a public sphere in which opinions can quickly solidify; if people are not swiftly 'undeceived' by the corporation, the allegations against it will be taken for facts. In this context, 'seen or read' is suggestive, too, evoking as it does a secondary public sphere in which not just active readers but also those in public spaces (the churchyard at Pauls, other concentrations of book-sellers, coffee houses and so on) who might simply observe the frontispiece of texts can be influenced by print.

Violet's pamphlet is laid out in something like chronological order, opening with his letter to John Benfield, clerk of the Corporation of Moniers, offering his services as an author, and the reply of the Corporation, asking him to "to vindicate our just Cause to the Common-wealth, against those scandalous lying pamphlets."[56]

The text also, though, reprints Blondeau's two libels, despite Violet's initial fears that they will quickly be "disperst into the hands of the ignorant multitude."[57] Violet is once more trusting to the active reader, presenting the libel so as to contest and discredit it, in the belief that they will not be taken in by it, but carefully weigh the evidence and reach the same conclusion as Violet himself, with the same confidence in the coiners at the mint.

Violet's text finishes with a direct answer from the 'company of moniers at the mint' to Blondeau's allegations. This short statement generally reaffirms what Violet has argued at greater length in the pamphlet, as well as reasserting the ways in which the corporation is regulated by the state with regards to both the quality of the metals used and the standardisation of the coins. It also reflects on the need to counter allegations made against the coinage, and to do so as a company:

> And before any determination of what the State would conclude on; *Peter Blondeau* a French man hath dispersed a false and scandalous Paper both at *Westminster* and at the Exchange in *London* and beyond Seas, in dishonor of the monies of the Nation; and charging the Officers and Moniers of the Mint with making monie contrary to their Indenture; a charge so false and scandalous, that hath inforced

> us the Provost and Moniers to reprint the said *Blondeau*'s Paper, and to give a short answer to the untruths and absurdities in it: And we humbly submit what we say to all Artists and knowing men in Mint businesse, whether the French man hath not declared in his printed Paper a great many untruths, with a great deal of impudence and ignorance. And we most humbly desire what we here say, to have the truth of it examined by the right Honorable the Committee for the Mint, and that their Honours would be pleased to give us such reparation as shall be by their great wisdomes thought fit.[58]

The pamphlet once more turns to the question of timing, this time suggesting that Blondeau's works are especially unfair since they are into print before any official decision or sanction can be made; the company of moniers argues that, by deliberately dispersing his paper at Westminster and the Exchange, Blondeau is seeking to use print to bypass traditional modes of authority and pressure those in government and commerce. Consequently, they must answer him as a company in print ('us'), and appeal to those 'knowing men' who understand their trade. In this way, the corporation seeks to influence the public sphere not only through their own participation, but in creating a specific type of audience.

Although the moniers at the mint were goldsmiths, the Goldsmiths' Company itself seems to have paid little attention to the allegations of Blondeau; neither his publications, nor those rebutting them, are discussed in the court minute books of the company. The Goldsmiths' Company did discuss a petition to Parliament in late 1652 against the present government of the company:

> After the reading of which order and petition and a mature debate concerning the same it was thought fit agreed and so ordered that a committee consisting of a certain number of wardens and assistants should be appointed by this court to prepare an answer to the said petition.[59]

The subcommittee quickly came up with a draft answer:

> At this court was read the draft of the petition prepared to be presented to the Parliament with the preamble thereof relating to the great trust reposed in the company by the state and then the rest of the petition in order to the better regulating the affairs of this company.[60]

Although the stress on trust and regulation does perhaps nod to the printed allegations of Blondeau, it is also a broad enough concern that it may well be unrelated, especially since the Blondaeu-Violet debate does not seem to enter into the consciousness of the Goldsmith's Court.

Nevertheless, the question of trust in public institutions, and corporations which touched on those institutions (such as coinage), was clearly a contentious one, and one which is examined in more detail in the next chapter.

Forts, investments and ontology

The final section of this chapter returns to the multinational companies and their detractors during the debates of the 1680s and '90s. As we have seen, by this time corporate discourse was well established, to the point of becoming rather cliched and repetitive. Nevertheless, tracing the use of a particular idea (in this case, the value of fortifications) can tell us much about the way in which corporations figured in the public imagination, and how they sought to manipulate opinion with small twists on old concepts or tropes.

By the end of the century, companies were increasingly shifting to a model of territorial holdings enclosed, or secured, by a fortification; this, they believed, offered stability for their traders and a check on the ambitions of local rulers and European rivals alike. However, what a 'fort' was differed from place to place, as did the potential effectiveness of fortification. For this reason, opponents of the companies were able to argue that not only were forts unnecessary in theory (emphasising contractual or treaty agreements with local rulers) but also they were impractical and indefensible.

The issue of forts, and the concomitant investments they necessitated and security that they provided, went beyond financial claims and counterclaims. In a sense, the debate over forts became something of an ontological or existential question for the corporations and their opponents. It was through forts and other real estate that the company itself became real, moving beyond its position as a convenient legal fiction to an actor in international trade in its own right. That is, by emphasising the nature and value of its holdings overseas, the corporation also emphasised that it was more than the vehicle for collective bargaining which had been, in its opponent's eyes, corrupted into a monopoly. As the strategies of overseas trading corporations gradually became entrenched over the course of the century, the debate turned from the export of bullion (and, by proxy, the need for a trade in 'luxuries' at all) to the best way to carry out global trade, and whether a company was even necessary.

Activities of fortification, land management and jurisdictional expansion were, as Stern has pointed out, important signposts on the road from trading company to state-like political actor, with the fort often integrated into urban planning in ways designed to increase the authority of the Company, and demonstrate its sovereignty.[61] Forts provided a physical anchor to company valuation, which would otherwise rely on estimations based on abstract activities such as the right to tax collection, or the value of import and export, as had been the case in the 1620s, with Thomas Mun's famously generous calculation of the East India trade being worth "the somme of 394223. l. 06. s. 08. d. advanced towards the general stock of the Kingdome."[62] By the 1690s the question of the real value of the Company became pressing, with moves to establish a new company, and ultimately, a commission established to unite the two stocks, requiring a real value be placed on the old company so as to compensate the shareholders. Capital investment in forts and other infrastructure ("Possessions, as Forts, Factories, Buildings, and Lands of Inheritance") was one of three key strands for valuing the 'dead stock' in India, the others being treaties with the Mughals and other local rulers, and revenue grants such as ground rent and other tax income, valued at around £40,000 per annum. The dead stock was valued by the old company at £350,000 in total, but the new company complained that they had not been given enough detail, but rather a paper containing only "The Names of several Forts, Castles, and Factories, with the Places where they are situated," and so "This Committee are not thereby enabled to Judge of their Value, for such Generals cannot be thought sufficient, on which to Purchase any Estate, much less an Estate at such a distance, and for which so great a Sum as 350000 *l.* is demanded."[63]

The corporate rhetoric envisaged fortifications after the Dutch model, able to command the countryside around them and produce awe and loyalty (or at least fidelity) in the natives of those countries in which they built:

> The said *Company* since their Incorporation have Erected Forts, Setled several Factories, Built Ships, Imployed many Seamen, and considerably Exported the Manufacturies of this Nation; and in the course of their Trade for so many Years, have not only actually lost Thirteen Ships, but been at above Two Hundred Thousand Pounds Charge: Which makes it evident that nothing but a *Company* and a *Joynt Stock* could have laid the Foundation of so considerable a Trade [. . .] it being impracticable to raise any considerable Trade in a remote Country, amongst Savage *Indians*, without Forts and Factories erected and setled amongst them.[64]

Opponents of the company tended to denigrate the forts. Naturally, though, these individual opponents did not have a unified strategy: Generally, these free traders sought to describe the forts as either not forts at all, or nevertheless ineffective against local forces, but they also questioned the need for forts, as well as the impact they had on corporate policy.

One anonymous pamphlet, probably an answer to the *Case of the Hudson's Bay Company* (or another like it; both are undated, but the *Impartial Account* does address the fairly generic issues raised in the *Case*), attempted to undermine the image of strong fortifications put about by the company, and inherent in the word 'fort':

> Those Forts pretended to be built by the *Hudson-Bay Company*, are no better than *Pig-Sties*, in *England*, nor of greater Strength; being a few *Pine-Trees*, squared and laid one upon another, and ramm'd only with *Moss*, to keep out the Wind.[65]

Indeed, the attack on the company turns on the naming of the structure, changing the name from 'fort' to pig-sty, as well as changing the geographical location from Hudson's Bay back to England; this double-pronged attack destabilises the company's particular claims for territorial governance and efficient global trading systems, rooting them instead in the parochial concerns of domestic pig farming. This is reinforced by the further detail of the fort/sty, which, by being 'rammed with moss' is poorly built and temporary (against the company's claim to permanence), and can only keep out the 'wind', not an attacking army. These structures could not provoke awe or loyalty in the native peoples, and consequently would protect neither the company's servants nor its trade.

Some opponents produced the parallel – yet slightly contradictory – argument that whether the forts worked or not was immaterial, since the best defence was a good trade which local rulers would wish to protect:

> The Turkey Trade is prosperously carried on by a regulated Company, without a Joint-stock or Forts. And nothing hinders but that the African Trade might be carried on in like manner. Nay we Trade safely even with the Pirates of Algier, Tripoli, and Tunis, who are the worst of Infidels. There is no Nation so Wicked, so Wild, and Barbarous; but that they will well-come and protect fair Traders that come to them; it being for their own benefit.[66]

The Levant trade was frequently the model for this sort of 'fort-free' trade, although trade to the Low Countries, Spain and France also featured prominently. Critics of the companies' policy on fortification relied on these precedents to proclaim a mutual self-interest in free, or at most, lightly regulated, trade. Such a position was intended to question the need for a company by undermining the need for fortification, and with it the joint stock which maintained the fort, and the monopoly.

Corporate writers reminded these critics that the areas in which trading took place were not as settled as the European states, and forts minimised the risks for traders and their goods from both local rulers and other European powers:

> Those Parts are divided into several Petty-Kingdoms, generally at War amongst themselves, and with whom no security can be had,

> but what Force maintains: And should we not have Forts and Castles to defend our Effects that lye there for a Market, and such as we buy, and lye ready for our Ships, they would be seized by the very Natives themselves, or by some Europeans with whom we may have War, and who have Forts and Castles upon those Coasts.[67]

By emphasising the diplomatic reality of the African coast, the writer is making an implicit claim for corporate experience of something quite unlike the context of intra-European trade. The management of the trade to Africa cannot be analogous to that of Spain, or even the Levant, since there is no large empire to negotiate treaties with, but rather a shifting set of small states which the RAC has learnt how to deal with. The writer also imagines something akin to an arms race among Europeans to build up fortifications in the area, and argues that, if the English forts are left unmaintained or abandoned, other European powers will take them over, "then the Trade, with our Forts and Castles, will be either lost to us, or carried on as Tributaries to those *Europeans* into whose hands those Defenses shall fall."[68] As European rivalries carried onto African soil, forts became important nodes in a global trading network imagined as being balanced across European states (and their proxy companies).

Still other writers implicitly recognised the power of fortification, but they attacked the building of forts as a distortion of company strategy. It led, they argued, to an increasingly militaristic stance which was incompatible with its goals as a trading collective:

> Forts or castles in India, if we have them, cannot defend us in case the Dutch, or French, or Indians be our enemies; but may tempt us (as it did the New Company) to offend them, or create a jealousie in the India princes of us, and by that means tempt them to offend us.[69]

Many of the pamphlets in the 1690s used the disastrous war against the Mughal Empire launched by the East India Company in 1686–89 as evidence of corporate overreach, and the failure of the joint stock to provide the stability in trade and diplomacy which it claimed as a key benefit over separate traders. In fact, as Emily Erikson has pointed out, the EIC "used their fortifications to defend existing settlements – not to engage in aggressive acts."[70] Hall was, perhaps, accurate in the sense that the war was born of a desire to confirm the "Company rights and authority and obtain independent, garrisoned colonies from which those rights could be protected," especially in Bengal and Siam.[71] That is, forts, however indefensible against other major powers, were in fact important symbols, markers of company jurisdiction more powerful as legal fictions than military positions.

The debate over the forts in the 1690s was in fact a reprisal of aspects of the *Sutton Hospital* case, in which Bacon argued that the corporation was "a purely imaginary body politic," while Coke rebutted that "this same immaterial and artificial person corresponds to a substantial, actually existing thing possessed of property."[72] The corporations of the 1690s, especially the EIC, adopted Coke's argument, while their opponents updated Bacon's, attempting to undermine corporate claims to property, and in so doing undermine any factual existence which could not be replicated by any other form of association, however loose.

Many of the questions over the forts turn on this very principle of real value – what manner of thing is the fort in reality? What value is derived from their presence? – and these questions occasionally collapsed into each other:

> The company thus possest of these Inchanted Castles, and believing themselves thereby invincible against all the world besides, make war with the great Mogull and King of Syam.[73]

Just as with Hall, this anonymous author argues that the corporate policy of fort-building leads to warfare. However, unlike Hall, who sees forts as indefensibly weak, yet nevertheless a destabilising influence on the geopolitics of the subcontinent, this author suggests that it is a misunderstanding of the very nature of forts which tempts the company into a martial policy. Roger Coke wrote a reply to the anonymous pamphlet, stressing the relation between the security of the fort, the trade and the state's interest in the trade: "These Customs ought to be imployed in Building Forts in proper places for securing the *English* Traffick in those Seas: And that when these Moneys are not so Imployed, they are due to the King."[74] Coke does not engage with the suggestion that the company sees forts as 'invincible' or 'enchanted', which is surely a tongue-in-cheek response to the corporate rhetoric on the necessity of fortifications, and their ability to hold powerful rulers in check, that we have already seen. But it also points to a more fundamental question, as this issue played out in the domestic public sphere: What was the nature of a fort, and how could that be fairly assessed at such a remove?

An anonymous pamphlet two years later, in 1693, brought together all of these arguments, demonstrating the way in which they had become well-established rhetorical positions:

> Forts and Castles are none at all, in Case the *Great Mogul* or other Princes in *India* will at any time Offend us. And for others (the *French* and *Dutch*, &c. if they be our Enemies) they cannot hurt us in any Port of the *Indies*, because there the Government, *&c.* will Protect us: And if they meet us at Sea, our Forts and Castles (if we have them) cannot defend us. So that Forts in *India* are, at best, no better to us in point of Security or Defence against Enemies, than Castles in the Air; but may do us much Hurt, for that they are likely

> to create a Jealousy of us in the *Great Mogul*, and other Princes of *India*, &c. and tempt us (as it did the New Company) to Contests, which will be fatal to us.[75]

Here, the 'inchanted' castles have become 'castles in the air', although the same point applies – they are somehow fantastic, belonging more properly to the realm of fiction than to reality. As well as combining standard political arguments on the forts, the pamphlet thus reveals the interplay between corporate debates and the evolution of political language more generally. Consequently, it reveals the integration between political economic and literary trains of thought, which early modern writers did not keep as separately as we might today.

Other writers developed the idea of fancy along the lines of 'speculation' or 'expectation', such as Richard Curteys, familiar with corporate structures thanks to his career as Bishop of Chichester and as a proctor of St John's, Cambridge. In a sermon preached before Elizabeth I, he warned of the dangers of theological or political speculation:

> Wée buylde Castles and toures in the ayre to get vs a name. So many heads, so many wittes, so many common wealthes. Plato his *Idaea*, Aristotles felicitie, and Pythagoras numbers, trouble most mens brayns. Wishers and woulders were neuer good housholders, deuisers and phansiers were neuer good Common wealthes menne.[76]

Curteys had something of a reputation as a scourge of unorthodoxy, so his opinion on political speculation is to be expected. Here again, though, the castle in the air has become linked with ideas of good or bad government, with Curteys insisting that those who are too imaginative cannot be valuable contributors to either the household or the commonwealth.

John Lightfoot, in his quasi-history of the bible which included a rebellion among apprentices, picked up the theme of the castle in the air as expectations and experimentation:

> They therefore getting away all the Armes their masters house would afford, betake themselves to a strong place in an Iland of *Euphrates*, and there publish and proclaime their rebellious resolution. Young men flocke in to them apace, men of the same desperate minds and fortunes, and after building some Castles in the ayre of future expectations, they begin to build a Fort in the Ile for their present securitie and rendevouz.[77]

Although Lightfoot retains the idea of the 'castles in the air' as speculative, the contrast with the 'real' fort is instructive. Having imagined the potential gains from their newly conquered island, the apprentices draw in like-minded fellows in order to turn the castle of the air into a fort on the ground – the parallels with early modern corporations and their buildings overseas are pretty clear.

In a sense, such terminology was almost inevitable, since 'castles in the air' was a commonplace early modern term for fancy or nonsense. Sir Philip Sidney, an influential poet, courtier, MP and adventurer overseas (first as a diplomat and then a soldier), used the term in his *Defence of Poesy*:

> And that the Poet hath that *Idea*, is manifest, by deliuering them forth in such excellencie as hee hath imagined them. VVhich deliuering forth also, is not wholie imaginatiue, as we are wont to say by them that build Castles in the ayre: but so farre substantially it worketh, not onely to make a *Cyrus*, which had been but a particuler excellencie, as Nature might haue done, but to bestow a *Cyrus* vpon the worlde, to make many *Cyrus's*, if they wil learne aright, why, and how that Maker made him.[78]

Sidney actually makes a distinction here between 'fancy' or imagination – a wholly abstract realm of the castles in the air – and poetry, which has the power, at least on some level, to reify that imagination. It does so because it transmits a version of the idea directly to its reader, making 'many Cyrus's' among its audience. In a sense, this question of making an imaginary form real is the same question which underlies the rhetoric on forts: Are the forts what they are imagined to be? And are the companies which make both forts and rhetoric themselves stable ideas?

The diarist John Evelyn wrote a pamphlet in 1667 (a decade in which he published a series of works concerned with what we might term the 'public good', including discourses on art and architecture, as well as a policy to reduce the smog in London by planting trees), arguing for a concerted engagement with public life. The work was a response to an essay of 1665 by George Mackenzie, a Scottish lawyer (later Lord Advocate), *A Moral Essay Upon Solitude*, which argued that contemplative retirement was the ultimate goal in life. Mackenzie's essay relies on the power of the imagination, best cultivated by a life away from pursuits of glory and fame in public service and spent instead in thoughtful solitude:

> That faculty [imagination] can mould *idea's* of thousands of species never yet created, that can bring forth moe monsters then *Africk*, and can produce moe novelties then *America:* and as we cannot but admire these productions, for their variety; So we cannot but love them, because they are our own. And thus, seing there can be no pleasure in that variety which is to be decerned in the world, but what our fancy takes, (for, what else is there in beholding real Castles, Navies, Courts or Cities, but a divertising of our fan|cies? for

> nature needs none of those) certainly, retirement hath in this the start of it's rival: for there, fancy is at fuller freedom.[79]

Part of Evelyn's work was given over to a defence of those who did not appear to be 'active' in the physical sense, such as architects or counsellors, and yet were an 'active' part of the commonwealth because their professions were intended to improve the general quality of life. Evelyn generally excoriates those who retire to idleness, and warns of a number of vices, including idle fancies:

> Ease and Solitude presents us with some pleasures that are not altogether so fit for our recreation, and as little suitable to our reason and stoical indifferency; nor seldom less dangerous and ridiculous in their objects than the most Publick Employment: For I find that one of the chief Prerogatives of our happyman (and whom by a contradiction to his Argument, he thinks ill defin'd by being tearm'd a little World) is by the advantage of his recess to mould Idëas of a thousand Species, never yet in being; and to use his own expression, produce more Monsters than Africa it self, more Novelties than America; to fancy Building, Navies, Courts, Cities, and Castles in the Air.[80]

This sort of imaginative retirement is contrasted in Evelyn's work to those whose practice it is to work with ideas (such as philosophers, poets and historians), because they turn their ideas to the public good.

Evelyn's addition of 'in the air' to the castles is designed to emphasise the ridiculousness of Mackenzie's position, which Evelyn argues undermines both philosophy and business interests. Evelyn is not apparently concerned that these 'novelties' and monsters will be harmful to the commonwealth; the issue is one of productivity. Nonetheless, the choice of language is revealing. Evelyn links the fanciful imaginative realm with Africa and America – following a tradition of seeing those places as strange or unusual, which will be explored further in Chapter 5, covering epic poetry – and adds navies and cities to the traditional castles in the air.

Evelyn is concerned with 'business' throughout, and closes his essay by returning to the theme of colonisation: "There a *Colony* planting an *Island*, and a barbarous and *solitary Nation* reduc'd to *Civility; Cities, Houses, Forts, Ships building* for *Society, shelter, defence*, and *Commerce*."[81] In 1651, Evelyn had moved to his wife's property at Sayes Court, an estate bordering the Deptford dockyard, which was significantly expanded during the time in which Evelyn lived nearby, allowing him a close view of the ships for defence and commerce which were produced there.

Indeed, for the companies, their ships, too, were a sort of 'castle in the air', or rather 'floating castles'. In a sermon preached before the

"Honorable Society of the East-Country Merchants resident in *England, Dantzick, Koningsberg*, and elsewhere," William Johnson spoke of the dashed expectations of those stranded at sea:

> But having spent all that day, with sore eyes, in expectation of an imaginary deliverance, in looking for a ship (or rather castle in the air) and seeing nothing come toward us, we began to despair.[82]

Johnson's audience well understood the perils of sea travel, and the imaginative power of a ship, both as a real artefact and in the metaphorical sense. The imagery of the ship was often combined with an image of government, as was the case for Nathaniel Johnson, discussing the importance of good kingship to the nation in 1686:

> All the World indeed must acknowledg we have a Royal, wise Pilot, who knows full well to steer the Soveraignty of the Commonweal. He hath weathered out high going Seas; so that neither their overwhelming liquid Mountains, nor the terrible Shot from the floating Castles have daunted him; magnanimity, unparallel'd Courage, and an Experience beyond most Crowned Heads, have raised him great Trophies of his Victorious toils: He is served with sage Councils, both private and National. So that all must confess we have less cause to fear any more dangers of Hurricanes and Shipwracks.[83]

Johnson fuses the corporate language on castles discussed here with Plato's idea of the ship of state (although reversed so that the pilot is trusted and revered). Here, the king is an experienced adventurer, not afraid of the perils of the seas – which, through the use of metaphors such as mountainous waves and floating castles, is extended into mastery of the land as well. The corporate ideas of ships, and the extension of sovereignty from their own floating castles to the land their castles occupied and overlooked, thus underpin ideas of government and political language.

Through the seventeenth century, trading companies began to negotiate just what right they had to speak in public, in what manner that was best undertaken, legally, politically and in the court of public opinion. In doing so, they brought corporate ideology directly into the public consciousness; directly and indirectly, literary and cultural productions were permeated with corporate ideas such as the circulation of bullion, the rights of the collective or the need for investment and state protection. The public were also frequently reminded of the risks of overseas trade, and thus the rewards which should be offered to traders who undertook dangerous voyages and withstood difficult conditions in the national interest. As the rest of this monograph demonstrates, such conceptual overlapping travelled in both directions as far as the corporation was concerned: Ideas generated within corporate discourse rippled out in society, and broader developments in political and social ideology were in turn refracted in that very corporate discourse.

Acknowledgements

A section of Chapter 1 originally appeared as "Blanching the Corporate Blush: Corporate Language in the Seventeenth Century Public Sphere" in the *Journal for Early Modern Cultural Studies* 18.4 (Fall 2018). I thank the University of Pennsylvania Press for permission to reprint that material here.

Notes

1 Jason Peacey, "Cromwellian England: A Propaganda State?" *History* 91, no. 302 (2006): 179.
2 William Ball, *A Briefe Treatise Concerning the Regulating of Printing Humbly Presented to the Parliament of England* (London: s.n., 1651), 24.
3 *A Briefe Treatise Concerning the Regulating of Printing Humbly Presented to the Parliament of England*, 4.
4 *A Briefe Treatise Concerning the Regulating of Printing Humbly Presented to the Parliament of England*, 7.
5 Anon, *The Objections of the Levant Company Answered* (London: s.n., 1650), 5.
6 See Barbara J. Shapiro, *Political Communication and Political Culture in England, 1558–1688* (Stanford, CA: Stanford University Press, 2012).
7 Peter Lake and Steven Pincus, "Rethinking the Public Sphere in Early Modern England," in *The Politics of the Public Sphere in Early Modern England*, edited by Peter Lake and Steven C. A. Pincus (Manchester: Manchester University Press, 2007), 3.
8 Martine van Elk, *Early Modern Women's Writing: Domesticity, Privacy, and the Public Sphere in England and the Dutch Republic* (Basingstoke: Palgrave Macmillan, 2017), 7.
9 Jurgen Habermas, *The Structural Transformation of the Public Sphere*, trans. Thomas Burger (Cambridge: MIT Press, 1989), 57.
10 Alexandra Halasz, *The Marketplace of Print: Pamphlets and the Public Sphere in Early Modern England* (Cambridge: Cambridge University Press, 1997), 163.
11 Habermas, *The Structural Transformation of the Public Sphere*, 22–3.
12 Levant Company charter of 43 Elizabeth [1601–2], in Cecil Thomas Carr, ed. *Select Charters of Trading Companies, 1530–1707* (London: Selden Society, 1913), 32.
13 BL IOR B/12 7th March 1628.
14 BL IOR B/12 12th March 1628.
15 David Colclough, *Freedom of Speech in Early Stuart England* (Cambridge: Cambridge University Press, 2005), 175 citing *CSPD* 1621 II.365.
16 Miles Ogborn, *Indian Ink: Script and Print in the Making of the East India Company* (Chicago: University of Chicago Press, 2007), 105.
17 BL IOR B/5, 16th February 1615.
18 For the detailed story of the attempted suppression of Kayll's pamphlet, and the attempts to punish the author directly through state apparatuses, see Ogborn, *Indian Ink*, 114–6.
19 Thomas Baker, *The Head of Nile, or, the Turnings and Windings of the Factious since Sixty in a Dialogue between Whigg and Barnaby*. (London: Walter Davis, 1681), 24.

20 William A. Pettigrew, *Freedom's Debt : The Royal African Company and the Politics of the Atlantic Slave Trade, 1672–1752* (Williamsburg, VA: University of North Carolina Press, 2013), 1–2.
21 William Wilkinson, *An Answer to the Book Written by the Guiney Company in Their Own Defence, for the Management of Their Trade in Africa* (London?: s.n., 1690), 1.
22 East India Company, *A Reply on Behalf of the Present East-India Company, to a Paper of Complaints, Commonly Called, the Thirteen Articles Delivered by Their Adversaries, to the Members of the Honourable House of Commons.* (London?: s.n., 1698), 2–3.
23 Anon, *An Answer to a Late Tract, Entituled, an Essay on the East-India Trade* (London: Thomas Cockerill, 1697), 7.
24 Marcus Nevitt, "Books in the News in Cromwellian England," *Media History* (2017): 10.
25 BL IOR B/8, 16th June, 1624.
26 BL IOR B/9, 2nd July 1624.
27 BL IOR B/9, 6th October 1624.
28 BL IOR B/9, 8th October 1624.
29 Anthony Milton, "Marketing a Massacre: Amboyna, the East India Company and the Public Sphere in Early Stuart England," in *The Politics of the Public Sphere in Early Modern England*, ed. Peter Lake and Steven C. A. Pincus (Manchester: Manchester University Press, 2007), 169. See also Edmond J Smith, "Reporting and Interpreting Legal Violence in Asia: The East India Company's Printed Accounts of Torture, 1603–24," *The Journal of Imperial and Commonwealth History*, early access (2018): 15–17.
30 BL IOR B/12, 20th July 1627.
31 BL IOR B/12, 20th July 1627.
32 Milton, "Marketing a Massacre: Amboyna, the East India Company and the Public Sphere in Early Stuart England," 181.
33 VOC, *Remonstrance of the Bewinthebbers or Directors of the Netherlands East India Company* (London?: n.p., 1624), sig. A3v.
34 BL IOR B/12, 20th July 1627.
35 BL IOR B/12, 5th September 1627.
36 BL IOR B/12, 5th September 1627.
37 BL IOR B/12, 19th November 1627.
38 BL IOR B/12, 18th April 1628.
39 BL IOR B/12, 18th April 1628.
40 BL IOR B/12, 21st April 1628.
41 BL IOR B/12, 21st April 1628.
42 BL IOR B/12, 21st April 1628.
43 BL IOR B/12, 25th April 1628.
44 BL IOR B/12, 5th May 1628.
45 BL IOR B/12 30th May 1628.
46 Robert Brenner, *Merchants and Revolution: Commercial Change, Political Conflict, and London's Overseas Traders, 1550–1653* (London: Verso, 2003), 64.
47 Thomas Violet, *A Copy of His Maiestys Most Gracious Letter to the Lord Major and Aldermen of His City of London* (London: s.n., 1647).
48 *A Copy of His Maiestys Most Gracious Letter to the Lord Major and Aldermen of His City of London.*
49 Anon, *The Clothiers Petition to His Majestie* (London: Peter Cole, 1642), 1.
50 *To the Right Honourable the Knights, Citizens and Burgesses in Parliament Assembled* (London: Peter Cole and John Sweeting, 1643), 1.
51 Richard Challenor, *Mr. Challenor His Confession and Speech* (London: Peter Cole, 1643), 6.

52 Peter Blondeau, *A Most Humble Memorandum from Peter Blondeau, Concerning the Offers Made to Him by This Commonwealth, for the Coining of the Money, by a New Invention* (London: s.n., 1653), Sig. A3r.
53 *A Most Humble Memorandum from Peter Blondeau, Concerning the Offers Made to Him by This Commonwealth, for the Coining of the Money, by a New Invention*, Sig. A7r-v.
54 Thomas Violet, *The Answer of the Corporation of Moniers in the Mint, at the Tower of London, to Two False and Scandalous Libells Printed at London, and Lately Come Forth without Date.* (London: Corporation of Moniers, 1653), 1.
55 *Answer of the Corporation of Moniers*, frontis.
56 *Answer of the Corporation of Moniers*, 3.
57 *Answer of the Corporation of Moniers*, 2.
58 *Answer of the Corporation of Moniers*, 24–5.
59 Goldsmiths Library, Court Minute Book 1651–54, 15th December 1652.
60 Goldsmiths Library, Court Minute Book 1651–54, 3rd January 1653.
61 Philip J. Stern, *The Company-State: Corporate Sovereignty & the Early Modern Foundations of the British Empire in India* (Oxford: Oxford University Press, 2011), 30–1.
62 Thomas Mun, *A Discourse of Trade, from England Unto the East-Indies Answering to Diuerse Objections Which Are Usually Made against the Same* (London: John Piper, 1621), 24–5.
63 Anon, *An Account of What Has Passed in the Treaty between the Old and New East-India Companies Towards an Agreement* (London?: s.n., 1699), 2–4.
64 *The Case of the Hudsons-Bay-Company* (London: s.n., 1690?), 1.
65 *An Impartial Account of the Present State of the Hudson-Bay Company* (London?: s.n.?, 1690?), 1.
66 *Considerations Concerning the African-Companies Petition* (London: s.n., 1696), 1.
67 *Considerations Relating to the African Bill Humbly Submitted to the Honourable House of Commons* (London: s.n., 1698), 1.
68 *Considerations Relating to the African Bill Humbly Submitted to the Honourable House of Commons*, 2.
69 Joseph Hall, *A Modest Offer of Some Meet Considerations, Tendered to the English About Their Coin and Trade, and Particularly to East India* (London: s.n., 1695), 2.
70 Emily Erikson, *Between Monopoly and Free Trade : The English East India Company, 1600–1757* (Princeton, NJ: Princeton University Pres, 2014), 12.
71 Stern, *The Company-State: Corporate Sovereignty & the Early Modern Foundations of the British Empire in India*, 122.
72 Henry S. Turner, *The Corporate Commonwealth: Pluralism and Political Fictions in England 1516–1651* (Chicago: University of Chicago Press, 2016), 17.
73 Anon, *An Apology for the English Nation* (London: s.n., 1691), 2.
74 Roger Coke, *A Reply to an Answer from a Friend, to the Apology for the English Nation, That the Trade to the East-Indies and Africa Should Be Free* (London: s.n., 1692), 7.
75 Anon, *Reasons Humbly Offered against Establishing, by Act of Parliament, the East-India-Trade, in a Company, with a Joint-Stock* (London: s.n., 1693), Sig. A2r.
76 Richard Curteys, *A Sermon Preached before the Queenes Majesty, by the Reverend Father in God the Bishop of Chichester, at Greenwich, the 14 Day of March 1573* (London: Henry Binneman, for Francis Coldocke, 1573), Sig. C4r-v.

77 John Lightfoot, *A Commentary Upon the Acts of the Apostles, Chronical and Critical, the Difficulties of the Text Explained, and the Times of the Story Cast into Annals* (London: R. C. for Andrew Crooke, 1645), 300.
78 Philip Sidney, *The Defence of Poesie* (London: William Ponsonby, 1595), Sig. C1r.
79 George Mackenzie, *A Moral Essay, Preferring Solitude to Public Employment* (Edinburgh: Robert Brown, 1665), 78.
80 John Evelyn, *Public Employment and an Active Life Preferred to Solitude and All Its Appendages* (London: I. M. for H. Herringman, 1667), 98–9.
81 *Public Employment and an Active Life Preferred to Solitude and All Its Appendages*, 116.
82 William Johnson, *Deus Nobiscum a Sermon Preached Upon a Great Deliverance at Sea* (London: John Crook, 1664), 102.
83 Nathaniel Johnson, *The Excellency of Monarchical Government, Especially of the English Monarchy* (London: T. B. for Robert Clavel, 1686), 338.

Works cited

Manuscript

BL IOR B/5
BL IOR B/8
BL IOR B/9
BL IOR B/12
Goldsmiths Library, Court Minute Book 1651–54

Print

Anon. *The Clothiers Petition to His Majestie*. London: Peter Cole, 1642.
———. *To the Right Honourable the Knights, Citizens and Burgesses in Parliament Assembled*. London: Peter Cole and John Sweeting, 1643.
———. *The Objections of the Levant Company Answered*. London: s.n., 1650.
———. *The Case of the Hudsons-Bay-Company*. London: s.n., 1690?.
———. *An Impartial Account of the Present State of the Hudson-Bay Company*. London?: s.n.?, 1690?.
———. *An Apology for the English Nation*. London: s.n., 1691.
———. *Reasons Humbly Offered against Establishing, by Act of Parliament, the East-India-Trade, in a Company, with a Joint-Stock*. London: s.n., 1693.
———. *Considerations Concerning the African-Companies Petition*. London: s.n., 1696.
———. *An Answer to a Late Tract, Entituled, an Essay on the East-India Trade*. London: Thomas Cockerill, 1697.
———. *Considerations Relating to the African Bill Humbly Submitted to the Honourable House of Commons*. London: s.n., 1698.
———. *An Account of What Has Passed in the Treaty between the Old and New East-India Companies Towards an Agreement*. London?: s.n., 1699.
Baker, Thomas. *The Head of Nile, or, the Turnings and Windings of the Factious since Sixty in a Dialogue between Whigg and Barnaby*. London: Walter Davis, 1681.

Ball, William. *A Briefe Treatise Concerning the Regulating of Printing Humbly Presented to the Parliament of England*. London: s.n., 1651.

Blondeau, Peter. *A Most Humble Memorandum from Peter Blondeau, Concerning the Offers Made to Him by This Commonwealth, for the Coining of the Money, by a New Invention*. London: s.n., 1653.

Brenner, Robert. *Merchants and Revolution: Commercial Change, Political Conflict, and London's Overseas Traders, 1550–1653*. London: Verso, 2003. 1993.

Carr, Cecil Thomas, ed. *Select Charters of Trading Companies, 1530–1707*. London: Selden Society, 1913.

Challenor, Richard. *Mr. Challenor His Confession and Speech*. London: Peter Cole, 1643.

Coke, Roger. *A Reply to an Answer from a Friend, to the Apology for the English Nation, That the Trade to the East-Indies and Africa Should Be Free*. London: s.n., 1692.

Colclough, David. *Freedom of Speech in Early Stuart England*. Cambridge: Cambridge University Press, 2005.

Curteys, Richard. *A Sermon Preached before the Queenes Majesty, by the Reverend Father in God the Bishop of Chichester, at Greenwich, the 14 Day of March 1573*. London: Henry Binneman, for Francis Coldocke, 1573.

East India Company. *A Reply on Behalf of the Present East-India Company, to a Paper of Complaints, Commonly Called, the Thirteen Articles Delivered by Their Adversaries, to the Members of the Honourable House of Commons*. London?: s.n., 1698.

Erikson, Emily. *Between Monopoly and Free Trade : The English East India Company, 1600–1757*. Princeton, NJ: Princeton University Pres, 2014.

Evelyn, John. *Public Employment and an Active Life Preferred to Solitude and All Its Appendages*. London: I. M. for H. Herringman, 1667.

Habermas, Jurgen. *The Structural Transformation of the Public Sphere*. Translated by Thomas Burger. Cambridge: MIT Press, 1989.

Halasz, Alexandra. *The Marketplace of Print: Pamphlets and the Public Sphere in Early Modern England*. Cambridge: Cambridge University Press, 1997.

Hall, Joseph. *A Modest Offer of Some Meet Considerations, Tendered to the English About Their Coin and Trade, and Particularly to East India*. London: s.n., 1695.

Johnson, Nathaniel. *The Excellency of Monarchical Government, Especially of the English Monarchy*. London: T. B. for Robert Clavel, 1686.

Johnson, William. *Deus Nobiscum a Sermon Preached Upon a Great Deliverance at Sea*. London: John Crook, 1664.

Lake, Peter and Steven Pincus. "Rethinking the Public Sphere in Early Modern England." In *The Politics of the Public Sphere in Early Modern England*, edited by Peter Lake and Steven C. A. Pincus, 1-30. Manchester: Manchester University Press, 2007.

Lightfoot, John. *A Commentary Upon the Acts of the Apostles, Chronical and Critical, the Difficulties of the Text Explained, and the Times of the Story Cast into Annals*. London: R. C. for Andrew Crooke, 1645.

Mackenzie, George. *A Moral Essay, Preferring Solitude to Public Employment*. Edinburgh: Robert Brown, 1665.

Milton, Anthony. "Marketing a Massacre: Amboyna, the East India Company and the Public Sphere in Early Stuart England." In *The Politics of the Public Sphere in Early Modern England*, edited by Peter Lake and Steven C. A. Pincus, 168–90. Manchester: Manchester University Press, 2007.

Mun, Thomas. *A Discourse of Trade, from England Unto the East-Indies Answering to Diuerse Objections Which Are Usually Made against the Same.* London: John Piper, 1621.

Nevitt, Marcus. "Books in the News in Cromwellian England." *Media History* (2017): 1–23.

Ogborn, Miles. *Indian Ink: Script and Print in the Making of the East India Company.* Chicago: University of Chicago Press, 2007.

Peacey, Jason. "Cromwellian England: A Propaganda State?" *History* 91, no. 302 (2006): 176–99.

Pettigrew, William A. *Freedom's Debt : The Royal African Company and the Politics of the Atlantic Slave Trade, 1672–1752.* Williamsburg, VA: University of North Carolina Press, 2013.

Shapiro, Barbara J. *Political Communication and Political Culture in England, 1558–1688.* Stanford, CA: Stanford University Press, 2012.

Sidney, Philip. *The Defence of Poesie.* London: William Ponsonby, 1595.

Smith, Edmond J. "Reporting and Interpreting Legal Violence in Asia: The East India Company's Printed Accounts of Torture, 1603–24." *The Journal of Imperial and Commonwealth History*, early access (2018): 1–24.

Smith, John. *The Generall Historie of Virginia.* London: I.D. and I.H. for Michael Sparkes, 1624.

Stern, Philip J. *The Company-State: Corporate Sovereignty & the Early Modern Foundations of the British Empire in India.* Oxford: Oxford University Press, 2011.

Turner, Henry S. *The Corporate Commonwealth: Pluralism and Political Fictions in England 1516–1651.* Chicago: University of Chicago Press, 2016.

van Elk, Martine. *Early Modern Women's Writing: Domesticity, Privacy, and the Public Sphere in England and the Dutch Republic.* Basingstoke: Palgrave Macmillan, 2017.

Violet, Thomas. *A Copy of His Maiestys Most Gracious Letter to the Lord Major and Aldermen of His City of London.* London: s.n., 1647.

———. *The Answer of the Corporation of Moniers in the Mint, at the Tower of London, to Two False and Scandalous Libells Printed at London, and Lately Come Forth without Date.* London: Corporation of Moniers, 1653.

VOC. *Remonstrance of the Bewinthebbers or Directors of the Netherlands East India Company.* London?: n.p., 1624.

Wilkinson, William. *An Answer to the Book Written by the Guiney Company in Their Own Defence, for the Management of Their Trade in Africa.* London?: s.n., 1690.

2 Trusting the corporation

At the heart of the early modern corporation's engagement with the public, and much of its private workings, was the issue of trust. Members needed to trust one another, and relied on the corporation to provide a framework to enable that trust, whether by establishing modes of behaviour, regulating credit and stock, or providing a forum for the resolution of disputes. The state, too, needed to trust that the corporation was behaving in accordance with its charter. Discussions of these matters tended to take place in private, although they did sometimes find their way into the press. Conversely, the question of the corporation's trustworthiness was of public interest to those who might invest in shares, since they needed to trust the corporation to manage their investment wisely, continue producing profits and ensure a level playing field among investors for the purchase of goods and distribution of benefits. This trust was built up by publicising the financial and political successes of the corporation, while detractors publicised allegations of misbehaviour in either financial arrangements or the appropriation of powers which did not properly belong to the company.

Questions of trust, in public and private, reveal the ways in which early moderns thought about the functions and values of the corporation. Issues of trust brought to the fore the legal fiction of the corporate body. While supporters of the companies stressed their ability to accumulate experience and provide long-term stability to a trade, others worried that the corporation might not be the immortal *persona ficta* it claimed to be: "Who will trust a Corporation, if its Duration and Existence be so fickle and infirm, that every Abuser or Misurer shall forfeit it?"[1] Putting one's faith in an institution required a belief that the institution would endure; proceedings like the *Quo Warranto* (in which the City of London was required to provide evidence for its claims to rights and privileges) reminded the public that the corporation existed by privilege of the state, which was revocable.

Economic historians have demonstrated the ways in which financial decisions in the seventeenth century reveal a growing trust in institutions, especially after the Glorious Revolution and the establishment of the Bank of England (and other banks devoted to private lending), as well as the gradual strengthening of common and property laws. In Britain, at least, the presence of significant creditors within elite groups (particularly the Whig faction) helps to explain the establishment of debt servicing mechanisms in the aftermath of the Nine Years' War. These powerful groups "wanted to reduce uncertainty surrounding public debt service" by transferring debt, through national institutions such as the Bank, to long-term commitments funded by a diverse range of taxation.[2] Consequently, as Douglass North has demonstrated, the willingness to lend to the government "increased by an order of magnitude," which "reflected a clear perception that the government would honour its agreements."[3]

This chapter builds on those conclusions, but from the point of view of popular thought rather than new institutional economics. It considers the broader question of popular and rhetorical understanding of that institutional trust – how did people conceptualise their trust (or lack of trust)? What metaphors and ideas circulated relating to trust and credit? How did they conceive of financial markets, the institutions which created and managed them, and the risks involved for investors as the century developed? And finally, how did those concerns over institutional risks manifest themselves in contemporary literatures?

In particular, this chapter is concerned with how the perception of creditworthiness was created in the public actions of corporate actors. Companies did this by stressing the power of their common borrowing, as well as security of the trade. Responses to these actions came in two sorts – one style of response was factual, arguing that a common seal meant no one was liable, or challenging the underlying finances of a company. The other sort was rhetorical, suggesting the company was corrupt in some way, either in the behaviour of its individuals, or in its rhetorical positioning (usually presenting its financial position as being better than it actually was). The second section thus deals with the way in which companies dealt with their status as a collection of individuals, and the difficulties that arose, for both the companies and their personnel. The question of real and perceived value is returned to in the final section, which looks at the practice of 'stock-jobbing' (talking up a stock beyond its actual expected returns to make a quick profit). In all three sections, I draw on the extensive correspondence of Sir James Bateman. Bateman was integrated into a range of financial markets at the turn of the century. He invested in a number of companies, including the New East India Company and later the South Sea Company, was a director of the Bank of England and the United East India Company, was responsible for securing funding for English forces on the continent, and was a commissioner for Greenwich Hospital, as well as becoming Lord Mayor of London in 1716–17. His correspondence shows the ways in which these questions of social reputation, economic reality and the difficulties of assessing credit and creditworthiness were interlinked in the early modern imagination.

One particular feature of the corporation, as opposed to individual traders, was its ability to borrow money on its common seal: in effect, the 'body corporate' taking a loan as a single entity. However, the imaginary potential of the 'corporation' acting as a person capable of taking a loan created uncertainty among investors and lenders alike. Who, exactly, was one lending to, and how could the creditworthiness of the corporation be established? A pamphlet discussing a scheme for fire insurance in the City of London, 15 years after the Great Fire, raised concerns about the relationship between the common seal of the City, its methods of security, and the consequences of other ways of raising funds:

> The Difficulty in Raising this *Fund*, is to be considered; for either the *Ground-Rents* do already belong to the *City*, or are to be *Purchased*. If they now belong to the City; It is not the Interest of the Citizens to Settle them for *Insuring of Houses*; because it will Lessen the Security of the *Chamber*, which is for the Payment of *Orphants* Portions; for although the Seal doth not Bind the *Land*, yet it is the *Land* and Revenue of the City, that gives Credit to the Seal, and makes it able to Satisfy.
>
> The *Ill Consequence* for the City to Alter their usual Security, for such a Designe, when there is no other reason, but that their seal is not sufficient Seecurity, is worth Consideration. *First*, It lessens the Credit of their own Seal, by preferring another sort of Fund in *Ground-Rents*, as a more *Vndoubted Security*. Which may prove a Consequence of some weight, because it is now trusted in as great a concern, which hath the same, if not greater reason, to expect as good Security.[4]

Here is an early example of the kind of discourse identified by North and others, with institutional borrowing based on the long-term, steady funding stream of assets and taxation (the 'land and revenue of the city') which assures investors that the City will be able to repay the loan. Indeed, the writer warns against using a specific form of income (ground rents), since earmarking funds in this way will make other lenders to the City nervous about the general creditworthiness of the institution – the apparent prioritising of specific sources of income over the general money-raising ability of the City would be enough to raise doubts in the minds of investors and creditors, and lessen their faith in the institutional structure of the City of London Corporation. Consequently, if they do not use their seal for all their borrowing, they cannot use it for any borrowing.

However, if the corporation borrowed money or accumulated debt on its seal (that is, the mark of its status as an impersonal and collective entity), or against a future stock, how could lenders and investors be sure of recouping their capital? Companies might well be able to raise revenue, but would they actually use it to service debt? While the companies presented their access to money markets as a strength, contemporary pamphlets warned that "it was unclear if the immaterial company was a trustworthy debtor."[5] One such pamphlet purported to be a letter from a country gentleman to a lawyer in the City, which began by noting that "the last Post brought me news of such factions and divisions in the East-India Company as (my friend says) have shaken their credit," and went on to ask for a legal opinion of that credit, since "a Neighbour of mine puts many scruples in my head about my security by their Common Seal."[6] It is worth noting that both of these concerns have come from other sources. The writer was doubtless attempting to suggest a broader frame of reference for his pamphlet by creating a sense of public interest, but these reports also suggest something of the ways in which ideas of creditworthiness and trust circulated among not just investors, but in news and in local networks by word of mouth. Craig Muldrew has shown how the early modern populace was "constantly involved in tangled webs of economic and social dependency . . . through the numerous reciprocal bonds of trust in all the millions of bargains they transacted."[7] Credit, creditworthiness and the social aspects of credit such as social hierarchies, wills and dependencies, were much discussed in person and in print.

The country gentleman would doubtless have been dismayed by the response, for the barrister in the city confirmed the scruples of the gentleman's neighbour in the strongest possible terms:

> I know they were cried up as infallible Security, and Lenders thought themselves obliged to the Company to accept their Moneys at Interest: this Reputation was such a Net, as caught the Fish by Sholes, and enabled them to borrow about 600000 ll. every Lender thinking he had so many Rich men in his Chest, when he had the Company's Seal there; but I am afraid you will scarce Credit me, if I tell you that their Seal is less Security for your Money, than the Word of any Sufficient Man in the Company; For their Common Seal binds not any one of the Company's
>
> Persons, nor Estates, either real or personal; you can neither Arrest, nor Implead great nor small amongst them upon their Common Seal; and if you should demand your Money of any particular person, he would but laugh at you, and bid you go to the Company with your Seal, for he owes you not a Groat.[8]

The lawyer does stress the strong reputation of the company: It is not clear whether it is the EIC themselves who have 'cried up' the 'infallible security', or whether it was other figures on the Exchange or in print, but nonetheless the letter does reflect a general sense that lending to the company is not only sensible but desirable, since it is unlikely to default. However, despite the financial soundness (or potential soundness) of such an arrangement, the pamphlet reveals an unease at this new form of lending to a company, rather than an individual who can be pursued. The lawyer goes on to note that while the company will not technically default on its debts, it will in practice be impossible to recover them because of the manoeuvrings of company men. He anticipates that the members of the corporation will use the inconsistency between corporate and personal liability to evade their debt – and, indeed, the phrases 'laugh at you' and 'bid you go to the company' suggest that this is a deliberate strategy rather than a legal oddity. Such a reading fits with the image of the company as fisherman, trawling up unwise lenders in a 'shoal' (or herding together, as today's equivalent metaphor for collective delusion in investment would have it) which is both clustered together and unaware of the danger it is creating by that very clustering. The lawyer also gives precedents from other companies such as the Grocers or Merchant Adventurers which had likewise disappointed their creditors, although he does say that the EIC are worse because they trade entirely on other people's money.

Given that the creditworthiness of the company was central to its business and political interests, a counter-pamphlet was perhaps inevitable; as the previous chapter demonstrated, companies were quick to respond when their reputation was threatened. Later that year *An Answer to Two Letters concerning the East-India Company* was issued anonymously. This pamphlet likewise took the epistolary form, with an additional note from the printer claiming the letter had fallen accidentally into his hands, and was being printed as a "Vindication of a Society, all whose Measures are just and honourable," but was "a service also to the Kingdom, to which so many Advantages are derived by them."[9] This declaration from the printer neatly sums up the pamphlet, which generally takes the standard attitudes that the East India Company has behaved well, traded successfully and so advanced the general stock of the kingdom.

The *Answer*'s particular strategy was to focus on relative reputation, defending the company by suggesting a scurrilous intent in the original, anonymous author(s) and publishers of the *Two Letters*:

> I have perused the said Letters, and can see no reason to believe that such Discourses should be published by any person whose Estate was entrusted to the said *Company;* or that had any real desire of receiving or giving satisfaction concerning the security of Money lent to them. No *Creditor* can be supposed to act so contrary to his own interest, as to make it his endeavour to weaken or lessen his security, by Exposing and Ruining his *Debtors Credit;* or teaching him a way to defraud himself, which is the Language of those Papers.[10]

The *Answer* seeks to undermine the author of the *Two Letters* with a two-pronged strategy. Firstly, it alleges deceit in the original claim to be an investor or creditor in the Company, since not only would such a pamphlet reduce the credit of the Company, but would also 'teach' them a way to 'defraud' their creditors; consequently, no one with any 'real desire' of receiving a return on their investment would publicise their 'doubt'. Secondly, with the rhetorical sleight of hand of taking this first deceit as fact, it suggests a reason for this subterfuge, which is to be found not in the Company's own affairs or behaviour, but in a mysterious 'cabal' of the traditional enemies of the corporation:

> It must therefore be some other Person then a *Creditor*, and some other Design than a doubt about *Security*, that occasioned the Publishing these Letters. There hath been a report that the *Dutch* had in Design to propose at the *Treaty* at *Nimegen*, a Restraint of the Importation of *Callico* into *Europe*, because it hinders the consumption of *French, Holland, Flanders*, and *German Linnens:* And lately some here did Decry the *East-India-Company* and Trade, because *Callico* (as they said) hindred the vent of *Fustians* and some other Native Manufactures. These corresponding so exactly, give ground to think they proceed from the same Councell, and the *Authour* of these Letters may be of that *Caball.*[11]

In this way, the *Answer* shifts the question of reputation back to the author of the letters, turning the anonymous nature of the original pamphlet back upon itself as a challenge to the very right to speak: Honesty and trustworthiness are not only necessary characteristics of the corporation, but are preconditions for entering into the public sphere. Such a move was a common one when the company or its representatives sought to deal with anonymous complaints. In Dudley Digges' response to *The Trades Increase* (discussed in the previous chapter), he alleged that the anonymous nature of the pamphlet hid the fact that it was a group of people set against the company: "some cunning and malitious persons, for priuate ends, or *lewder* purposes infused the *Quicksiluer* that set that running head a work."[12]

However, in adopting this strategy the *Answer* also reveals a shift in the conceptual understanding of the public sphere, now imagined as a set of competing self-interests. Publishing is no longer a way of stimulating debate or sharing information (as the *Two Letters* positions itself), but only as a strategy for increasing or decreasing the value of one's own credit or investments, and consequently the credit of the EIC itself. It is likely that the author of the *Answer* was part of the East India Company, or hired on their behalf, especially since this conceptualisation of the print marketplace as a space of claim and counterclaim designed to advance particular interests or reputations fits with the strategies of corporate printing which were outlined in the previous chapter.

Given this positioning, the fact that the author of the *Answer* does not seek to dispute the central allegation of the *Two Letters*, that the company does not necessitate a liability among its investors, is remarkable. The extraordinary claim discussed previously, that the *Two Letters* would teach the EIC how to defraud its creditors, relies upon the premise that such a 'fraud' would be possible, and the only reason the company does not behave in that manner is because they either have not thought of it, or it is not acceptable as part of common understandings of debt and credit. Reproducing the paragraph regarding borrowing on the seal from the *Two Letters* I have cited previously, the *Answer* asks, "Who is there so ignorant, but knows this? [. . .] I dare say not one of forty that have lent money to the *Company* thought so."[13] In fact, he argues, investments in the company are not made because it has more capacity to insure against risk (which any investment must be subject to), but because it has the joint stock to secure the loans, and a proven capacity to repay them. The *Answer* does, though, respond to allegations of fraud among leading members of the company:

> As to dishonest practices, is it Rationally to be supposed that a Number of men can so easily engage in wicked and cheating actions? The *Government* of the *East-India stock* is committed to 26 *Persons*, and no Affair can be Transacted without 13, so that if the Major part be Persons of Honesty and Conscience, you are secure; nothing can be done unworthily. Yea if there should be but one Honest man of 13, yet you are sure, seeing such an act of knavery, as would defraud the *Creditors*, would be detected.[14]

Here, as throughout the pamphlet, the corporate form is invoked as a reason to trust the East India Company more than a private individual; trust is increased, and risk diluted, by the constant oversight of the court of assistants legislated for by the company themselves. In fact, the idea that even one honest man would be enough to prevent an 'act of knavery' would be tested to destruction in the two decades following the *Letters*, as the concentration of corporate power in a few hands, particularly those of Josiah Child, led to allegations of "oligarchy, or arbitrary government."[15] A petition of 1691 alleged that the directors of the EIC had "managed the [trade] only for their private gain, without any regard to the publick Good," and such sentiment was widespread in the 1680s and '90s as the Company began to take on an increasingly state-like role, even declaring war, while opposition in Britain, particularly discussions over a new East India Company, gathered pace.[16] In the 1670s, though, these issues were some way off, and the appeal to the corporate form might well have carried some weight; discussions of the form of the East India Company in particular were centred on how best to ensure access to the trade, most particularly in the distinctions between joint stock and regulated companies.

Regardless of the defence given in the *Answer*, the issue of the creditworthiness of the corporate form continued to circulate in print. Discussions over a 'new' East India Company often centred on the parlous financial situation of the Old Company, with one pamphlet announcing that the "present company or joint stock is only an imaginary fund, not having any real stock of its own left to carry on the trade."[17] Such concerns, though, were not limited to the East India Company. On 27 July 1694, the Bank of England was granted its charter by William and Mary after raising £1.2 million as a stock. Contemporary pamphleteers, though, repeated the dire warnings of the *Two Letters* for those considering investing in the Bank:

> It deserves also to be seriously thought upon, by all that lodge Monies in their hands, that when they think they have Trusted a Corporation, they may find that they have no such Body Corporate to implead for what they have Lent, but must be forced to sue so many Distinct, and several Individuals as are Contributors to the *Bank* [. . .] From whence it is obvious that in order to a Person's recovering one single 100 *l.* he may be to Sue and Implead four or five hundred several Men, and that by distinct and separate *Actions*, which is infinitly worse, than to sit down contentedly with the Loss of the Mony.[18]

As the lawyer had assured the country gentleman 20 years earlier, this question of credit once again turned on the distinction between the corporate entity and its members, so much so that it would be better simply to give up on the investment than to try and recover it from the 'four or five hundred' shareholders. Legally, a scant difference, but a significant one in practice, since when debt was due the corporation became an immaterial shell, which might be sued but held nothing of its own to be sued for. The corporation's right to authorise actions, and consequently its creditworthiness, as Henry Turner has argued in his reading of *Leviathan*, lay not in the fictional person of the corporation, but in its "governors, whose authority is backed by the state."[19] Consequently, although the joint stock might provide creditworthiness in a technical sense, it could not provide it in the moral sense: trusting a corporation meant trusting those 400 or 500 men who made up the body corporate to behave honourably, and rather than providing safety in numbers, as defenders of the corporations had suggested in the 1670s, the sheer quantity of parts of the corporate body made it impossible to trust.

Such a distinction between person and corporation, and their relative trustworthiness, was a fundamental one. It arose because of the conception that the corporation was nothing more or less than a set of networked individuals who relied on their connections (personal, family and corporate) for profit and as markers of trust. As a consequence, the corporation had a crucial role in both establishing its own credit, but more fundamentally, acting as a guarantee (in the social, rather than financial sense) for its members. A corporation could be trusted if it was an effective regulator of the debt and dealings of its employees. In this way, customers could trust a merchant, even if they had not dealt with him before; because he belonged to a company, he would in theory follow its norms and practices, and redress could be sought if necessary from the company itself.

Trust networks and office holders

The East India Company minutes record that in March 1693 Thomas Papillon, former director of the company and MP for Dover, petitioned for the company's help in securing a bond held in trust:

> Thomas Papillon Esq. on the behalf of his nephew Samuel Papillon moving the Court that the £500 credit in the name of Thomas Nicholson which was by deed made over to George Papillon deceased in trust for Samuel Papillon his son may not be transferred, nor any Dividends thereupon paid to any person without notice given to the said Mr Thomas Papillon, the Court directed the Acceptant Generall to take notice thereof, and to act therein accordingly.[20]

Here, the corporation acts as a balance on the complex network of bonds and debt between the Papillon family – key, if not uncontroversial, nodes within the EIC network – and Thomas Nicholson. Papillon's request demonstrates the company's ability to regulate, at least to some extent, its servants and their financial arrangements. We have already seen the ways in which the creditworthiness of the company depended on good individuals, and Papillon's intervention here shows how those individuals often relied on the company, as a reification of the merchant community, to establish and regulate reliable credit networks.

Perry Gauci has argued that trust played a key role in this sort of small network generation among the merchant community, especially when deciding how and to whom to expand networks of investment, including taking on new apprentices; trust "would clearly have been a pivotal issue in determining the relationship between master and apprentice, especially if the former wished to send the youngster abroad to continue his education."[21] For this reason, many merchants preferred to take apprentices from kinship networks, or those from gentle backgrounds when large bonds could be secured against the credit of the family. The master and apprentice developed a symbiotic bond, too, since the reputation of one could affect the other: Most obviously this came from apprentices misbehaving, but being apprenticed to a reliable and reputable master was a significant career boost, which continued even after the apprenticeship was concluded.

A merchant's reputation was thus a crucial determinant of how trust- or creditworthy he was, and so such an attribute was a vital commodity to be protected. We have already seen how anonymous pamphleteers played with this notion of reputation to undermine opposing views on creditworthiness and political economy more generally. For the East India Company, the Amboyna massacre, and the subsequent printed dispute, was the origin of the corporate strategy to aggressively defend its reputation in print; as the previous chapter showed, the EIC were well aware of the potential damage to their reputation from what they saw as Dutch slander, and the pamphlets they produced replicate their internal discussions on the issue:

> Our losses are without compare, to lose our liues and liberty, to lose our goods, to lose our trade and trafficke, and now lastly in our owne Countrey to lose the honest reputation of men, of Englishmen, of English Merchants, of the English company of East-India. This is a losse irrecouerable, as an Heathen Historian writeth; *Maiora sunt fame & fidei damna, quam que sarciri possunt:* The losse of a good name, the losse of trust and credit are losses irrecouerable.[22]

Here, reputation is almost fungible, one of many things in which the company deals, although, of course, it is considerably more valuable than 'goods' or 'traffic' since it is the base on which those things rest. Ceri Sullivan has shown the ways in which an early modern merchant became a "locus of fixed value in the trading system on the basis of his word," and this was even more true for the corporation, which had to guarantee not only itself, but also its members, and those who dealt either with the company as a whole or its individual members.[23] Reputation and trust thus cascaded out from the corporation through the early modern trading economy.

These matters were a consideration for individual traders within a corporate network, too, for they had to have an eye on both their own and their company's credit. John Fardoe, an EIC servant in India, was accused of stealing four bags of cloves, and petitioned for the case to be dealt with in public:

> Now forasmuch as matters of such moment, ought not to be suppressed hushed up and concealed, that concerns life and loss of good name and credit. I humbly demand and crave a public trial in your powerful session; and if I be found guilty to have like merit without mercy; If acquitted, to do me justice for these injurious slanders accordingly.[24]

Fardoe clearly feared the consequences of a private trial, although whether that was to do with the application of law or internal influence we cannot say, although he is clearly concerned about the 'suppression' of facts within the company. His good name and credit can only be restored, in any case, by a public acquittal, and appropriate redress for the 'slanders' against him. Unfortunately, the response to this petition seems not to have survived, and Fardoe vanishes from the records; we can probably assume that some sort of private action took place, whether a trial or Fardoe leaving the Company's service. Here, the internal workings of the company are thrown in to relief – remaining a creditworthy network of individuals paradoxically occasioned a certain type of private 'justice' designed to keep crimes (real or imagined) from the public consciousness.

The logical consequence of this system was that the concern for reputation should outweigh the short-term benefits of bad practices such as reneging on debt or cheating on a deal. Sir James Bateman was responsible for securing Exchequer Bills to remit money to Richard Hill, Deputy Paymaster for the army, in the Low Countries during the Nine Years' War. Because of this, we have frequent correspondence between the two, at a time when various forms of state-backed credit instruments were being brought to the marketplace, offering a useful overview of the way these instruments were used and considered. Bateman frequently wrote to Hill lamenting his difficulty in securing appropriate credit for the army, often because the Bills were either delayed in printing or, more often, sold to other merchants and brokers ahead of him:

> It seems that the Lords are now offered something more and they would be off from the bargain with us – which with submission I think is not very genteely done and in my judgement contrary to their own interests, for who will deal with them another time if they break contracts as they see convenient.[25]

Bateman's letter demonstrates not just his frustration about this particular deal, but a more general concern about business practices. The rather barbed 'genteely' plays on the social status of the Lords, but perhaps also points to a more general sense about the way business should be done, with concerns over reputation taking precedence over short-term gains. As Bateman argues, doing business in this way is not just morally better, but financially superior too, since a reputation for honest dealing leads to future business, while breaking a contract means no one will 'deal with them another time'.

However, the Lords did let him down, and in a further letter to Hill a fortnight later Bateman returned to his frustration over the ways in which the Exchequer Bills were managed:

> Since there is no dependence on either their words or minutes though the last was formerly esteemed as a sacred and secure as any bonds

> could be between man and man, but the breach of such positive agreement will lessen their esteem with all private men.[26]

Once again Bateman decries the practice of reneging on deals, this time invoking not just the 'words' of the Lords, but also their 'minutes', the supposedly authoritative and immutable records of decision-making. Bateman's point about the loss of faith 'private men' will have in the Lords points to a division between merchants (debt traders, as in this case) and government, perhaps reflecting broader concerns about the honesty and reliability of institutions.

Around the same time as Bateman and Hill were corresponding privately, public statements on the corporations increasingly turned towards the same questions of fraud and duplicity. Sharp corporate practices undermined the company's stated position as an immortal body corporate eager to protect its reputation, with opponents bringing a range of complaints, including aggressive tactics (internally and externally), monopolistic tendencies and even fraud:

> Some of the prevailing Members in the Committee have lately introduced a new way of Selling a very great part of the *Companies* Goods to themselves, by *private Contracts*, to the great Prejudice of the usual Buyers at their publick Sales, and so in few Years have acquir'd vast Estates, by Defrauding all the other Adventurers, contrary to their Oaths and the Trust repos'd in them.[27]

Unlike Bateman's complaints on open back-pedalling, the allegation here is that the company is dishonest when no one is looking – in fact, precisely *because* no one is looking. The self-regulation which earlier in the century was axiomatic – even if, as in the case of Fardoe and others, it was never as honest and well regulated as the company suggested – has been superseded by the opportunity for profit which comes from controlling the supply chain.

In fact, the question of who watches the watchers was a vexed one for corporations. As governing organisations, they fiercely defended their right to self-regulation, "policing almost every aspect of their members' behaviour and conduct" and in so doing "strengthened their own reputations as rigorous self-governing institutions."[28] However, that same desire for internal procedures left them open to attacks like the anonymous pamphleteer mentioned previously, since if corporate officers were corrupted then neither the generality of members, the wider public nor often even the state could do much to hold them to account. One petition from William Craddock in 1598 makes this complaint in clear terms:

> The merchants in this suit being accuser, judge and executioner in their own cause, in affecting their private lucre, have exceeded the

> ample charters granted by the King of this realm & confirmed by her majesty have dealt therein contrary to the laws of the realm and all course of justice, and therefore the petitioner hath appealed from their sentence to the trial of her majesty's laws and to your Lordship's censure.[29]

For Craddock, the existence of corporate justice has had the effect of creating a kangaroo court, in which those out of favour with the company cannot be successful. Although Craddock was able to engage in some jurisdiction-shopping, in his appeal to Sir Thomas Egerton, a Privy Councillor (and future Lord Chamberlain) and Keeper of the Seal, the petition demonstrates the chilling effect that corporate self-governance could have, and how remote it might become from the laws of England in which it was supposed to operate: Indeed, overstepping the provisions of the charter clause allowing laws so long as they were not repugnant to the laws of England was a frequent complaint by those who opposed corporate jurisdiction, especially overseas.[30]

The goldsmith Thomas Violet, whose schemes were discussed in the previous chapter, reflected on the difficulty of Elizabeth I's trusting of office holders who worked in the Royal Mint, a position notoriously sensitive and open to abuse:

> For, though in other things shee would hear them; yet when it concerned themselvs, and upon the point of her Revenue, shee would not trust wholly the greatest of her Officers, but had her instruments to give her true Information, a sure waie for a State never to bee deceived, and a rule fit for these times. This storie is much after this manner recorded of Queen *Elizabeth*, for a piece of high Prudence.[31]

Violet's recounting of this story is partly an attack on the Goldsmiths' Company specifically, but also reveals a deeper anxiety over self-regulation generally. The fact that he is returning to a piece of state control – the use of 'instruments' to test the honesty of those believed to be exporting bullion without permission – from half a century earlier, and suggesting that it is somehow axiomatic, underlines both how consistent concern over corporate honesty has been, and perhaps how ineffective or sporadic attempts to regulate corporations have been.

In many ways, the best form of control the state had over corporations was their charters. Because they had to be granted, and then renewed at regular intervals, charters were a mechanism by which the state could set limits on corporate power, whether by financial obligation or limitations on their activities. In the same pamphlet, Violet comments on the negotiations for the establishment of the Company of Wire-Drawers (artisans who span gold and silver into threads for clothing and other decoration):

> Besides, the Gold-Wier-drawers before any Excise was thought of, did offer unto the late King, and his heirs for ever, one thousand pounds a year, and two pence the Ounce, to have a Corporation, as I shall make it appear. But the deceits so grosly practised by many of them, was so clearly proved that then at that time the State would not trust them with a Corporation, as I have formerly declared.[32]

In this case, despite an offer of consistent revenues for the Crown, the question of trust was too great for a corporation to be established, as the degree of independence offered would make their 'deceits' harder to identify and prosecute. In other cases, competing schemes or patents might infringe on a charter, and these disputes were resolved in the courts, or more usually by lobbying either the royal court or Parliament to reinforce or reissue a charter. Deciding between the two schemes was often a matter of relative value to the awarding body, as was often the case with rivals to, and/or factions within, the major international companies such as the East India or Royal Africa Companies. A letter from the RAC to its factors in Monserrat made this point:

> Some Members of Parliament being persuaded (by the insinuations of persons who have more regard to their own Private interest than the public) that the present African Companies trade is prejudicial to the plantations, especially in relation to their being furnished with Negroes, we recommend your obtaining a petition, by what planters you can obtain.[33]

The company was clearly concerned enough by those persons lobbying Parliament to attempt to shore up its position; notably, though, instead of making a public point about the private interests of those putative new traders, they sought to amass private interests of their own from among the colonists in the West Indies, presumably on the basis that a sufficient agglomeration of private interests became a public good.

The decisions about control and regulation might also take into account precedence, and relative trust, a point made by the masters of Trinity House in a pamphlet against a patentee who had set up a rival lighthouse:

> Whereas it is auerred and deliuered, that the Patentee hath bene at 25 or 30 hundred pounds vpon the charge of his structures, or houses built at *Winterton:* we answer, that the like structures or houses may be built for 150 pounds, or thereabouts. And for the surplus of charges, we professe, not to vnderstand it, neither do we thinke that the Patentee can giue an account thereof.
>
> In point of care, may any be equall to vs? we aduenture our liues, our estates, yea all our meanes within the compasse of these channels:

> our hopes in all depend vpon the knowledge of channels, sands, and the well keeping of sea-markes. His Maiestie reposeth the trust, the care and charge of his Nauie royall (in point of conduction and pilotage) to vs; we say, to vs onely: neither will his Ma: repose this trust in any other Corporation or Companie in this kingdome. If all these weightie motiues be not of force, to settle more care in vs, then in any other, for the well keeping of sea-markes, let vs suffer, and be hanged at the gates of the Kings Court, for example to others.[34]

The masters stress the long-term 'trust', 'care' and 'charge' which has been placed in them over the piloting of the Royal Navy, and the exclusivity of this trust, which has not been placed in 'any other Corporation or Company'. The rhetorical flourish of a proposed hanging, should anyone else be found more trustworthy, underlines the good-faith efforts of the company of Trinity House, who will behave properly without competition or oversight simply as a consequence of the 'weighty motives' of royal trust. The speculation which opens the pamphlet, that the patentee has either overcharged or mis-accounted for the building of rival structures, also speaks to the question of trust, and was a serious charge in its own right. Not only did it bring to mind the monopolistic practices of patent exploitation so frequently condemned in Parliament and print, but also it suggested a commercial untrustworthiness too, since a failure to keep proper accounts was a primary reason for denying a merchant access to credit.

Accounts became increasingly important to justify trust in merchants, and especially those who operated overseas, where account books were the only real way the company had of keeping track of their servants' dealings. One anonymous pamphlet, calling for a new East India Company, wrote of the Old Company that "they want three of four years books from India," which the writer saw as an "impardonable crime, [which] renders their servants worthy of severe castigation."[35] To be unable to properly judge the trade that took place in India defrauded investors, other traders and consumers alike, and by allowing these account books to go missing (or by actively hiding them) the company was colluding in the fraud. This was a breakdown in trust between the Old Company and the commonwealth as a whole, for which missing accounts overseas were simply emblematic. However, it was not a failing of the corporate structure, since the author believed a new corporation would solve these issues; controlling servants overseas was perfectly possible, so long as the company's rules were properly enforced.

Corporate office holders were not just important within the corporation, and for those seeking to trade with them, but also fulfilled a vital ambassadorial function. The Levant Company sponsored an ambassador in Constantinople, but his position was not always easy, having to juggle between the demands of the nation, the company and local laws and customs.[36] The ambassador needed royal authority to negotiate *capitulations* (treaties or declarations granting trading privileges) with the Ottoman rulers, as well as authority from the company to keep order among its servants, although they were frequently undermined on both counts. The Levant Company wrote to the community of merchants in Constantinople in 1641 to deal with a rumour they were becoming a "faction" conspiring against the Ambassador, reminding them that "in such divisions our affaires may much suffer."[37]

Whether king or company had ultimate authority over the ambassador was a vexed question. In 1636, the Company wrote to Sir Peter Wyche – who had been ambassador to the Ottomans since 1628 and was in fact waiting for his successor, Sir Sackville Crowe, to arrive – regarding a dispute they were having on the matter of consulage.[38] Consulage was a tax levied on English ships carrying a stranger's goods to Constantinople, which had been granted to the English by the Sultan in a *capitulation* of 1580. The revenue technically belonged to the king, but was traditionally kept as a perk by the ambassador, and both Wyche and the Company laid claim to the proceeds. Wyche professed to have "quietly injoyed it for some years," although the Company claimed that this was not by right, but a *de facto* appropriation of their resources at too great a distance for them to challenge:

> And we may justly challenge your discretion, that you, who are resident there to doe us right, & protect the Nation, should soe farr forget your selfe, and the obligacion you owe to the Company as to bring our Consuls to Turky Justice, for your owne lucre. We conceive that neither your self, nor any of the Grand Seignor's ministers can be competent judges in the matter.[39]

The Company stressed that the first duty is to 'do us right', with 'protect the nation' something of an afterthought that is subordinate to (perhaps even part of) the 'obligation' to look after the company's affairs. The company has been damaged in Wych's pursuit of lucre not just because he has taken their money, and consequently upset the balance between king and company, but because he has done so by involving an Ottoman court ('Turky Justice'). Wyche wrote back to the company in October, apparently after hearing of "very scandalous" accusations made against him at a Levant company meeting, asserting that his rights came from the king, and superseded the company:

> The cause of these scandelous aspertions, are because I have maintayned his Majesties right & prerogative in the business of the strangers consolage, & would not give waie to Mr Bernard the Consull at Smirna, to please anie farther against it, who presumed to apeare before Turkish justice in oposition of his Majesties Ambassador

> usinge the name of the Merchants, against the Authoritie of his Majestie as if the Turkish Ministers ought to have decided betwixt our Soveraine and his subjects.[40]

Wyche makes a counterclaim against the company's claim to sovereignty by appealing to the crown, although he, too, accepts that these disputes ought to be kept within the company rather than referred to outside courts (outside both jurisdictionally and territorially). Ironically, Wyche's response crossed with a letter sent by the Company, demanding to see the documentation for just such a claim:

> You may please once more to take notice that your possessing & injoying [the consulage] was never once consented to by us, no not so much as by our silence, having in all or most of our letters, since you did assume it, absolutely disclaimed your proceeding therein and prayed you to desist. Only we omitted one thing, which we desire to be satisfied in namely to know what authority you have from his majesty for collecting therof, and that you will find us a copie.[41]

Like many companies, the Levant merchants place their trust in writing, relying on paper copies of accounts, letters and contracts to conduct their business and form an institutional memory; indeed, as they suggest here, they would later rely on their letters and account books to make the claim in Parliament that they had always enjoyed the privilege of stranger's consulage, and every letter they send to Wyche in the period stresses their unhappiness at his attempts to keep the money for himself. Consequently, the claim of a piece of writing that would severely affect their business (since the consulage charges were a key revenue stream) to which they do not have access is a troubling one, both for this particular case, and the general completeness of their own archive.

Crowe did eventually take over from Wyche in 1638, but the tension between company and state did not end there. During the Civil Wars, Crowe attempted to shut down the business in the Levant because he felt the directors of the company were too closely aligned to the Parliamentary cause.[42] The company sent out Sir Thomas Bendish, who managed to have Crowe imprisoned and to take over the ambassadorship:

> We doe also thank your Lordship for your endeavour at Smirna, though we conclude that factory resolute in denying any thing but what suits with thier owne humor; else we suppose they would have yeelded to some of our orders provided for their regulation.[43]

Once again the company has failed to adequately control its servants, with separate networks of power being established in factories away from Constantinople when there was little power to coerce them to follow the company's direction. Even the intervention of the ambassador, with his own networks of power and authority, has been insufficient to quell the faction developing at a distance.

The fact that corporations were composed of multiple networks continued to cause problems for those who sought to work within them or speak on their behalf. One letter between factories in India reveals the difficulties of ensuring trade is properly organised within the company structure:

> Yours of the 22nd December from Ballasore came to our hands the 11th March by Capt. Knox wherein we are sorry to read your discontent and the distraction of the company's affairs in your parts by being managed by others than their servants.[44]

The company's affairs were damaged once the management of them went outside the carefully controlled structures of the EIC, with its insistence on accounting, letter-writing and a chain of accountability stretching back to London (even if this was not always enforced perfectly). The same problems continued in the Levant. James Brydges, 8th Baron Chandos, having been elected ambassador by the Levant Company, arrived in Constantinople in July 1681. Just two months later, he wrote to the Levant Company to complain that their decisions were undercutting his embassy:

> But I must needes say I was extreamly surpris'd to heare from all hands att both Smyrna & Aleppo that you had chosen your Generall Ships before you understood what was the issue of my negotiation here which was a direct contradiction to his Majestys Letters, & made very contemptible much I had say'd of that nature by authority of his Majestys Letter whih ware deliver'd, & your owne instructions, & whether when the King wishes the Visir in his Letters to beleive what his Ambassador from time to time say'd & your actions prove the Ambassador a misreporter in matter of fact, is your reall interest, I humbly submit to the great wisdome of the Court, my duty is to obey, not dispute, & will allwayes according to the creditt & power given me, doe you all the faithfull service I am able.[45]

Brydges is clearly primarily concerned about his reputation here, stressing that he has been made a 'misreporter in matter of fact' and his speech has been made 'contemptible'. Clearly, having an ambassador undermined in this way permanently eroded his ability to conduct diplomatic business – rather like Bateman's observations on the behaviour of the House of Lords, it is the long-term 'credit' of his position which is deemed to be of far greater importance than any short-term benefits (or, in this case, potential mismanagement). Brydges chides the company for their lack of understanding of his work and negotiations, and their impatience in reaching decisions, which have damaged his reputation with the Vizier, and consequently the trade itself.

Office holders thus had a double office – they were responsible for their own honest behaviour, but also had a broader duty to ensure as far as they could that the company's affairs were managed appropriately and without scandal. This necessitated clear hierarchies and careful thought before acting, as well as a respect for the written word. As Miles Ogborn has shown, the East India Company developed careful ways of reading letters, combining their "concerns with abuses of office [. . .], following orders, and giving respect," which resulted in particular ways of writing from their servants overseas.[46] These examples from the Levant Company demonstrate the potential pitfalls in communication networks when those principles were not followed. To be a corporate officer was to behave well, write well and present one's actions to both private and, ultimately, public scrutiny. Only then could officers be trustworthy. Trust was established through personal relationships, written communication and record keeping, and the corporation mediated all these relationships, making it a crucial tool for the creation and upkeep of trust networks, and a facilitator of credit relationships in Britain and overseas.

Public good and reputation

Thus far, my discussion has focused on the (broadly) institutional factors within corporate structures and ideologies which generated – or undermined – trust in those institutions. Consequently, the discussion has considered the community within the corporation, or the wider mercantile community which dealt with them, as well as their public statements on the broad benefits of corporate activity. However, as the issues faced by the ambassadors suggest, corporations also faced questions of the public good at an internal level, whether through the establishment of a 'corporate society', as in Virginia, Madras and so on, or in matters of regulation when they had an impact beyond the behaviour of corporate members.

As the previous chapter showed, companies frequently positioned themselves as defenders of the public good. In particular, they claimed to be vehicles for the general increase in prosperity, as their economic activities (beneficial improvements to employment and manufacturing) rippled out into society, whether in charitable activities, or the ability of widows and orphans to support themselves through the stock. Private letters, though, reflected a concern over the division between public and private good, both in perception and fact. As well as his role at the Bank of England, Sir James Bateman (discussed previously in the context of treasury bills) was also an investor in the New East India Company, and there too he shared concerns over public responsibility and creditworthiness, in every sense of the word. The New EIC had been set up to compete with the Old Company in 1687; in practice, however, the same groups of merchants dominated both Companies, and there was little real commercial competition between the two (they would eventually combine to form the United East India Company in 1709), although relationships between the separate companies and the public good provoked substantial debate in print. Writing about a proposed merger of the Old and New East India Companies in 1699, he noted that:

> Our India Company is now going to treat with the Old I am afraid it will not have the desired effect of a happy union though the generality on both sides seem to desire it. But I doubt some of our great managers will obstruct it. A little time will show us what we may expect.[47]

Despite the bulk of investors being (at least in Bateman's view) in favour of a merger, the 'great managers' – directors and major shareholders – seem likely to block the merger in their own interest. In this letter, that seems a matter of private corporate governance, but later correspondence made it clear that Bateman saw this as a broader concern:

> It would as you say be very happy if the 2 Companies could unite before the Parliament meets, but there is no prospect of it. The Old are very confident their party is now strong enough to get off the 5% next sessions. This jangling will obstruct public affairs and the good in general I fear will not be so much minded as the particular interest of private parties.[48]

Understanding one's own gain as a public good was a fairly standard reading of the political economy, and Bateman's complaint that the 'good in general' is being ignored may simply reflect the risk to his own investment. Nevertheless, the letters do reflect a concern over how widely wealth is being spread, and the way in which decisions are taken within the corporation – Bateman's concern that decision-making is being undertaken for a privileged few at the top of the company was a reasonable concern for investors who trusted those managers to return profits for everyone. The elision of 'what is good for the membership of a corporation' with 'what is good for the broader economy' was a rhetorical position, but also a natural consequence of an understanding of corporate management as promoting the 'general good'.

In fact, the merger of the Old and New Companies provoked concerns on all sides as to the quality and reputation of those involved, as well as concerns over whether they could or would act in the public interest. Josiah Child, a director and unquestionably a 'great manager' of the Old

East India Company, wrote to Thomas Papillon regarding the Parliamentary process of charter renewals and proposed mergers:

> By what I have said already you will see I think the present Act of Parliament no good foundation to erect a lasting East India Company upon, that can withstand the craft and force of the Dutch or French in India; neither do I think the gentlemen entrusted with the New Company's affairs sufficient for such an undertaking.[49]

Like Bateman, Child has a model of the director as a 'public good' figure, although in his case that is a defensive posture against the encroachment of other nations, rather than a positive vision of general economic benefits (notwithstanding that the two could and frequently did go together). The public good thus becomes a matter of international statecraft, reinforcing the links between corporate and international politics, and consequently between the corporation and the state.

The vexed question of locating a public good at the intersection between corporate and state interests was hardly unique to the 1690s, of course. Captain John Bargrave, a planter in Virginia, unsuccessfully petitioned first the Privy Council and then Parliament against Sir Thomas Smythe in April 1621, accusing him of establishing a tyrannical government in the colony, and asking for a commission to examine the government in Virginia.[50] He was evidently already working on that issue, since he had prepared a new set of laws, mediating between the crown, the company and the planters, which he presented to the company at a court on February 22, 1621, although these were never printed.[51] An undated copy survives in manuscript with a set of annotations, the author of which is identified on the manuscript as Sir Edwin Sandys. These notes focus on the interaction between the state and the planters, and how to ensure that the institutions of crown and company can best work for public good, noting that:

> It is the saying of Pliny the younger in his oration to Trajan the emperor that men for the most part are of that disposition that they desire and show things honest and dishonest as they are profitable unto them. Wherefore in determining matters of policy commodity as well public as private is of great moment.[52]

This commentator argues that, since what is deemed good is tied up with what is profitable, policy-making cannot distinguish between public and private. Contemporary tracts on political economy argue that it is perfectly possible, even desirable, for private companies to incur losses so long as the commonwealth gains. Here, though, is a perhaps more realistic, or cynical, understanding of policy-making, which the commentator argues, agreeing with Bargrave's laws, must be undertaken with private and public profit in mind. Only when everyone benefits will policy, and policy-makers, be deemed 'honest'. By setting policies for the general and individual good, and dividing profits among the owners, workers, crown and company, "the Plantation may be increased and cemented to the state's heart, and an increasing public stock gained and the king's rent paid."[53]

Such an understanding of political economy requires a nuanced awareness of the interplay between public and private finance. Returning to the pamphlet concerning the common seal of the Bank of England discussed previously, we see the question is not just one of trust in a single institution's creditworthiness, but in the network of institutions making up the political economy of early modern England:

> But the Case of the *Bank* of *England* is much otherwise, seeing beyond the making good the Interest of 1200000 *l.* neither the Government nor the Kingdom are obliged to see one Farthing either Principal or Interest paid of all that this New Corporation Erected into a Bank, shall obtain Credit, and become indebted for. Nor is there the least connexion betwixt their subsisting as a *Bank*, and the Nations continuing safe and opulent; yea the sooner that comes to be dissolved, the more flourishing the Kingdom will be, and only such as have trusted them will be affected by their Fall.[54]

For this anonymous author, the risk to investors comes because the bank is divorced from other public institutions. Because neither the 'government' nor the 'kingdom' are obliged to guarantee the credit taken out by the Bank, it is significantly riskier for those who invest. As D'Maris Coffman has shown, the public took some time to fully accept the new institutions which guaranteed state debts, and this pamphlet is an example of such scepticism.[55] Similarly, because the Bank (in the author's opinion, at least) does not contribute to the security or the wealth of the nation – in fact, it has a negative effect since it holds back its 'flourishing' – it can, will and must be allowed to fail. Such an argument runs counter to the thesis of North and Weingast, who show that since all loans to the Crown went through the Bank, the "government had thus created an additional, private constraint on its future behaviour."[56] Consequently, the risk element of lending to the state decreased, reflected in falling interest rates, and the establishment of secondary private credit markets which relied on the crown loan. These financial markets were, in effect, backed by the crown, and meant that this anonymous pamphleteer was doubly wrong – not only did the Bank usher in a new financial flourishing, it also helped to strengthen the bonds between institutions, and, crucially, public trust in that network of institutions which made up the political economy of the 1690s.

Stock

The establishment, and success, of the joint-stock model added an extra element to the question of public faith in corporate actors in this period. The purchase of stock required trust in the public and private actions and statements of a corporation: Were those managing the joint stock trustworthy? Could they be trusted to make good decisions to generate returns on the stock? Faith in the company was one thing, as we have seen, but investors also had to be sure that the stock they were buying represented good, or at least reasonable, value. Towards the end of the century, gazetteers and stock-lists began to be published with daily updates in the prices of various key stocks (and many others moved in parallel to the main stocks such as the Bank and East India Company). Alongside this information, though, came fears of price manipulations, especially in the practice of stock-jobbing, the purchase and quick sale of a share for a profit. Not only did this inflate the price of a share for genuine investors, but it also had the potential to create bubbles, as the upwards pressure on shares prices meant they became out of proportion to the actual value of the company or the dividends they accrued. Sir James Bateman also noted the price fluctuations in key stocks:

> Bank stock rise to 118% and New E India to 98% and almost all other things in proportion and to the wonder of every man for such sudden and large jumps is strange and I think grounded on no reason to be advanced so much in one day.[57]

Bateman's letters also reveal a consistent worry about stock-jobbing (although he does not use the term) in treasury and banknotes, reporting on a number of occasions that he cannot purchase them himself because the price is wrong (in this case, the discount given for using the note instead of cash). The same concern about prices was replicated in Daniel Defoe's essay on projectors (investors who pursued profit at the public's expense[58]), in which Defoe argued that the same impulse for a quick profit lay behind both stock-jobbing and some types of projecting:

> They made the whole *Exchange* the Gamesters, and rais'd and lower'd the Prices of Stocks as they pleas'd; and always had both Buyers and Sellers who stood ready innocently to commit their Money to the mercy of their Mercenary Tongues.[59]

The image of the stock-jobber as a parasitical creature, always ready to deceive the innocent or honest men, was a popular one, as was the idea that stock-jobbers were dishonestly playing both sides (both 'buyers and sellers') by access to better information, whether real or imagined. As a consequence, Defoe identified the same disparity between actual and perceived value in shares:

> So have I seen Shares in Joint-Stocks, Patents, Engines, and Undertakings, blown up by the air of great Words, and the Name of some Man of Credit concerned, to 100 *l.* for a 500th. Part, or Share, some more, and at last dwindle away, till it has been Stock-Jobb'd down to 10, 12, 9, 8 *l.* a Share, and at last no Buyer; that is, in short, the fine new word for Nothing-worth, and many Families ruin'd by the Purchase.[60]

Defoe is here describing no artificial bubble, in which prices are inflated by the association the stock has (whether factually or otherwise) with 'creditable' men and its predicted success. The shares reach a ludicrous price on the basis of these associations, before the bubble is burst by the 'stock-jobbers' who have presumably made a fortune selling the shares in the first place. In fact, Defoe sees (with some despair) that the true correspondence is not between the share and its inherent or predicted value, but between the share and the 'credit' of those who seek to talk it up and encourage investment. Although the stock-jobbers pervert this relationship, Defoe does not challenge the validity of an investment based on the credit of other investors, but simply warns his readers to be aware of those wrongly using the 'name' of such men.

Although the earliest printed use I have found of the phrase is 1604, it was not until the 1690s that the phenomenon of the 'stock-jobber' caught the public attention.[61] Pamphlets from this decade repeatedly emphasise the points of Bateman and Defoe, in particular that the 'flipping' of stock did not add anything useful to the country, but in fact drew capital away from worthy projects:

> Searching Mines, Improving Land, Exercising Manufactures, Forreign and Domestick Traffick, are Noble Enterprizes, which denote a private Man publick spirited: by these the Poor are imploy'd, the Revenues increased, the Honour and Reputation of the Nation's inhanc'd, and his Success affords equally satisfaction and applause: whereas, if one *Stock-jobber* get an Estate, another is undone, the Curse of the Sufferer accompanies it, and himself is despised by all Lookers-on: here's no *Poor* imploy'd, nor *Customs* or *Excise* paid.[62]

For this anonymous writer, stock-jobbing takes capital out of productive circulation – improving proto-industrial processes generates employment, employment trade, trade generates customs which can be reinvested in mining and manufacture – instead creating a zero-sum game, in which the stock-jobber 'wins' by sinking someone else's capital into an estate which is either entirely unproductive or at least does not circulate money in a way perceived to be advantageous. Anne Murphy has shown the myriad ways in which "a new class of speculators and stock-jobbers were able to create risk and take advantage of the market's flaws and inadequacies" in order to "draw investment away from trade."[63] Contemporary pamphlets, too, made the link between stock-jobbing and other forms of speculation and market manipulation:

> Some Years ago People were in warm pursuit after Plate-wrecks, and when that failed, the same Humour had recourse to Stock-Jobbing, and notwithstanding the vast Losses and Disappointments therein, no less than the whole Nation and the Legislative Power thereof, immediately fell headlong from thence into Lotteries, and from that Extremity we fell to another Excess, of Banking; and now all these proving either Abortive, or being at stand, the Humour inclines to Interloping; and of this also, at the Cost of some body or other, we are now in a fair way to be convinced.[64]

Many of these activities are 'rush' activities, in which the first few people in the marketplace might well make money before either the resource is exhausted (plate-wrecks), the practice is too widely known or understood (stock-jobbing, banking), the market is saturated (lotteries) or the authorities clamp down (interloping). Linking these activities together, the anonymous pamphleteer creates a 'type' of the financial rogue, moving from one illicit or dubious scheme to another before they can be found out.

The sense of the stock-jobber as unfairly gaining from others' losses was naturally more acute in times of war, a point a 1699 pamphlet on 'public credit' (in both the sense of a national bank but also honour) made especially clear:

> Some Gentlemen who have suffered much under the great and necessary Charge of the War, are without difficulty prevailed upon to be angry, especially when they see an overgrown Stock-jobber's Estate swelled to such a Bulk in so small a time, by dealing in the Funds. From Envy to Ill-will is an easy step, which being once taken, all Arguments seem of weight that side with our Passions: how easy is it to convince such a one that Publick Credit is of the last ill Consequence, that it makes a Nation prodigal, Stock-jobbers only fat, and Gentlemen lean; and (as some have ventured to speak out plainly) that it ought to be destroyed, that we may never be trusted again.[65]

The writer warns against the (seemingly) reasonable anger against those who have profited from the misfortune of those gentlemen who have had charge (financial and personal) in the Nine Years' War being allowed to spill over into other financial dealings: The fact that some people have manipulated stock in the past – perhaps the very exchequer notes that so exercised Sir James Bateman – must not be allowed to sour the public on further stock and credit when it is in the national interest.

The issues of stock-jobbing, and its relationship to honour and warfare, were brought to the stage by Thomas Shadwell in a play staged in 1692 and published posthumously the next year as *The Volunteers, or, The Stock-Jobbers*. Shadwell was made Poet Laureate after Dryden's removal from the post, and while he has traditionally been identified as a Whig, Steven Pincus has argued that he is best understood as a Trimmer: a staunch critic of Toryism, but no radical either, instead holding to "the idea of mixed monarchy as enshrined in the ancient constitution."[66] For this reason, the play moves away from traditional ideas of honour which "centred on loyalty to the king" and towards "abstract versions like patriotism and the public good."[67] Although the play features Major General Blount, an old Cavalier whose neighbour is Colonel Hackwell, a former Roundhead, the two do not revisit that conflict but share a mutual appreciation for the law, the public and those who serve in the military in particular. The central plot sees their children, Hackwell junior and Eugenia, (eventually) marry, although the 'blocking' comes not from their opposing politics, as might be expected – in fact, Blount is particularly keen to ensure the match – but from Hackwell's new wife, who seeks to disinherit his son in place of her own children.

The 'volunteer' of the title is Welford, admired by other characters for his martial skill, ability to endure hardships and the very fact he has volunteered for combat rather than taking an officer's rank to direct proceedings from behind the lines. Welford serves with Hackwell junior, and spends the play successfully wooing Hackwell's sister Clara (supported by Blount) against the background threat of his regiment being deployed to Flanders. As the title suggests, financial and romantic matters are intertwined throughout the play, such as the sparring between Hackwell junior and Eugenia as they discuss their love letters and ultimate match in terms of relative fortunes:

Hackwell jun: Your father is generous and compassionate; and sure, with that great Stock of your own, you must inherit all his virtues

Eugenia: Could you think that your bills were to be answered at sight, like Bills of Exchange?[68]

Here the pun is on stock by activating three of its meanings: it is lineage, and possessions, but also an expectation of future value through inheritance. Eugenia's response continues the interplay between finance and emotion: In attempting to draw a line between the behaviour of credit merchants and the loving expectations highlighted by the reference to inheritance in the previous line, Eugenia accidentally demonstrates that the same kind of calculation may be behind them both. Love letters and Bills of Exchange are both sets of writing designed to be trustworthy, and used in expectation of future gains – Eugenia making Hackwell wait, in fact, is a hard-headed part of the courtship process as she waits to determine what stock he will have from his own father and stepfather, who look like they will deny him his fortune.

Later in that same scene, after the young suitors have left, Colonel and Mrs Hackwell are introduced by two sharpers ("a new name for a rogue and a cheat," according to the *Dramatis Personae*) to two stock-jobbers; at Mrs Hackwell's insistence, they suggest a series of investments for the couple to make:

1 Jobber: Why, it is a mouse trap, that will invite all mice in, nay rats too, whether they will or no; a whole share, before the patent, is fifteen pound; after the patent, they will not take sixty; there is no family in England will be without 'em.

2 Jobber: I take it to be a great undertaking: but there is a patent likewise on foot for ones walking under water, a share twenty pound.[69]

The image of the mouse trap is a particularly rich one. It was, after all, an everyday necessity which no family would be without, so a patentee would naturally expect to reap a large and consistent profit. But it also points to the exploitative nature of the stock-jobbers, luring in unsuspecting investors. In fact, animal metaphors were common for those who decried the practice of stock-jobbing. George White, while an EIC director, wrote of "a strange sort of insects call'd stock-jobbers, who devour men on our exchange, as the locusts of old did the herbage of Egypt."[70] An anonymous pamphlet a few years later:

> They are kept in good Hands, and the Stock-Jobbers, those Moles, those Underminers, and Destroyers, not suffer'd to come amongst them, the Jack-Daws have been too hard for the Rooks, (as those Gentlemen are call'd;)[71]

Both of these metaphors stress the destructive nature of the jobbers, who undermine honest projects and eat away good capital. But the anonymous pamphlet goes further, suggesting a risk from the very presence of the jobbers, who are 'not suffered to come among' good businessmen, with a second animal metaphor placing them as rooks kept away by jack-daws – two members of the corvid family, who look similar, perhaps suggesting the difficulty in telling honest men and jobbers apart. Like the mice who are drawn in 'whether they will or no', the presence of jobbers is presented as an insidious and inescapable threat once they are established.

The Hackwells and the stock-jobbers continue their conversation, with Col Hackwell picking up this idea by stressing the only value of these impossible-sounding projects is to make him money, rather than be useful:

Mrs Hackwell:	That would have been of great use to carry messages under the ice this last frost, before it would bear.
Hackwell sen:	Look thee, lamb, between us, it's no matter whether it turns to use or not; the main end, verily, is to turn the penny in the way of stock-jobbing, that's all.
2 Jobber:	There is likewise a patent moved for, of bringing some Chinese rope-dancers over, the most exquisite in the world; considerable men have shares in it; but verily, I question whether this be lawful or not?
Hackwell sen:	Look thee brother, if it be to a good end, and that we ourselves have no share in the vanity or wicked diversion thereof, by beholding of it, but only use it whereby we might turn the penny, and employ it for edification, always considered that it is like to take and the said shares sell well; and then we shall not care, whether the aforesaid dancers come over or no.[72]

The jobber's drawing on anonymous, but 'considerable men' as a form of security, would have been familiar to anyone versed in the corporate writings of the period. As in the pamphlets on the dangers of lending to corporations analysed previously, one form of credit (reputation) is transformed into another (invest-ability). Hackwell's replies fit with the "popular images of puritans as hypocritically austere figures," an image particularly suited to the stage and intensified in the latter part of the seventeenth century.[73] Here, the hypocrisy of profiting from the entertainment condemned as 'wicked diversion' is coupled with the second hypocrisy, that so long as the shares increase in value, Colonel Hackwell has no interest in whether the performers actually arrive – that is, he does not care for truth so long as his own cause is advanced. This hypocrisy is reinforced in the closing lines of the scene, when Hackwell arranges a further 'consultation' with the jobbers, in order "to settle matters as to lowering and heightening of shares."

The climax of the play once again draws together financial and romantic matters, as Hackwell's exultation in his profits leads to the discovery of his wife's adultery. Stepping out of the ball to a darkened room, Hackwell rejoices in the success of his investments:

> I have gotten pretty well out of the paper, and other patents, and made a pretty sum of them:- I have shares in some that cost me nothing, but were given me to prevent my caveats: those I'll keep a while; but for the linen, we have agreed when that shall rise – and then I'll wriggle myself out of that.[74]

However, Hackwell's gloating is interrupted by his wife and Nickum, one of the sharpers who introduced the couple to the stock-jobbers, who have stolen away to continue an affair. She, too, gloats, that soon her husband will "settle all his Estate" upon her, when he will leave her. Colonel Hackwell interrupts them, and kills Nickum in a swordfight. Mrs Hackwell is the subject of the play's joke, here, since she is immediately told that her daughter has made an unsuitable match to a dancing teacher, and leaves the stage lamenting her "complete ruin." Nonetheless, the juxtaposition of Hackwell's financial schemes with his wife's amorous ones invites the audience to find some sort of moral equivalence in their 'wriggling'. Just as the adulterers break down social norms and threaten established social structures, so too do the stock-jobbers threaten established financial systems – in both cases, the good of the individual is put before the whole, with potentially disastrous consequences for the commonwealth.

In his hypocrisy and financial chicanery, Hackwell recalls the corporate religious figures of Ananias and his brethren who become involved in "venture" and "projection" for the philosopher's stone in Jonson's *The Alchemist.*[75] Just like the East India Company, Ananias justifies his behaviour by claiming he acts "with widows' and with orphans' goods" (II.v.47). He asks Subtle, who is pretending he can transmute cheap metal goods from other orphans into gold, whether the parents of the orphans were godly, in an exchange which is a telling reflection on trust networks:

Ananias: Were the orphans' parents Sincere professors?
Subtle: Why do you ask?
Ananias: Because We are then to deal justly, and give, in truth, Their utmost value.
Subtle: 'Slid, you'd cozen, else An if their parents were not of the faithful? I will not trust you, now I think on't, Till I have talked with your pastor.
(II.v.56–62)

Ananias suggests that godliness ought to be a key driver in creating trust, and crucially that this should extend to commercial matters, where the brethren will 'deal justly' with one another and give honest 'values' to commodities. Jonson satirises the faith-based mercantile network as the play develops, and their trust is revealed to be just as negotiable as every other moral stance put forward in the play. Nevertheless, this would not have been an unusual concept for early modern audiences, who were familiar with the success of religiously oriented trading groups, such as Huguenot families in London, Quaker networks across the Atlantic and even Muslim combines across the Indian Ocean.[76] Perhaps most prominent of these were Jewish networks, linked to gold, banking and Amsterdam in the early modern imagination, and often the bearers of displaced anxiety about the functioning of the economic system more generally.[77] While these godly groups did not necessarily behave badly to those outside of their networks (indeed, they probably behaved more or less the same inside and outside of the faith[78]), both dramatists and petitioners portrayed these groups as inside-facing threats to the mercantile community more generally.

Subtle's apparent shock, though, is a characteristically cynical manoeuvre, designed to draw in Tribulation Wholesome, Ananias's pastor, who he correctly suspects will be more manipulable than the zealous young man. Their conversation on their return to see Subtle confirms as much, with Ananias insisting that "the sanctified cause/should have a sanctified course," but Tribulation completing his half-line with the cutting "Not always necessary" (III.i.13–14). Tribulation then confirms that the brethren are ready to "lend their willing hands to any project" (III.ii.13). The conversation between Tribulation and Subtle lays bare the hypocrisy in the brethren which Subtle suggested in the earlier scene: First, Tribulation confirms that they seek "to grow soon and profitably famous" (III.ii.101), and then he and Subtle work out a legal loophole for their scheme. Tribulation asks "this act of coining, is it lawful?" and is delighted when Subtle assures him that it is not coining, but casting, remarking "Ha! You distinguish well./Casting of money may be lawful" (III.ii.153). Ananias resignedly notes that the "brethren may approve it lawful, doubt not" (III.ii.158), and so the hypocrisy is confirmed while also drawing the audience's attention to the potential economic problems of unlimited coining.

The characters of *The Alchemist* are obviously not investing in stock. But they are investors, or what would later be termed projectors, seeking a scheme to get rich at the expense of others. In this regard, *The Alchemist* and its contemporary plays reflect a general anxiety over a marketplace in which use-value is gradually becoming divorced from price, where capital makes money not because something is productive (or even traditionally unproductive ways such as usury), but because people simply believe it is valuable.

Jonson picked up this theme in other works, such as *Volpone*, in which a series of inheritance hunters are gulled into paying to be added to the will of an apparently dying old man (although the titular Volpone is no such thing). In another of his disguises, this time as a mountebank to sell his snake-oil healing potion, Volpone cries to his audience that "I ask you not as the value of the thing, for then I should demand of you a thousand crowns."[79] This is ironic, of course, since the stated price of six crowns is still much more than its actual value. Volpone claims he is substantially undercharging, despite a list of eminent authorities who can swear by the potion, because of his "affection" for the crowd, and eventually reduces it further to sixpence as "a pledge of your loves."[80] In effect, Volpone reduces the financial price of the item in exchange for an emotional price.

His performance in that scene, and throughout the play, relies on smoothly eliding the differing ideas of value and credit that I have been discussing in this chapter. This exploitation of the gap between perceived value and actual value was replicated in the stock market even at the start of the seventeenth century, and serves as a precursor to the share bubbles in East India and South Sea stock. Corporations created trust, and they created value; but they also created risk, and a disjunction in the economy between real and abstract notions of value which reverberated through early modern literature, and which we are still negotiating today.

Notes

1 Anon, *The Case of the Quo Warranto against the City of London* (London: s.n., 1690), 113.
2 Ryan Saylor and Nicholas C. Wheeler, "Paying for War and Building States: The Coalitional Politics of Debt Servicing and Tax Institutions," *World Politics* 69, no. 2 (2017): 398.
3 Douglass C. North, *Institutions, Institutional Change and Economic Performance* (Cambridge: Cambridge University Press, 1990), 139.
4 Anon, *An Enquiry, Whether It Be the Interest of the City to Insure Houses from Fire* (London: Printed for the Gentlemen of the Insurance Office, 1681), 4.
5 William A. Pettigrew and Tristan Stein, "The Public Rivalry between Regulated and Joint Stock Corporations and the Development of Seventeenth-Century Corporate Constitutions," *Historical Research* 90, no. 248 (2017); "The Public Rivalry between Regulated and Joint Stock Corporations and the Development of Seventeenth-Century Corporate Constitutions," 355.
6 Anon, *Two Letters Concerning the East-India Company* (London?: s.n., 1676), 1.
7 Craig Muldrew, *The Economy of Obligation: The Culture of Credit and Social Relations in Early Modern England* (Basingstoke: Palgrave Macmillan, 1998), 97. On constructing credit networks, see also Nuala Zahedieh, "Making Mercantilism Work: London Merchants and Atlantic Trade in the Seventeenth Century," *Transactions of the Royal Historical Society* 9 (1999); Natasha Glaisyer, "'A Due Circulation in the Veins of the Publick': Imagining Credit in Late Seventeenth- and Early Eighteenth-Century England," *The Eighteenth Century* 46, no. 3 (2005).
8 Anon, *Two Letters Concerning the East-India Company*, 3.
9 *An Answer to Two Letters Concerning the East-India Company* (Bristol: s.n., 1676), 14.
10 *An Answer to Two Letters Concerning the East-India Company*, 14.
11 *An Answer to Two Letters Concerning the East-India Company*, 1.
12 Dudley Digges, *The Defence of Trade* (London: William Stansby for John Barnes, 1615), 2.
13 Anon, *An Answer to Two Letters Concerning the East-India Company*, 1–2.
14 *An Answer to Two Letters Concerning the East-India Company*, 4.
15 Philip J. Stern, *The Company-State: Corporate Sovereignty & the Early Modern Foundations of the British Empire in India* (Oxford: Oxford University Press, 2011), 150.
16 Anon, *A Petition against the East India Company* (London: Thomas Braddyll and Robert Everingham, 1691), 1.
17 Anon, *Reasons Humbly Offered against Grafting or Splicing* (London?: s.n., 1690), 1.

18 *Some Considerations Offered against the Continuance of the Bank of England in a Letter to a Member of the Present Parliament* (London?: s.n., 1694), 3.
19 Henry S. Turner, *The Corporate Commonwealth: Pluralism and Political Fictions in England 1516–1651* (Chicago: University of Chicago Press, 2016), 215.
20 BL IOR B/40, 29th March 1693, fol. 180r.
21 Perry Gauci, *The Politics of Trade: The Overseas Merchant in State and Society, 1660–1720* (Oxford: Oxford University Press, 2001), 72.
22 Bartholomew Churchman, *An Answer to the Hollanders Declaration, Concerning the Occurrents of the East-India* (London: Nicholas Okes, 1622), 2.
23 Ceri Sullivan, *The Rhetoric of Credit: Merchants in Early Modern Writing* (Madison, NJ: Fairleigh Dickinson University Press, 2002), 27.
24 BL Egerton 2086, Petition of John Fardoe to Humfrey Fitzherbert, Captain and chief commander for the Hon Company of Merchants trading to the East Indies, Aboard The Gift, 14 October, 1620.
25 Huntington, Bateman Correspondence, HM78007, Bateman to Richard Hill, 11 May 1697.
26 Huntington, Bateman Correspondence, HM78009, Bateman to Richard Hill, 25 May 1697.
27 Anon, *A Brief Account of the Great Oppressions and Injuries Which the Managers of the East-India Company Have Acted on the Lives, Liberties, and Estates of Their Fellow-Subjects* (London?: s.n., 1695), 2.
28 Jennifer Bishop, "Speech and Sociability: The Regulation of Language in the Livery Companies of Early Modern London," in *Cities and Solidarities: Urban Communities in Pre-Modern Europe*, ed. Justin Colson and Arie van Steensel (Abingdon: Routledge, 2017), 209. On the failures of regulation and development of new regimes in the Merchant Adventurers, see also Thomas Leng, "Interlopers and Disorderly Brethren at the Stade Mart: Commercial Regulations and Practices Amongst the Merchant Adventurers of England in the Late Elizabethan Period," *The Economic History Review* 69, no. 3 (2016).
29 Huntington, Ellesmere, EL2352, Petition of William Craddock (relates to April & May 1598).
30 For example, the imposition of martial law in St Helena was widely regarded as a case of corporate legal overreach by the East India Company; see Philip J. Stern, "Politics and Ideology in the Early East India Company-State: The Case of St Helena, 1673–1709," *The Journal of Imperial and Commonwealth History* 35, no. 1 (2007).
31 Thomas Violet, *The Advancement of Merchandize* (London: William Du-Gard, 1651), 34.
32 *The Advancement of Merchandize*, 118.
33 TNA T70/57, RAC to Montserrat (Edward Parsons and Samuel Horne), 5th March 1696/7.
34 Trinity House, *The Answer of the Masters of the Trinity-House, to the Special Objections of the Patentee, to the Keeping of Winterton Lights* (London?: s.n., 1621), 1.
35 *Reasons Humbly Offered against Grafting or Splicing*, 2.
36 The same was also true in India, where the EIC sporadically supported diplomatic efforts; see Rupali Mishra, "Diplomacy at the Edge: Split Interests in the Roe Embassy to the Mughal Court," *Journal of British Studies* 53, no. 1 (2014).

37 TNA SP105/111 Levant Company to English Merchants in Constantinople, 19 March 1641, f. 97r.
38 See Mark Charles Fissel, "Early Stuart Absolutism and the Strangers' Consulage," in *Law and Authority in Early Modern England: Essays Presented to Thomas Garden Barnes*, ed. Thomas G. Barnes, Buchanan Sharp, and Mark Charles Fissel (Newark: University of Delaware Press, 2007).
39 TNA SP 105/111, Levant Company to Wyche, London, 3 June 1636, fol. 3v-4r.
40 TNA SP 97/15, Wyche to the Levant Company, Constantinople, last of October, 1636, f. 101r.
41 TNA SP105/111, Levant Company to Wyche, 1st September 1636, f. 11v.
42 See Jason Cameron White, "Royal Authority Versus Corporate Sovereignty: The Levant Company and the Ambiguities of Early Stuart Statecraft," *The Seventeenth Century* (2017).
43 TNA SP 105/112, Company to Bendysh, 18 May 1648, p. 40.
44 BL IOR E/3/26 Nicholas Buckeridge and George Morton at Bandar Abbas to the Agent and factors in Bengal, April 2 1659, p. 59.
45 BL Stowe 219, Chandos to My Lords and Gentlemen, Pera, 23 September, 1681, fol. 10r.
46 Miles Ogborn, *Indian Ink: Script and Print in the Making of the East India Company* (Chicago: University of Chicago Press, 2007), 98.
47 Huntington, Bateman Correspondence 78022, Bateman to Richard Hill, 20 February 1699.
48 Huntington, Bateman Correspondence 72030, Bateman to Richard Hill, 3 October 1699.
49 Josiah Child to Thomas Papillon, 22 October, 1698, in A. F. W. Papillon, ed. *Memoirs of Thomas Papillon, Merchant* (Reading: Joseph Beecroft, 1887), 90.
50 See W. Noel Sainsbury, ed. *Calendar of State Papers Colonial, 1574–1660* (London: Longman, 186), 29; "Reply of Sir Thomas Smythe and Alderman Johnson to the Petition of John Bargrave, 1621," *The Virginia Magazine of History and Biography* 6, no. 4 (1899).
51 Susan M. Kingsbury, ed. *The Records of the the Virginia Company of London: The Court Book*, 4 vols. (Washington, DC: Government Printing Office, 1906), I.444.
52 Huntington HM 962, John Bargrave, A Treatise Showing How to Erect a Publique and Increaseing Treasurie, c. 1633, fol. 4r.
53 Huntington HM 962, John Bargrave, A Treatise Showing How to Erect a Publique and Increaseing Treasurie, c. 1633, fol. 4r.
54 Anon, *Some Considerations Offered against the Continuance of the Bank of England in a Letter to a Member of the Present Parliament* (London?: s.n., 1694), 3.
55 D'Maris Coffman, "Credibility, Transparency, Accountability and the Public Credit under the Long Parliament and Commonwealth, 1643–53," in *Questioning Credible Commitment: Perspectives on the Rise of Financial Capitalism*, ed. D'Maris Coffman, Adrian Leonard, and Larry Neal (Cambridge: Cambridge University Press, 2013).
56 Douglass C. North and Barry R. Weingast, "Constitutions and Commitment: The Evolution of Institutions Governing Public Choice in Seventeenth-Century England," *The Journal of Economic History* 49, no. 4 (1989): 821.
57 Huntington, Bateman Correspondence, HM78028, Bateman to Richard Hill, 12 Sep 1699.
58 On the issue of projecting and its relationship to the early modern investment economy, see Koji Yamamoto, *Taming Capitalism before its Triumph: Public*

Service, Distrust, and 'Projecting' in Early Modern England (Oxford: Oxford University Press, 2018).

59 Daniel Defoe, *Several Essays Relating to Accademies, Banks, Bankrupts, Charity-Lotteries, Courts of Enquiries, Court Merchants, Friendly-Societies, High-Ways, Pension-Office, Seamen, Wagering, & C* (London: Thomas Cockerill, 1700), 30.

60 *Several Essays*, 12–13.

61 Elizabeth Grymeston, *Miscelanea* (London: Melch. Bradwood for Felix Norton, 1604), 11, 'The Ballad'. The OED incorrectly places the first usage at 1626, but gives the ballad in Grymeston as an example from its citation in Defoe's Ye True Born Englishmen in 1701.

62 Anon, *Plain Dealing* (London: S. Eddowes, 1691), 6–7.

63 Anne L. Murphy, *The Origins of English Financial Markets: Investment and Speculation before the South Sea Bubble* (Cambridge: Cambridge University Press, 2009), 1.

64 Anon, *Some Considerations Upon the Late Act of the Parliament of Scotland, for Constituting an Indian Company, in a Letter to a Friend* (London: s.n., 1695), 4.

65 *The Importance of Public Credit* (London: s.n., 1699), 2.

66 Steven Pincus, "Shadwell's Dramatic Trimming," in *Religion, Literature, and Politics in Post-Reformation England, 1540–1688*, ed. Donna B. Hamilton and Richard Strier (Cambridge: Cambridge University Press, 1996), 265.

67 Christopher J. Wheatley, "Thomas Shadwell's the Volunteers and the Rhetoric of Honor and Patriotism," *ELH* 60, no. 2 (1993): 398.

68 Thomas Shadwell, *The Volunteers, or, the Stock-Jobbers a Comedy* (London: James Knapton, 1693), II.i.

69 *The Volunteers, or, the Stock-Jobbers a Comedy*, II.i.

70 George White, *An Account of the Trade to the East-Indies* (London: s.n., 1691), 5.

71 'Person of Honour', *Angliae Tutamen, or, the Safety of England* (London: For the Author, 1695), 27.

72 Shadwell, *The Volunteers, or, the Stock-Jobbers a Comedy*, II.i.

73 Rachel Willie, *Staging the Revolution: Drama, Reinvention and History, 1647–72* (Manchester: Manchester University Press, 2015), 203.

74 Shadwell, *The Volunteers, or, the Stock-Jobbers a Comedy*, V.iii.

75 The Alchemist II.v.65–6 in Ben Jonson, *The Alchemist and Other Plays*, ed. Gordon Campbell (Oxford: Oxford University Press, 1995). Further references are given in the text.

76 Gary Stuart de Krey, *A Fractured Society: The Politics of London in the First Age of Party 1688–1715* (Oxford: Clarendon Press, 1985), 143–4; S. D. Smith, "The Account Book of Richard Poor, Quaker Merchant of Barbados," *The William and Mary Quarterly* 66, no. 3 (2009); Patricia Risso, *Merchants and Faith: Muslim Commerce and Culture in the Indian Ocean* (Boulder, CO: Westview Press, 1995).

77 Francesca Trivellato, "Credit, Honor, and the Early Modern French Legend of the Jewish Invention of Bills of Exchange," *The Journal of Modern History* 84, no. 2 (2012).

78 For example, for the argument that Quaker networks were not ethically distinct from wider commercially practices, see Ester Sahle, "An Investigation of Early Modern Quakers' Business Ethics," *LSE Economic History Working Papers* 216(2015).

79 Volpone II.ii.169–70 in Jonson, *The Alchemist and Other Plays.*

80 Volpone II.ii.173 and 203 in *The Alchemist and Other Plays.*

Works cited

Manuscript

BL Egerton 2086
BL IOR B/40
BL IOR E/3/26
BL Stowe 219
Huntington, Ellesmere EL2352
Huntington, HM78007–78028
Huntington, HM 962
TNA SP 97/15, 105/110, 105/112
TNA T70/57

Print

Anon. *An Answer to Two Letters Concerning the East-India Company*. Bristol: s.n., 1676a.

———. *Two Letters Concerning the East-India Company*. London?: s.n., 1676b.

———. *An Enquiry, Whether It Be the Interest of the City to Insure Houses from Fire*. London: Printed for the Gentlemen of the Insurance Office, 1681.

———. *The Case of the Quo Warranto against the City of London*. London: s.n., 1690a.

———. *Reasons Humbly Offered against Grafting or Splicing*. London?: s.n., 1690b.

———. *A Petition against the East India Company*. London: Thomas Braddyll and Robert Everingham, 1691a.

———. *Plain Dealing*. London: S. Eddowes, 1691b.

———. *Some Considerations Offered against the Continuance of the Bank of England in a Letter to a Member of the Present Parliament*. London?: s.n., 1694.

———. *A Brief Account of the Great Oppressions and Injuries Which the Managers of the East-India Company Have Acted on the Lives, Liberties, and Estates of Their Fellow-Subjects*. London?: s.n., 1695a.

———. *Some Considerations Upon the Late Act of the Parliament of Scotland, for Constituting an Indian Company, in a Letter to a Friend*. London: s.n., 1695b.

———. *The Importance of Public Credit*. London: s.n., 1699.

Bishop, Jennifer. "Speech and Sociability: The Regulation of Language in the Livery Companies of Early Modern London." In *Cities and Solidarities: Urban Communities in Pre-Modern Europe*, edited by Justin Colson and Arie van Steensel, 208–25. Abingdon: Routledge, 2017.

Churchman, Bartholomew. *An Answer to the Hollanders Declaration, Concerning the Occurrents of the East-India*. London: Nicholas Okes, 1622.

Coffman, D'Maris. "Credibility, Transparency, Accountability and the Public Credit under the Long Parliament and Commonwealth, 1643–53." In *Questioning Credible Commitment: Perspectives on the Rise of Financial Capitalism*, edited by D'Maris Coffman, Adrian Leonard and Larry Neal, 76–103. Cambridge: Cambridge University Press, 2013.

Defoe, Daniel. *Several Essays Relating to Accademies, Banks, Bankrupts, Charity-Lotteries, Courts of Enquiries, Court Merchants, Friendly-Societies, High-Ways, Pension-Office, Seamen, Wagering, & C.* London: Thomas Cockerill, 1700.

Digges, Dudley. *The Defence of Trade*. London: William Stansby for John Barnes, 1615.

Fissel, Mark Charles. "Early Stuart Absolutism and the Strangers' Consulage." In *Law and Authority in Early Modern England : Essays Presented to Thomas Garden Barnes*, edited by Thomas G. Barnes, Buchanan Sharp and Mark Charles Fissel, 186–223. Newark: University of Delaware Press, 2007.

Gauci, Perry. *The Politics of Trade: The Overseas Merchant in State and Society, 1660–1720*. Oxford: Oxford University Press, 2001.

Glaisyer, Natasha. "'A Due Circulation in the Veins of the Publick': Imagining Credit in Late Seventeenth- and Early Eighteenth-Century England." *The Eighteenth Century* 46, no. 3 (2005): 277–97.

Grymeston, Elizabeth. *Miscelanea*. London: Melch. Bradwood for Felix Norton, 1604.

House, Trinity. *The Answer of the Masters of the Trinity-House, to the Special Objections of the Patentee, to the Keeping of Winterton Lights*. London?: s.n., 1621.

Jonson, Ben. *The Alchemist and Other Plays*. Edited by Gordon Campbell. Oxford: Oxford University Press, 1995.

Kingsbury, Susan M., ed. *The Records of the the Virginia Company of London: The Court Book*. 4 vols. Washington, DC: Government Printing Office, 1906.

Krey, Gary Stuart de. *A Fractured Society: The Politics of London in the First Age of Party 1688–1715*. Oxford: Clarendon Press, 1985.

Leng, Thomas. "Interlopers and Disorderly Brethren at the Stade Mart: Commercial Regulations and Practices Amongst the Merchant Adventurers of England in the Late Elizabethan Period." *The Economic History Review* 69, no. 3 (2016): 823–43.

Mishra, Rupali. "Diplomacy at the Edge: Split Interests in the Roe Embassy to the Mughal Court." *Journal of British Studies* 53, no. 1 (2014): 5–28.

Muldrew, Craig. *The Economy of Obligation: The Culture of Credit and Social Relations in Early Modern England*. Basingstoke: Palgrave Macmillan, 1998.

Murphy, Anne L. *The Origins of English Financial Markets: Investment and Speculation before the South Sea Bubble*. Cambridge: Cambridge University Press, 2009.

North, Douglass C. *Institutions, Institutional Change and Economic Performance*. Cambridge: Cambridge University Press, 1990.

North, Douglass C., and Barry R. Weingast. "Constitutions and Commitment: The Evolution of Institutions Governing Public Choice in Seventeenth-Century England." *The Journal of Economic History* 49, no. 4 (1989): 803–32.

Ogborn, Miles. *Indian Ink: Script and Print in the Making of the East India Company*. Chicago: University of Chicago Press, 2007.

Papillon, A. F. W., ed. *Memoirs of Thomas Papillon, Merchant*. Reading: Joseph Beecroft, 1887.

'Person of Honour'. *Angliae Tutamen, or, the Safety of England*. London: For the Author, 1695.

Pettigrew, William A., and Tristan Stein. "The Public Rivalry between Regulated and Joint Stock Corporations and the Development of Seventeenth-Century Corporate Constitutions." *Historical Research* 90, no. 248 (2017): 341–62.

Pincus, Steven. "Reply of Sir Thomas Smythe and Alderman Johnson to the Petition of John Bargrave, 1621." *The Virginia Magazine of History and Biography* 6, no. 4 (1899): 378–81.

———. "Shadwell's Dramatic Trimming." In *Religion, Literature, and Politics in Post-Reformation England, 1540–1688*, edited by Donna B. Hamilton and Richard Strier, 253–74. Cambridge: Cambridge University Press, 1996.

Risso, Patricia. *Merchants and Faith: Muslim Commerce and Culture in the Indian Ocean*. Boulder, CO: Westview Press, 1995.

Sahle, Ester. "An Investigation of Early Modern Quakers' Business Ethics." *LSE Economic History Working Papers* 216 (2015).

Sainsbury, W. Noel, ed. *Calendar of State Papers Colonial, 1574–1660*. London: Longman, 186.

Saylor, Ryan, and Nicholas C. Wheeler. "Paying for War and Building States: The Coalitional Politics of Debt Servicing and Tax Institutions." *World Politics* 69, no. 2 (2017): 366–408.

Shadwell, Thomas. *The Volunteers, or, the Stock-Jobbers a Comedy*. London: James Knapton, 1693.

Smith, S. D. "The Account Book of Richard Poor, Quaker Merchant of Barbados." *The William and Mary Quarterly* 66, no. 3 (2009): 605–28.

Stern, Philip J. "Politics and Ideology in the Early East India Company-State: The Case of St Helena, 1673–1709." *The Journal of Imperial and Commonwealth History* 35, no. 1 (2007): 1–23.

———. *The Company-State: Corporate Sovereignty & the Early Modern Foundations of the British Empire in India*. Oxford: Oxford University Press, 2011.

Sullivan, Ceri. *The Rhetoric of Credit: Merchants in Early Modern Writing*. Madison, NJ: Fairleigh Dickinson University Press, 2002.

Trivellato, Francesca. "Credit, Honor, and the Early Modern French Legend of the Jewish Invention of Bills of Exchange." *The Journal of Modern History* 84, no. 2 (2012): 289–334.

Turner, Henry S. *The Corporate Commonwealth: Pluralism and Political Fictions in England 1516–1651*. Chicago: University of Chicago Press, 2016.

Violet, Thomas. *The Advancement of Merchandize*. London: William Du-Gard, 1651.

Wheatley, Christopher J. "Thomas Shadwell's the Volunteers and the Rhetoric of Honor and Patriotism." *ELH* 60, no. 2 (1993): 397–418.

White, George. *An Account of the Trade to the East-Indies* London: s.n., 1691.

White, Jason Cameron. "Royal Authority Versus Corporate Sovereignty: The Levant Company and the Ambiguities of Early Stuart Statecraft." *The Seventeenth Century* (2017): 1–25.

Willie, Rachel. *Staging the Revolution: Drama, Reinvention and History, 1647–72*. Manchester: Manchester University Press, 2015.

Yamamoto, Koji. *Taming Capitalism before its Triumph: Public Service, Distrust, and 'Projecting' in Early Modern England*. Oxford: Oxford University Press, 2018.

Zahedieh, Nuala. "Making Mercantilism Work: London Merchants and Atlantic Trade in the Seventeenth Century." *Transactions of the Royal Historical Society* 9 (1999): 143–58.

3 The world's exchange

The first two chapters have demonstrated the ways in which corporations engaged, more or less directly, with the commonwealth, in their use of print, the development of a unified 'body corporate' and their role in regulating trade and personal relationships. The remaining three chapters of the book examine the corporation on a more conceptual level. They are concerned with the effects of corporate activities on ways of thinking, or what Raymond Williams called "structures of feeling." The term is particularly apposite, since part of what Williams meant by it was the unification of analysis of cultural changes with "the changes covered by the disciplines of politics, economics and communications."[1] My analysis in these chapters draws on the changes corporations instituted in the political economy of early modern England (at least in part), but considers them as they were refracted into contemporary writing. I take as my starting points three key aspects of transnational corporate activity – the idea of a national trade, the structuring of that trade and the duty to spread the Gospel – and consider how those aspects of corporate life helped shape, and were in turn shaped by, popular discourses.

This chapter deals with the structure of trade, and in fact the concept at the very heart of trade: the exchange. 'Exchange' was (and still is) a conceptually heavily loaded term: It involves an assessment of value, and thus placing two or more kinds of things into a relational system; it could be entirely practical (one good swapped for another in the same physical location), or, increasingly, take place entirely in the space of representation through either money or credit; it could be mutually beneficial, or a source of deceit and mistrust; it could be productive or destructive. Exchange is the point at which the imaginative possibilities of ownership or purchase collapse into a specific event – a price is fixed, the worth of an object is decided, abstract notions such as credit or future returns are made real and given value.

This chapter therefore begins by considering the shift in meanings of exchange, and especially its expansion from the direct swap of two goods to a broader network of credit-facilitated global trade, in part through writings related to the activities of the East India Company. These pamphlets, and the other writings they generated in response, helped to create the idea of 'productive exchange'; that is, exchange which added a value, either to the things being exchanged, or the economy as a whole, so that the circulation of goods and money came to be seen as a goal in itself. This idea of productive exchange was critiqued in contemporary literary sources, such as Milton's 1634 *Masque Performed at Ludlow Castle (Comus)*, and the role of exchange and circulation in that text is analysed in light of those political economic debates.

The second part of the chapter considers London as a site of global exchange. The Royal Exchange, built in 1571, provided a specific place for merchants to do business, adding to a growing sense of London as a global trading centre. As well as expressing their delight in the global goods brought to London, writers began to reimagine London's history from the Romans onwards into a narrative of mercantile importance, and utilised these historical or geographical studies to address contemporary concerns over wealth, power and governance. Conceiving London in this way drew together a number of 'structures of feeling': national pride, awareness of global trading routes, and political economy, all of which found their way into literary texts such as translations and city comedies.

Exchange

The word 'exchange' is first recorded in its sense of swapping one thing for another in 1483 by the *Oxford English Dictionary*, although it did not become common in English until the middle of the sixteenth century. In 1538, Thomas Elyot produced a Latin-English dictionary in which he used the word in what would become its standard form, "an exchange of money," and most of his other uses have the narrow remit of banking and foreign currency transactions.[2] The word 'exchange' thus has, in its initial incarnation, a specific sense of foreign exchange, an exchange that takes place across national and cultural boundaries. However, in the same volume Elyot makes reference to "bargain by exchaunge,"[3] which suggests the sense we would now recognise of a transaction swapping goods, or goods for money.

In fact, the idea of exchanging one set of goods for another had become so commonplace by the early seventeenth century that it had become axiomatic, with the minister William Sclater arguing that tithes could be paid in other forms since "exchange is no robbery in this kind."[4] Sclater's usage suggests that this is already a common phrase, and the *Oxford Dictionary of Phrase and Fable* gives the phrase as being recorded from the mid sixteenth century, although the first recorded usage I have found is from 1592: "treaties had and fair exchanges coy."[5] Late sixteenth century writers still saw the exchange as an exchange of things at its core, viewing currency as a necessary intermediary, but not an object of exchange in itself:

> The coin is stricken to be the tokens for exchange of things between man and man: yet it is the wares that are necessary for mans use, that are exchanged in deed, under the outward name of the coin.[6]

In 1582, the schoolmaster John Mellis of Southwark produced an expanded edition of a textbook which had supposedly originally been written by Robert Recorde and John Dee, *The Ground of Arts*. He claimed that his additions were to the benefit of those who "trade in merchandize," and the new, third, part of the book does indeed give examples for calculating profit and loss, translating different systems of measurement and coinage, as well as computing the gains or loss by exchanges.[7] The treatise offers a fairly simple outline of coins of other realms, and how to calculate equivalent value between English, French and Flemish currency. However, an entire chapter is dedicated to "Rules of Barter, and Exchanging of Merchandise."[8] This chapter offers detailed examples of how to conduct trade which is partly done by barter and partly by sale for money, delivered as problems in which the relative value of the transaction is to be discovered by the student or reader:

> A Venetian hath in London 100 pieces of silke, to put away for ready money at 3 lb the piece. But in barter he delivers thē for 4 lb the piece, taking wools of a Felmonger at 7 lb 10 s the C. weight which was worth no more but 6 lb the C. in ready money: The question is now, what wools pay for the silks, and which of them win or lose by the barter.
>
> *Answer*. 100 pieces of silks at 3 lb, is 300 lb: and at 4 lb is 400 lb: Then to find what wools pay for the Silke: Saye by the rule of three direct: If 7 ½ d buy me 1 C. weight, what 400 lb? work, and find 53 ⅓ C. weight of wool: Now to find the estate of their gain or loss, caste up his wool at 6 lb the C. (for so much they were worth ready money) and you shall find 320 lb, which is 20 lb more than the silks were to be sold for in ready money: whereupon the Venetian gained 20 lb by the Barter.[9]

Although these are, presumably, arithmetical problems rather than specific examples, they nonetheless demonstrate the realities of mercantile life, as well as the relationship between varied forms of exchanges. Currency exchange is over-simplified, and although Mellis refers to the potential fluctuation of currency, his models assume a static exchange, with no value to be created by anticipating those fluctuations: "Exchange is no other thing then to take or receive money in one city, to render or pay the value thereof in an other city."[10] Instead, profit for Mellis comes through the balance of barter and ready money payments in any particular transaction, as well as the potential to hold goods or credit for potentially more profitable transactions in the future.

Mellis's problems demonstrate the extent to which ready money was valued by late sixteenth-century merchants, as well as the fact that payments often had to be made in kind or on credit, as a consequence of what Carl Wennerlind has termed "the scarcity of money problem."[11] The model of barter, and the general understanding of exchanges as material things, could not be replaced by an exchange system in which currency existed as an object of exchange in itself, because there was simply not enough physical currency in circulation to generate such an understanding of coin. Instead, money became a commodity because of its quality as what Foucault termed a "universal sign" in his analysis of the ideological tension between accumulation and representation.[12] That is, coinage has value not because of the intrinsic value of the gold or silver which comprises it, but because it is a way of measuring the value of all other objects. As a consequence of these developments, new ways of regulating exchanges had to be found. Most prevalent was allowing credit to stand in for physical coinage (that is, performing the same symbolic function as coin); but debt could also be traded, expanding personal credit instruments into objects of exchange in their own right.

As the seventeenth century developed, exchange itself came to be seen as a producer of additional value. The examples given previously of the late sixteenth century take the exchange as the moment value is determined and solidified, so that profit and loss is calculated at the moment of exchange. However, proponents of global corporate activity reconfigured this formula, arguing that the process of exchange was in itself productive.

Against a background of the anti-trade and anti-monopoly pamphlets discussed in Chapter 1, merchants began to articulate in print their sense of how the economy worked in practice, and theoretical models for its improvement. They tended to move away from wealth based on the acquisition of bullion to a model of an international economy based on a series of global trades, as international markets became increasingly integrated. At the heart of these models, therefore, was the concept of exchange, both in its general sense of trade, and in the specific sense of changing coin. Malynes, for example, although he bemoaned the loss caused to England by currency exchanges, nonetheless argued that the circulation of materials on a global scale by the East India Company was demonstrably beneficial:

> For if pepper doe but cost two pence halfpenny the pound in the Indies, and that ten shillings employed therein will require but 35 shillings for all charges whatsoever to deliver it in London; where it is usually sold for above 20 pence: It followeth by consequence, that

> there must be a very great gain [. . .] For when the said Indian commodities are sent from England into Turkie, Livorne, Genoway, the Low Countries, Marselleis and other places, and are sold for ready money: The same is employed again upon Corints, Wines, Cotton-Wool and Yearne, Galles and divers other Commodities, wherewith the ships being reladen [. . .] So that wee may very well affirm, that by this trade the treasure of the realm can greatly be increased and augmented.[13]

Malynes thus sees the East India trade not as a drain on bullion in return for luxuries, but rather as a profit-generating trade precisely because it generated surplus value in the re-export of materials bought so cheaply in India. By virtue of the well-organised East India trade, keeping down the cost of bringing spices and other exotic materials back across the globe, England is actually able to mitigate the losses it would otherwise incur in the foreign currency markets. Indeed, so beneficial (yet difficult) does Malynes consider this trade that he accepts that it "may bee thought convenient to have joint stocks for remote places, as the *East Indies* and *Persia*" despite the anti-corporate, anti-monopoly position which is otherwise maintained throughout his pamphlet.[14]

Malynes's acceptance that 'remote places' might need a joint stock points to the trans-locationality of the exchange systems developed in the early modern period; that is, they function as exchange systems with only the scantest regard for geographical specificity. Even among the traders to these places, geography was initially understood, as Malynes's terminology of 'East Indies' and 'Persia' suggests, only in the broadest regional sense; this was reinforced by charters which offered monopolies over huge swathes of the globe, such as the East India Company's first charter, which allowed them to voyage

> By way of traffic and merchandize to the *East-Indies*, in the countries and ports of *Asia* and *Africa*, and to as many of the islands, ports and cities, towns and places, thereabouts, as where trade and traffick may by all likelihood be discovered, established or had.[15]

To an extent, of course, the range of the charter is a consequence of the necessity of discovery on the voyages, but that, too, speaks to the way in which these trading zones were conceived of as fairly homogenous regions. 'Trade and traffic' was equally possible in the East Indies, Asia and Africa, and the Company was expected to establish a trading network which stretched across those spaces. In practice, of course, that proved impossible for much of the century, but the sense of London as a city at the heart of a global trading network did not diminish.

Alongside this economic imperative came an opportunity for a cultural claim to London's status as a European or even global trading city. The playwright John Lyly, in *Euphues and his England*, a hugely influential study of form and wit – indeed, the "best-selling and most widely read literary work of the period"[16] – contains a digression on London's status:

> The chiefest [city in England] is named *London*, a place both for the beauty of building, infinite riches, variety of all things, that excelleth all the cities in the world: insomuch that it may be called the store-house and mart of all *Europe*.[17]

Lyly's text considers London on a number of scales at once – it is at once full of infinite riches and variety, yet closes with the rather bathetic description of the city as a storehouse. It is the chief city of England, although despite its wealth just a 'Mart' in a European market-system; yet even here, Lyly's phrase 'all Europe' does hint at a grander status within that system. The necessity for his audience to keep multiple levels of meaning in play perhaps reflects the dizzying new status of London as a city, at once familiar yet also part of a growing global network.

The Merchant Taylor John Stow created his survey and history of London from a "sense of patriotic duty," offering a description of London which, while not uncritical, nonetheless accentuated its wealth, civic power and influence.[18] Like Lyly, he characterised London as a great commercial city, but Stow went further by emphasising its connectivity with the rest of the trading world beyond Europe by specifying the goods which pass through it:

> At this city merchant strangers of all nations had their keys and wharves: the Arabians sent gold: the Sabians spice and frankensence: the Scithian armour, Babilon oile, Indian purple garments, Egipt precious stones, Norway and Russia Ambergrese, & Sables, & the French men wine.[19]

The list of commodities is striking in its luxury – these are superfluous goods (many of which would soon be provided in greater abundance and at lower prices by the great trading companies). On one hand, this risks activating a narrative of dangerous exoticism, although Stow does not incline in this direction. Rather, Stow hints at the idea of a global exchange, in which commodities that are abundant (and thus not luxuries) in one country can be sent to another where there is a lack, in return for the abundance of that second country.

The conception of trade as a perpetual, worldwide system of exchange was reinforced by corporate discourse throughout the seventeenth century. Companies sometimes sponsored official ambassadors, most famously Sir Thomas Roe, first in India and later the Ottoman Empire; alternatively, merchants carried royal letters of introduction to new territories, for example Richard Chancellor on the first voyage of what would become the Muscovy (Russia) Company in 1551. Elizabeth I's rationale for international trade (and, in part, the establishment of the overseas trading companies) was that economic growth came through redistribution of nature's plenty. In her letter to the King of China in 1583, she argued for a demand-led international marketplace, in which the plenty of England is transported out in return for the importation of those things which England lacks, but are plentiful elsewhere:

> For by this means we perceive, that the profit which by the mutual trade on both sides, al the princes our neighbors in the West do receive, your Imperial Majesty & those that be subject under your dominion, to their great joy and benefit shall have the same, which consisteth in the transporting outward of such things whereof we have plenty, & in bringing in such things as we stand in need of. It cannot otherwise be, but that seeing we are borne and made to have need one of another, & that wee are bound to aide one another, but that your Imperial Majesty will well like of it, & by your subjects with like endeavor will be accepted.[20]

Elizabeth's model is, at least in part, a fantasy, in which lack and oversupply can be perfectly balanced. This is a fantasy, though, not of nature's bounty but of human organisation; mankind is 'borne and made to have need of one another', and so the abundance of nature can be well distributed if only the right sets of international trading partners are found. Despite the practical difficulties in establishing such a delicately poised balance of trade, Elizabeth nonetheless presents this demand-driven system as the ideal economic model to maximise the 'profit on both sides'.

Free trade as international redistribution remained current as a piece of political economy long after Elizabeth's initial optimism at the opening of trade routes had developed into a steady trade. The legal scholar Hugo Grotius's *Mare Liberum*, first published anonymously in 1609, argued that the seas were under no natural dominion of any state, nation or individual, and consequently there could be no restriction to trade on the seas. The proximate cause of Grotius's work was the seizing of a Portuguese trading ship by the Dutch East India Company in the East Indies in 1603, part of a broader monopoly-breaking campaign waged by the Dutch (both the VOC and the Republic) against the Portuguese in India and the Indian Ocean. Grotius's argument for freedom to travel in order to trade, therefore, was a specific political intervention which became a broad intellectual argument. To make that argument, Grotius drew on the first principles of natural liberty:

> I will base my argument on the following most specific and unimpeachable axiom of the Law of Nations [. . .] Every nation is free to travel to every other nation, and to trade with it.[21]

Grotius takes his first principles from God's will as it is expressed in His creation, and here he was "indebted to medieval voluntarists."[22] Consequently, Grotius looked to the natural state of trade, as expressed in the distribution of goods and agriculture (in both their actual and potential states). He follows his statement of the axiomatic 'Law of Nations' with his understanding of natural resources:

> God Himself says this speaking through the voice of nature; and inasmuch as it is not His will to have Nature supply every place with all the necessities of life, He ordains that some nations excel in one art and others in another [. . .] so by the decree of divine justice it was brought about that one people should supply the needs of another.[23]

Although Grotius does not necessarily see this system in terms of a perfect balance, he shares his commitment to mutual supply with Elizabeth, and the long tradition of divinely ordained international (which was increasingly becoming global) resource allocation. Exchange becomes the way in which nations (or other groupings of people) interact with one another, helping to supply mutual wants as well as offering societal and political benefits – not least the prevention of the entirely self-sufficient or autarkic state, cut off from world affairs and tending away from the cooperation and harmonious balance that exchanges promoted.[24]

In his pamphlet giving the conditions for a just war, Grotius restated his commitment to free trade as a natural right, and emphasised the social benefits of international commerce: "No man hath right to obstruct the way of Commerce to any Nation with any other that is remote; because the permission of Trade is for the interest of human society."[25] It followed that even war was justified if it was done to open up trade, since to deny international commerce was to deny the will of God in mutual supply, as well as the liberty of His subjects to undertake His commands and benefit (in access to needful goods and in mutually beneficial intellectual exchanges) from the world-system which He had devised.

In practice, Grotius's commitment to 'free trade' as we might understand the term today was less than absolute, for he defended the Dutch ability to establish exclusive contracts with non-European powers in the East Indies on the grounds that it was legitimate to exclude everyone from a trade once it was secured for one nation, but the Portuguese had been specifically excluding some nations but not others. Trade, that is, should be for all or none.[26] The Dutch exclusion was defended by Grotius as necessary to secure the trade (an argument to which corporate pamphleteers in England and the Netherlands had frequent recourse) – the commitment to the military defence of global trade, and long-distance international relations, meant that a true monopoly was justified, even necessary, so long as it did not artificially inflate prices beyond the actual cost of securing and transporting the goods.

The idea of universality in trade was thus an intellectual position which considered goods as part of an integrated global economic system with theological and political ramifications. In his 1617 reflection on the justification for travel, Bishop Joseph Hall repeated the idea of the providential global balance as an exemption for mercantile adventure:

> Some commodities God hath confined to some countries, upon others he hath with a full hand poured those benefits, which he hath but sprinkled upon some. His wise providence hath made one country the granary, another the cellar, another the orchard, another the arsenal of their neighbours, yea of the remotest parts.[27]

Five years after Hall, Gerard Malynes noted that even in a fictional country which had no need of outside goods, trade would still be preferable to self-sufficiency:

> Insomuch, that although they could have lived without them in regard of commodities: yet charity, humanity, and *policy* willeth us to maintain friendship with our neighbours, and rather to give them part of our blessings, then not to deal or communicate with them [. . .] But God caused nature to distribute her benefits, or his blessings to several *climates*, supplying the barrenness of some things in one country, with the fruitfulness and store of other countries, to the end that interchangeably one Common-weale should live with an other. And therefore is *traffic* and *trade* so much to be maintained and defended.[28]

Malynes's model does not even touch on profit (although his treatise clearly is interested in the increase of England's wealth), concentrating instead on the 'charity' and 'humanity' provoked by neighbours trading with one another. The fantasy of perfect abundance, though, is quickly dismissed, and Malynes joins instead with Elizabeth's fantasy of a perfect redistributive system which matches supply and lack to mutual benefit.

Such a model reconceptualises global trade as a moral, even divine, imperative, and a range of authors "imaginatively re-constructed pre-Flood trade and technology in light of the mercantilist theory of economics."[29] Some, like the preacher John Flavel (who is discussed in more detail in the next chapter) were explicit about the revelatory potential of global trade:

> The most wise God hath so dispensed his Bounty to the several Nations of the World, that one standing in need of anothers Commodities, there might be a sociable Commerce and traffick maintained amongst them all, and all combining in a common League, may, by the help of Navigation, exhibit mutual succors to each other.[30]

Here, trade becomes an enriching of the soul, as well of the nation. Following God's plan, made evident by the distribution of commodities, leads to peaceful international relations and mutual growth. Irenicism and commerce become inevitably linked. These international exchanges remained a core defence of corporate activity, even as its mechanisms, such as the export of bullion, came under attack:

> But to live well, to flourish and grow rich, we must find means, by trade to vent our superfluities; therewith to furnish and adorn us with the treasure and those necessary wares, which foreign nations do afford.[31]

Mun argues, in effect, that the overseas corporation serves the public good by creating a balance of trade in which dangerous superabundance is converted to other, essential, goods, for the benefit of the whole nation, who flourish in the new trades and industries that create employment and further exports.[32] As Istvan Hont has shown, international commercial competition remained "a primary state activity," with the defence or increase of trade a guiding principle of military and state organisation.[33]

The language of the mutual benefit of exchange underlying international commerce was not restrained to the transnational merchants who defended their monopoly, the aspiring traders who decried it or political thinkers such as Grotius. Radical groups, in particular, adopted the terminology of economic debates, and their preoccupation with supply, want and lack can be seen through this corporate lens. Gerald Winstanley, defending the rights of the 'Diggers' to common land, questions the basis of trade via money:

> For after our work of the Earthly community is advanced, we must make use of Gold and Silver, as we do of other metals, but not to buy and sell withal; for buying and selling is the great cheat, that robs and steals the Earth one from another [. . .] And therefore, the main thing we aim at, and for which we declare our resolutions to go forth, and act, is this, to lay hold upon, and as we stand in need, to cut and fell, and make the best advantage we can of the woods and trees, that grow upon the Commons, to be a stock for our selves, and our poor Brethren, through the Land of *England*, to plant the Commons withal.[34]

At the heart of his communitarian vision are the same questions of need and supply that motivated the corporate writers we have already examined, as is the idea of establishing a shared stock (of lands and natural resources, rather than money). Yet Winstanley differs from those writers by imputing a moral dimension to exchange, where 'need' becomes a question not of 'lack', but of individual requirement and sustenance. As a consequence, the freedom to trade is subsumed into a broader freedom to survive, even if that means distorting or remaking the marketplace so that exchanges work on a moral, as well as purely market, level.

The Levellers, too, borrowed the terms of economic debate for their own social programme, "seeing monopolies at work not just in commerce, but also in religion, law and ultimately politics."[35] One of their leaders, William Walwyne, considering the linguistic training required to become a clergyman, argued that "they have hereby made it a difficult thing to be a minister, and so have engrossed the trade to them selves."[36] Just as the Diggers had, Walwyn uses social issues to question the economic rationale underpinning market conditions (in this case monopoly), and to propose an alternative model predicated on fairness rather than pure 'efficiency', although he would probably not have recognised a stark distinction between those aims.

Similar questions played out on the stage, as plays began to register and critique the global trade on which London's booming wealth depended. Indeed, the stages themselves were frequently a result of the developing corporate economy, either in their construction or their audiences. In *The Knight of the Burning Pestle*, characters continually refer to the presence of trade and overseas activity. The chivalric romance that Rafe attempts to construct is repeatedly, bathetically undermined by reference to his trade as a grocer. The pestle itself, of course, is on his shield as a constant 'remembrance of my former trade' (I.276). Other characters, not least the squire/prentice, also undermine his self-image in a manner reminiscent of the *Quixote*: 'Right Courteous and Valiant Knight of the Burning Pestle here is a distressed damsel, to have a half-penny worth of pepper' (I.310–12). The civic chivalry which the play satirises, if not openly mocks, is thus interwoven with the economic reality of the trades which support it.

Arguably the most self-consciously bourgeois of the genre, and therefore unsurprisingly the comedy most concerned with the corporations of the City of London, was Dekker's *Shoemaker's Holiday* (1599). The central character, Simon Eyre, is a contradictory type of new merchant. He is generous with his support for his workers (and, later, the citizenry of London), yet simultaneously a shrewd operator who, whether buying the stock of a frightened merchant or taking the place of a recently deceased holder of civic office, is unafraid to turn another's misery into his own profit. Indeed, the play turns on that tension between economic and social capital, or, more precisely, the ability of the characters to transform one into the other.

Eyre is offered the quick sale of a ship laden with the exotic goods of corporate (probably the Levant Company) trade: "sugar, civet, almonds, cambric" and so on, which his workers estimate to be worth "two or three hundred thousand pounds."[37] The reason given is that the "merchant owner of the ship dares not show his head," presumably indicating trouble with the authorities of London or the out-ports, and so offers "a bargain in the commodities," even going so far as to allow a sale of the goods before payment is made to him.[38] In fact, as David Scott Kastan notes, the deal is so good as to obviate the "expenditure of 'readie monies' that mercantilists feared," ensuring that luxuries and wealth are kept in, then spread around, London in equal measure.[39]

As well as squaring the circle of bullion exports, Eyre, his wife and his workers all comment on the potential of this deal to transform luxury goods into the literal and social capital necessary to procure advancement in London's government. Hodge tells him that if he goes through with the deal, he "cannot choose but be a lord at least." His wife, Margery, feels "honour creep upon me" and "a certain rising in my flesh," and the rather crude suggestiveness of social and personal 'rising' serves to reinforce the (perceived) links between public and private advancement.[40] Indeed, so confident is Eyre in the social value of the deal that he dresses in his finery, and it is evident from Firk's comment, comparing Eyre to "a threadbare cloak new turned and dressed," that this is a transformation emphasising wealth and status.[41] So stark is the difference, and so much have clothes (and the wealth they signify) made the man, that Hodge proclaims "now you look like yourself, master," saying that only now will people stand aside for Eyre and give him his proper title of " 'Right Worshipful' " (probably referring to his status as a master of the Right Worshipful Company of Cordwainers, although proleptically hinting at his future mayoralty). As Andrea Lawson has argued, the clothes that Eyre puts on to secure this deal, alongside other exchanges in the play such as gift-giving, have the effect, *pace* Kastan's ideas of the play's unification, of emphasising the "disharmony between the gentle and working classes."[42]

The Merchant of Venice also explicitly elides purely economic transactions with a moral economy, in this case one of friendship, love and revenge. As has been frequently noted, the Christians of the play are less interested in economic returns than they are in using their wealth to provide for and support one another; this support is then returned to them in their own need, so Antonio's loan to Bassanio is (provisionally) repaid in Portia's offer to redeem his debt to Shylock, just as Bassanio is generous to Graziano once he has secured his own wealth. As Karen Newman has pointed out, while Venice and Belmont may appear to be oppositional landscapes of business and love, the process of exchanging is not limited to the city:

> What is important is the structure of exchange itself which characterizes both the economic transactions of Venice and the love relationships forged at Belmont. Venice and Belmont are throughout the play compared and contrasted, but the syntax of exchange itself functions in both locales; indeed, it seems universal.[43]

The language of the play, too, continually moves from the economic to the moral. Images of money, credit, debt, worth and hazard are constantly invoked only to remind the audience that it is the moral, not the monetary, that is worthwhile. For example, after Bassanio has correctly chosen the lead casket, his exchanges with his new fiancé are filled with commercial terms used of emotion and personal value. Portia says that for his sake she would increase her worth:

> I would be trebled twenty times myself
> A thousand times more fair, ten thousand times more rich,
> That only to stand high in your account
> I might in virtues, beauties, livings, friends,
> Exceed account. But the full sum of me
> Is sum of something which, to term in gross
> Is an unlessoned girl.[44]

Portia offers a summary of her worth via economic terms such as 'account', 'sum', 'livings' and 'gross'. She had earlier compared her growing love to interest ("scant this excess" [III.ii.112]), and Bassanio describes the marriage as "my new int'rest" (III.ii.220). Despite the proliferation of these terms, the scene (and the play more generally) resists the easy understanding of its characters in economic terms; rather, the use of those terms invites the audience to grasp at a truth of character which goes deeper than the merely economic to a moral economy in which debt, obligation and value is determined by community and communally minded actions. No sooner has the marriage begun to be celebrated than economics intrude again, in the news that Antonio's ventures have failed; even here the financial ruin is transmuted into Bassanio's moral failure in having "engaged my friend to his mere enemy" (III.ii.261), once more allowing the play to demonstrate the deeper morality underpinning its questions of exchange and engagement.

A similar movement can be observed in reverse in Jonson's *Bartholomew Fair*, though, as with so much of the fair, the morality revealed is not the idealised Christian charity of Venice but its obverse: corruption and venality. The characters of the play continually sacrifice their morality for economic gain, and no character better exemplifies this than the widow Purecraft, who, in order to woo Quarlous, reveals her schemes on behalf of herself and the Puritan church: She is a "holy widow" in order to exploit her suitors for "feasts and gifts," but also serves as a "maker of marriages." Her marriages are of two sorts, either rich widows who are enticed to give "a third part of their wealth" to the church, or young virgins who are encouraged to "steal from their husbands" once they have converted them.[45] The moral and social institution of marriage is reduced to an economic transaction – a standard satirical comment on social organisation, but one which also reveals the intersection between financial gain and moral decay on which the play turns.

John Milton's 1634 *Masque Presented at Ludlow Castle* (better known as *Comus*) turns on this very question between economy and morality. In the masque, the eponymous enchanter captures a virtuous young lady, takes her back to his palace and tries to seduce her; her chastity protects her from his amorous advances, and eventually her two brothers burst in and drive the enchanter off. This is, of course, a well-worn trope.

Yet, despite the fact that he has magically secured her to a chair, Comus turns to intellectual, rather than physical intimidation, in order to have the lady become a willing partner in seduction. He offers her a "cordial julep" to quench her thirst and restore her body after her time spent wandering in the woods.[46] Anticipating her rejection, he notes that she would be breaking her bond with nature by not taking care of her 'borrowed' body:

> Why should you be so cruel to yourself,
> And to those dainty limbs which Nature lent
> For gentle usage, and soft delicacy?
> But you invert the covenants of her trust,
> And harshly deal like an ill borrower
> With that which you received on other terms,
> Scorning the unexempt condition
> By which all mortal frailty must subsist,
> Refreshment after toil, ease after pain
>
> [678–86]

The imagery Comus uses brings to mind a more practical and economic 'covenant' than the metaphorical granting of life by nature, suggesting the lady is not keeping up her end of the bargain on mortgaged property. She has taken possession of a body on 'other terms' (that is, keeping it alive and well), but, like an improper borrower, neglects to maintain what she has borrowed, let alone increase its value.

This image would be fairly surprising by itself – borrowing and covenants hardly seem to us to be the kind of "liquorish baits" (699) that the Lady claims she will continue to reject – but Comus continues on his economic theme to more abstract notions of use-value and consumption:

> If all the world
> Should in a pet of temperance feed on pulse,
> Drink the clear stream, and nothing wear but frieze,
> The all-giver would be unthanked, would be unpraised,
> Not half his riches known, and yet despised,
> And we should serve him as a grudging master,

As a penurious niggard of his wealth,
And live like Nature's bastards, not her sons,
Who would be quite surcharged with her own weight,
And strangled with her waste fertility.
[722–8]

Comus links the economic necessity of consumption to a moral one, on two grounds. Firstly, God would go 'unthanked' and 'unpraised' if mankind were not enjoying the full range of his bounty. Moreover, the long-term effect of this would be for mankind to come to believe that God was deliberately withholding wealth, and so serve 'grudgingly'. Comus's startling suggestion is that only through consumption can we properly appreciate the 'riches' of the natural world, and only by consuming those riches can mankind have a proper relationship with God. Consumption has a second value, too, since it counters the superabundance of nature, which would otherwise become a dead weight, where man's 'waste' of her gifts becomes, in a curious combination of imagery, a crushing burden which ultimately strangles her.

There is a curious echo here of Calvin's discussion of nature's gifts in his *Institutes*, in which he suggests that food (and by extension God's other creation) was created not just for sustenance, but also for delight:

> Therefore let this be a principle that the use of gods gifts swerves not, when it is referred unto the end appointed of God, for God hath created all things for our good, and not to our destruction. Now if we consider to what end he hath created food, we shall find that he meant to provide not only for necessity, but also for delectation. So in apparel comeliness, in herbs, trees and fruits, besides divers uses, we have diversity of taste, colour, smell and shapes.[47]

Calvin argues that the use-value of food goes beyond even the 'refreshment after toil' that Comus outlines, with a stress on the sensory experience of nature which is meant to be enjoyable in itself, and meant to be used in many ways. However, if this is an authority Comus is attempting to co-opt for his argument, his is only a partial reading. Calvin immediately goes on to warn against the very thing to which Comus bends the *Institutes*, the "lust of the flesh":

> Notwithstanding on the otherside we must diligently prevent the lust of the flesh, which unless it be brought in order doeth by and by break out. First of all it shall be bridled with one bridle, if we set down, that all things are therefore created for vs, that we may know the author thereof, and give him thanks for his tender kindness toward us.[48]

Calvin counteracts precisely the argument that Comus is making – it is not consumption *per se* that lets us thank God, but rather thoughtful meditation on His gifts even as they are enjoyed. The 'lust of the flesh' comes when consumption is fetishised as an end in itself.

Finally, Comus turns his economic arguments back to the overtly sexual, comparing the spending of coin to pleasure:

> List Lady be not coy, and be not cozened
> With that same vaunted name virginity,
> Beauty is Nature's coin, must not be hoarded,
> But must be current, and the good thereof
> Consists in mutual and partaken bliss,
> Unsavoury in the enjoyment of itself.
> If you let slip time, like a neglected rose,
> It withers on the stalk with languished head.
> [736–43]

In some ways, this is a standard *carpe diem* argument, enhanced by the subsequent image of a rose withering on the stalk. But the choice of 'coyn' is unintentionally revealing on Comus's part. The comparison to a miser or 'hoorder' is simple enough: If beauty is not spent, it will be wasted, like a flower whose season is up. It is the addition of 'currant', though, which is the crux of Comus's argument. There is a subtle, yet significant, difference between beauty as specie to be spent, used and lost, and something which is to be circulated. Comus attempts to use this economic motif to shift the debate away from a virginity which is binary (preserved/given up) to a new system of morality in which sexuality does not come at a bodily price at all.

The addition of 'current' seems to add to this, in a fairly unsavoury way, by drawing on the arguments in favour of usury:

> Yet for money, as it is current money, there is no manner of use to be made of it, but only in parting from it [. . .] Yet this money, for this use, shall be to the usurer fruitful, and profitable, and never the weaker or worse for the using.[49]

Current money, Fenton suggests, is even more valuable than hoarded money, since it cannot be used up but rather increases by being spent (that is, lent); by 'circulating' her beauty, Comus implies, the Lady will not be weakened but strengthened.

Catherine Gimelli Martin has acutely tracked the similarities between this section of the debate and the rejection of Mammon by Guyon in the *Faerie Queene*. Both Guyon and the Lady "foil the false guide's attempt to convince them that since mother nature is an endless storehouse and retailer [. . .] mankind must follow her licentious 'ensample.'"[50] Martin sees this as part of a broader pattern of (non-Puritan) active reason within both the masque and Spenser's poem, in which individuals are saved only after their temperance has allowed them to overcome temptation. Without wishing to deny the importance of this Spenserian connection, I suggest that the material temptation of the lady has other, more compelling, resonances in contemporary economic theory and practice.

It is revealing that the Lady explicitly engages with Comus's economic argument at this point. Rather than rejecting his arguments on purely moral grounds – as she had done earlier on the fitness of his palace and the necessity of refreshment – the Lady rejects not just the immoral arguments, but the economic vehicles used to advance them:

> Imposter do not charge most innocent Nature,
> As if she would her children should be riotous
> With her abundance she good cateress
> Means her provision only to the good
> That live according to her sober laws,
> And holy dictate of spare temperance.
> (761–6)

This, the first part of the Lady's rejection of Comus, mirrors the rejection of Mammon in the *Faerie Queene*. Guyon, too, gives the example of a temperate natural world corrupted by greedy mankind: "with how small allowaunce/Vntroubled Nature doth her selfe suffise" (*FQ* 2.7.15). However, Spenser's knight ultimately rejects the advances of Mammon on moral grounds alone – wealth, especially superabundance of wealth, is dangerous because it encourages covetousness, and consumption beyond need, and so for our corrupt world it is better not to be tempted by vast natural wealth. The Lady, though, goes on to offer an alternative economic model:

> If every just man that now pines with want
> Had but a moderate and beseeming share
> Of that which lewdly-pampered Luxury
> Now heaps upon some few with vast excess
> Nature's full blessings would be well-dispensed
> In unsuperfluous even proportion,
> And she no whit encumbered with her store
> (767–73)

Here, the agency for the apportionment of nature's goods goes away from nature herself, and to those who develop a system for the distribution of those bounties – unlike Guyon's general warning against avaricious consumption (in the metaphor of mining), the Lady specifically attacks those "few" who heap up the majority of nature's goods. Thus, the economic attack shifts from a general human exploitation of the earth to a capitalist system which distributes unevenly.

Blair Hoxby sees the Lady's response to Comus here both as a defence of her chastity and as a refusal to participate in the kind of economy that Comus describes, in which constant exchanges lead to increased consumption and production:

> The Lady's argument is predicated on the economy's being static rather than dynamic: distribution will be the sole important factor in an economy only if growth is not an important consideration.[51]

While I generally agree with Hoxby's reading of this scene, I suggest he underestimates the Lady here. She does not see the choice in so stark a set of terms (dynamic growth/static stagnation), nor does she simply passively refute the terms of Comus's argument. Rather, she offers an alternative model of a working economy, which is redistributive, but, crucially, has just the same amount of consumption as Comus's model does. When the Lady tells him that nature will be 'no whit encumbered with her store', she is unequivocal that her system involves consumption at a level which will eliminate the dangerous superabundance that Comus warns against; however, by spreading that consumption to 'every just man', the Lady effectively posits a proto-Keynesian model of a demand-led and redistributive economy against Comus's calls for a trickle-down system based on those blessed by nature spending whatever they have for the good of the economy generally.

That the Lady's is an equally dynamic system as Comus's can be seen from contemporary arguments over redistribution. The Lady's apparently incongruous defence of an alternative economic system makes more sense in the context of contemporary debates on the morality of exchange. She has recognised that Comus is not simply presenting a *carpe diem* argument, but one that also draws on ideas of circulation – in order to thoroughly discredit his moral argument, she must undercut his economic one as well.

The Lady refutes the capitalist logic of Comus by invoking a moral virtue, temperance, allied with a utopian/Arcadian idea of a plenty which denies the need for the exchange and surplus value on which Comus's argument relies. Although she acknowledges lack, she counters, anticipating the arguments of the Diggers and Levellers, that nature has sufficient if it just well-dispensed. By removing herself from the marketplace of lack, supply and continual circulation, the lady is able to refute Comus's argument on both economic and religious grounds simultaneously. This connection between corporate activity and religion is considered in greater detail in Chapter 5, but for the rest of this chapter I return to the sense of productive exchanges and interaction which structured mercantile life and descriptions of the city of London.

Londonopolis

In 1571, the Royal Exchange building was opened in London by Elizabeth I. This grand space was the first major commercial development in England, and combines in its very name both senses of exchange: global currency swaps and material trade. The Exchange, which Lyly in his *Euphues* called "a glorious *Burse*" soon came to occupy an important imaginative space as a place "for the meeting of merchants of all countries, where any traffic is to be had."[52] Natasha Glaiyser has tracked the "resonances the Exchange had in images of London," and she argues that "The exchange was important in its own right, not only for its role in trade but also because its image was constructed, both in words and pictures, to represent the whole of the trading world in miniature."[53]

Such a picture was not always positive, of course. S.R., who claimed on his title page to be a Cambridge student, combined the Exchange with Paul's and Westminster as places of vice:

> Three places at London, wherein 3. notable vices reign.
> In the Royall exchange.
> In Pauls
> In Westminster hall.
> Usury.
> Simony.
> Bribery.[54]

Although this text is clearly designed as a series of witty exercises, all of which revolve around creating thematic trios, the combination of spaces undertaken here is revealing. While the government, church and commercial communities were hardly new targets for accusations of corruption, the insertion of the Exchange reveals how quickly it became synecdochic for that mercantile community, and perhaps points to something of its function in governing or regulating trade.

The need for a physical mercantile space also reflects the practical necessities of trade, especially international trade, in early modern London. Most sales were conducted by face-to-face bargaining, with prices fluctuating based on both supply and currency exchanges (the theoretical responses of economic writers to changing prices is discussed subsequently). As a consequence, as Laurence Fontaine has observed, "the arrangement of stores according to specialisation was crucial," not only to allow buyers a quick investigation of relative price and quantity, but also so that "the whole profession [of merchants] could exercise an initial form of control over the conduct of individual members."[55] Merchant guilds, of course, had always sought this form of control, but the Exchange offered new opportunities (and challenges) for regulators and traders alike.

With new companies, trades, goods and buildings, it is no surprise that the self-conception of London shifted as well. The idea of London as an entrepot, a global centre of exchange, was developed throughout the seventeenth century. This was in some ways a simple expression of civic and national pride, and in others a recognition of a new reality of political economy, in which overseas investment and constitutional innovation went hand in hand. Part of this trend can be seen in new histories of the city, which stress its historical trading status to create a history of the city which emphasised its position as an important centre of European trade.

Richard Hakluyt began his survey of English voyages by cataloguing the presence of London, and English merchants more generally, in other great histories, noting that his reader:

> May learn out of Venerable *Beda*, that almost 900 years past, in the time of the *Saxons*, the said city of *London* was *multorum emporium populorum*, a mart-town for many nations [. . .] There may be plainly see in an ancient testimony translated out of the *Saxon* tongue, how our merchants were often wont for traffics sake, so many hundred years since, to cross the wide seas, and how their industry in so doing was recompensed.[56]

After providing an entire page of similar examples, Hakluyt closes by eliding those histories with his own editorial practice, because "After all these, out of 2. branches of 2. ancient statutes, is partly shewed our trade and the success thereof with diverse foreign nations in the time of *K. Henry* the sixth."[57] The move from historians of repute to his own activity in collecting statutes is subtle, but serves to place Hakluyt in that tradition at the same time as establishing London's illustrious history. These narratives were not just designed to burnish the reputation of London, but to provide evidence of London's "providential place in the world: past, present and future."[58]

Robert Batchelor has argued that there was a shift in the kind of histories available in early modern London. The sixteenth century saw an emphasis on centralisation; however, in the seventeenth century

> Devolution of authority required by shifting patterns of exchange, multipolar and overlapping trading networks, and extension of exchange relations beyond the distance of easy communication caused a proliferation of objects ranging from manuscript histories to more technical achievements such as popular printing or instrument and map-making designed to address such problems.[59]

Although Batchelor is interested primarily in the new objects (especially maps) produced as a consequence of this shift, he is correct to observe that histories began to change too. Histories of London began to appear, most famously Stow's *Survey* (1598), which was discussed previously in the context of global commodities. There were many reasons for these histories, of course, not least the growing interest in antiquarianism more generally. But as Parry notes in his survey of the chief antiquarians, the new histories "had a power over the past, for they were able to determine which parts of it were vital and should be held in respectful attention."[60] These surveys of London met the corporate needs of the seventeenth century by developing the notion that mercantile activity had always been the rationale (and preserve) of London, as well as emphasising corporate independence from authority.

Stow emphasises the commercial power of London, and its contribution to the rest of the English economy:

> By advantage of the situation it disperseth foreign wares (as the stomach doth meat) to all the members most commodiously. By the benefit of the river of Thames, and great trade of merchandize, it is the chief maker of mariners, and nurse of our Navy: and ships (as men know) bee the wooden walls for defence of our realm.[61]

Stow's digestive metaphor points towards London's status as a middle point – it takes in the 'meat' from outside of the body (England), 'digests' it internally and then spreads the benefit around the rest of the country-body. In the same passage, Stow also regurgitates the contemporary ideal in which mercantile expansion is inevitable, ever-increasing and a tangible benefit to English foreign policy:

> It spreadeth the honor of our country far abroad by her long navigations, and maketh our power feared, even of barbarous Princes. It only is stored with rich merchants which sort only is tolerable: for beggarly merchants, do bite too near, & will do more harm than good to the realm.[62]

Stow, like Hakluyt, supports his assertions about the present state of London by stressing the history of commerce within the city

> For Tacitus, who first of all authors nameth it Londinum, saith that in the 62 after Christ it was albeit, no colony of the Romans, yet most famous for the great multitude of merchants, provision, and intercourse.[63]

Even ancient London was famous for its merchants. This passage from Tacitus continued to excite historians of London, and James Howell went further than Stow in his 1657 *Londinopolis*:

> It was a notable character, which Cornelius Tacitus, (that famous register of time, who had lived here many years) did give of London about fifteen hundred years ago, *Londinum copiâ Negotiatorum, &*

> *Comeatu maximè celebre*, London a most renowned mart for multitude of merchants, and commerce. If she deserved such a character in those days, what would she merit now? who being compared to what she was then, may be said, in point of magnitude, to be as a large volume in Folio, to a book in Decimo Sexto: And, in point of trade, as in an East Indy Carrack, to a Quinbourough Oyster ketch.[64]

Howell's explicit comparison to classical London – a comparison encouraged throughout his text, not least by the title – helps to create a teleological history in which trade is London's destiny. The comparisons emphasise this continuity, since the objects (books and ships) are of the same basic sort, while stressing a startling jump in scale. This is reinforced by his choice of ships in the final comparison, with the new London represented by a trade ship designed for global travel out of London, and the old London by a local ship used to deal specifically with a single, domestic product. There is also, of course, a shift from production in the case of the oyster ship to the process of exchanging which the carrack is designed to enable and streamline.

The myth-making persisted well into the seventeenth century. Camden's 1637 *Brittannia* contains frequent references to merchants operating all over the British Isles, but he too finds classical precedent:

> Suetonius with constant resolution, passing through the midst of his enemies, went to Londinium, a town verily by the name that it carried of a Colony, nothing famous, but for concourse of merchants, & provision of necessaries most of all other frequented.[65]

This Suetonius is not the biographer, but Gaius Suetonius Paulinus, governor of Britain. For Camden, London's 'fame' comes from nothing but the fact that it is frequented more than any other place by merchants. Camden's London thus derives its status because of its position as a domestic entrepot, but, in the context of the other new histories of the city, it is not hard to extrapolate a future for London as a European, or even global, 'mart-town', in precisely the way that Lyly had articulated in 1580.

As well as the work of global traders, writers turned to the Thames, as both a practical and imaginary figure, to underpin their characterisation of London's pre-eminence. Shipping on the Thames was a crucial link between London and the world, but also served as a valuable metaphor for the distribution of the fruits of trade into London, and then around Britain. The sixteenth song of Drayton's poem *Poly-Olbion*, based on *Britannia*, discusses the provident location of the Thames, and the positive effect this has on English trade:

> What seed doth any soyle, in *England* bring, that I
> Beyond her most increase yet cannot multiply.

Besides; my sure abode next goodly *London* is,
To vent my fruitfull store, that me doth neuer misse.[66]

Drayton gives a link from mercantile culture to perpetual exchange – London is a place that will deal with any overabundance by creating productive trading relationships.

John Denham developed Drayton's idea of London as a site of superabundance in his geographical poem on the Thames:

So Thames to *London* doth at first present
Those tributes, which the neighbouring countries sent;
But at his second visit from the East,
Spices he brings, and treasures from the West;
Findes wealth where 'tis, and gives it where it wants,
Cities in Desarts, woods in Cities plants,
Rounds the whole Globe, and with his flying towers
Brings home to us, and makes both Indies ours:
So that to us no thing, no place is strange
Whilst thy faire bosome is the worlds Exchange.[67]

Denham's Thames is one which has two modes of looking outwards, first to Europe and on 'his second visit' to the rest of the global trading network. The Thames works to redistribute wealth across the globe, in the same manner as those theorists of a providential balance of trade, finding wealth wherever it happens to be placed, and relocating it to where it is necessary. But Denham's poem reconfigures that balance – perhaps making explicit what was only implicit before – so that it is England which takes a disproportionate benefit: the trading model delivers 'both Indies' to London's control, as well as uniting the world's 'treasures' in England.

Denham's phrase was probably deliberately echoed by one William Smith, who wrote a lengthy poem in quatrains to James, Duke of York, after his naval defeat of the Dutch in 1665. The poem begins with praise of his military skill before moving to the assistance of the Thames in the fight, and closes with a broader paean to the city:

And thou, oh stately *City*, whose fair face
Minerva, Mercury, Bellona grace,
Whose *Arms* and *Arts* astonish'd *Europe* owns,
Whose *Trade* the frigid and the torrid *Zones*,
Whose double-named River kindly brings
(As Tribute) useful, and all precious things,
Rich *Indian* Harvests, what is rare or strange,
Whilest his transparent Stream's the *Worlds Exchange*.[68]

The double-naming of the river (Thames and Isis) points to its origins inland; although, as the current in Smith's poem seems to be flowing downstream, to bring in the Indian harvests and other trade goods, also suggests a flowing out of London to Oxford and beyond. There is also a classical allusion here, to the "double-named" river in Ovid's *Ex Ponto* (1.8.11), placing London in a long tradition of trading and imperial cities, and I consider the role of such cultural translation subsequently.[69] Similarly, in a poem dedicated to Cromwell, William Godolphin turned to a maritime metaphor:

> But since that *Power* which now informs our Age,
> Hath reconcil'd the Strength, and quell'd the Rage
> Of the disturbed Sea, the Fire, the Wind,
> And (what is more) the Tempests of our Mind.
> Far now our Ships their Canvas Wings shall stretch,
> And the World's wealth to richer *England* fetch.
> Till greater Treasures overspread our Coast
> Than *Tagus* or *Pactolus* Sands can boast.
> With this Design our busie Vessels range
> About, to make our *Isle* the *World's Exchange*.[70]

Godolphin seems to conform to the standard set of praise for Cromwell, that he has calmed turbulent times and imposed peace. But Godolphin makes more of a connection between these two states than a purely temporal one. His poem moves from a discussion of raging winds and tempests to an image of a ship sailing (presumably with the calm winds), linking the metaphors of peace and war. So too the 'Design' that impels England's 'busy vessels' may well be a reference to the maritime imperialist policy pursued by the republican government, commonly known as the 'Western Design'. As Michael Braddick points out, the navigation system was the same mechanism by which "Barbados and Virginia were made to submit to the Free State [. . .] became also the means to regulate and direct the trade of the colonies."[71]

At the same time the poem adopts the common idea of England as the 'world's exchange'. Here England is compared with classical places of wealth and trade, as well as the comparative 'richer' being allowed to modify either simply England ('richer than before') or also the World ('England is richer than the rest of the world'). In either case, it is clear that, for Godolphin, England's wealth relies on the importation of worldly goods which become English once they 'overspread our coast'.

In 1681, Robert Hearne adopted the phrase as part of a political-historical tract outlining the danger of disagreements and disloyalty under the guise of a history of the Civil Wars:

> And what a late learned writer said, speaking in the praise of a land, and the admirable blessings of it, may be said of England; and I shall apply it, according to his words: A land (says he) of

> strength, of plenty, and of peace; where every soul may sit beneath his vine, unfrightened at the horrid language of the hoarse trumpet, unstartled at the warlike summons of the roaring cannons: A land, whose beauty hath surprised the ambitious hearts of foreign princes, and taught them by their martial oratory, to make their vain attempts. A land, whose strength reads vanity in the deceived hopes of conquerors, and crowns their enterprizes with a shameful over-throw. A land, whose native plenty makes her the world's exchange; supplying others, able to subsist without supply from foreign kingdoms: In it self, happy; and abroad, honourable. A land, that hath no vanity; but, what's the sweetest of all blessings, peace and plenty; that hath no misery, but is propagated from that blindness, which cannot see her own felicity. A land, that flows with milk and honey;[72]

Although Hearne quotes with no specific reference to the source text, the material from the 'late learned writer' he cites so approvingly as a praise of England was written with a somewhat different purpose in mind. It was a part of *Boanerges and Barnabas*, a text first written by Francis Quarles, a poet and royalist propagandist, in 1644. This volume, popular enough to be translated into Dutch and German, was a collection of essays on sinful characters: each character is introduced with an apology or defence, after which some corrective bible verses are given, and the character soliloquises upon them before offering an apology. However, 'The Secure Man's Triumph', in which this passage appears, was not in the first edition, but was quietly added, along with a number of others, in the second edition of 1646.

The fuller version of the passage that Hearne gives as 'praise of a land' actually comes from the secure man's apology and description of his state; Quarles' secure man soon realises that he has made the error of overconfidence which leads to 'an improvident carelessness', although Hearne does not include this change of heart.[73] By removing the 'praise' from this context, Hearne obviates the moral message in favour of a martial and economic triumphalism.

The passage recurs in the Levant merchant John Praed's text on trade of 1697, in which Quarles, and *Boanerges and Barnabas*, are specifically cited. Here too, though, it is used not as a sign of overconfidence, but as a realistic assessment of the nation's strength. Indeed, so confident is Praed in his nation that he sees domestic stability as the catalyst for overseas conquest and colony:

> Her prince might say to us concerning the Empire, as Joshua did to the Children of Israel concerning Canaan, how long are you slack to go to possess the land, which the Lord God of your Fathers hath given you?[74]

Although Praed goes on to discuss the need for reforms in religion, justice and trade, these are usually given in terms of a 'restoration' of ancient or customary practices, not innovations, something akin to the hearkening back to a 'golden age'. Indeed, using the concept of the 'world's exchange' to look back to an imagined age of trade and plenty was relatively commonplace, as in this text published only under the initials S.E:

> England, whose former plenty, and freedom, of commerce, hath sounded as echoes of triumph to all nations round about her: and in despite of envy or their emulating her happiness, made her trade the worlds exchange.[75]

As with the histories generally, these narratives are used to establish precedent for current positions. But they also carry something of the nostalgia identified in the genre by Nicholas von Maltzahn, who notes that the continued existence and circulation of founding myths "assisted claims to an insular autonomy since times immemorial and promised the recovery of Britain's ancient prestige."[76] A similar manoeuvre occurs in these mercantile writers, who seek to associate themselves with the glorious past, and in so doing offer themselves as the means to a more glorious future.

For these writers, the celebration of global trade is harmonised with the idea of Anglicisation. For Denham, the Thames 'brings home' the Indies, and 'makes [them] ours', phrasing which suggests a celebration both of the exchanges with far-flung places, but also the English ability to naturalise them in London which prevents the 'strange'-ness of both objects and places. Similarly, although Smith's Thames is filled with 'what is rare or strange', they are transformed into acceptable tribute, given value only through English ideas of what is 'useful or 'precious'.

Dramatic representations of the Thames had a similar function, such as the puppet show play-within-a-play of Jonson's *Bartholomew Fair* which, under the guise of making it "a little easy and modern for the times," transposes the Thames into the setting for a puppet-performance of Hero and Leander:

> As for the Hellespont I imagine our Thames here; and then Leander I make a dyer's son, about Puddle Wharf; and Hero a wench of the Bankside, who, going over one morning to old Fish street, Leander spies her land at Trig stairs and falls in love with her.[77]

The space, of course, is meaningless, in the sense that as a fictive setting it could as well have been Abydos as London, a conceit the play has already alluded to in its opening scene: "When't comes to the fair once, you were as good go to Virginia, for anything there is of Smithfield."[78]

Although the moment is slyly self-reflective, pointing for a moment at the artifice required to 'recreate' a place on stage, it also opens the broader question of space with which the play is concerned. The fair functions as a place of (more-or-less) lawless exchange, and it does so because of its own nature rather than any geographical specificity. It does not matter to the plot where the characters are, so long as it is sufficiently commercial and liberal to allow them to scheme, trick and traffic with one another. The choice of London for the puppet scene, then, serves to reinforce this sense of the city as an open space onto which many stories can be written, and a place where everything can be exchanged. The commercial aspect of the performance is reinforced by having both Hero and Leander move about in boats, rather than by swimming as in Ovid's original, perhaps a reference to increased water traffic on the Thames: the linking of shipping (whether the great ocean-going trading ships, or the local herring fishers providing the food Hero unexpectedly seeks out) with wealth was a long-established conceit by the time Jonson was writing.

The idea of 'Englishing' as a mode of accommodating the foreign was a commonplace. In his translation of book two of Virgil's *Aeneid*, John Denham argued that Virgil's language ought to be naturalised to a contemporary English: "Therefore if *Virgil* must needs speak English, it were fit he should speak not onely as a man of this Nation, but as a man of this age."[79] By the time Denham was translating Virgil (a manuscript version was circulated in 1636, although the printed version did not appear for 20 years), 'to English' had become a synonym for 'to translate', as for example in Chapman's poem *Euthymiae Raptus* in which the ghost of Homer implicitly endorses his efforts at translating, saying, "I, invisibly, went prompting thee/To those fair greens where thou didst English me."[80] Moreover, commendatory poems attached to intercultural writing of this period figured translation in economic terms, not as conquest, but as plunder. For foreign texts to engage with (or be engaged by) England and Englishness, they must be (literally as well as figuratively) brought to England.

Two of the poems celebrating Chapman's work as a translator are illustrative: Ben Jonson's 'To my worthy and honoured friend Mr George Chapman' and Michael Drayton's 'Chapman the Translator'.[81] Both of these poems figure Chapman as a type of conquistador, or corporate adventurer, who travels to foreign lands and returns with valuable possessions. Jonson's commendatory poem on Chapman's translation of Hesiod explicitly engages with a discourse of overseas commodity extraction: 'What treasure hast thou brought us! And what store, still dost thou arrive with, at our shore' (4–5). However, this discourse is complicated slightly by the fact that it is Chapman himself who must create the treasure, as he has to 'refine old Hesiod's ore' (1–2), having already 'wrought in rich Homer's mine' (3). For Jonson, translation is, in every sense of the word, refining. Foreign poetry gains value when it is properly translated into English, so much so that translation can be called Chapman's 'trade' (11), although the use of the term alongside the economic metaphors also points to the system of global exchanges that allow such a production. Similarly, Drayton's poem represents Chapman as a plunderer of Greek treasures: 'Chapman, who hath brought to us Musaeus, Homer and Hesiodus, out of the Greek, and by his skill hath reared them to that height' (6–10). Like Jonson, Drayton stresses the dislocation of the texts, and the work that Chapman has undertaken to naturalise them. It is notable that even within a colonial discourse it is the act of translation, not the cultural violence, which is deemed most noteworthy.

Anne Coldiron's model of an early modern print marketplace shaped by its engagement with the foreign is perhaps useful here. She notes that translations in the sixteenth century 'all bear marks of friction, traces of one culture resisting the other while appropriating material from it.'[82] This, she argues was in part a result of the effect of foreign, particularly French, influence on the budding print marketplace in England, visible not only in the type of texts produced, but also in their physical characteristics such as binding or woodcuts. In the highly self-conscious paratexts attached to translations we can see evidence of such engagement; these paratexts do not present translation in simple nationalistic or colonial terms, but rather as a much more subtle process of interaction between two valorised cultures.

For this reason, translations (and in particular, the self-reflexive prefaces to translations) demonstrate both the confidence of the new corporate traders 'Englishing' the commodities of the globe, and the sense of productive exchange demonstrated in ambassadorial and economic writings. Moving from a foreign language to English adds value, creates a new audience (or marketplace) and reinforces the idea that English writers and merchants can remake European or global spaces from London.

This chapter has thus shown the ways in which the idea of exchange was changed by corporate ideology during the seventeenth century, and in particular the abstracting of the process to include conceptual ideas such as debt, circulation and identity. These ideas were examined in literary texts of the period, which considered the moral and social elements of exchange, as well as reflecting new, or newly significant, forms of civic and national identity. The next chapter picks up the idea of 'Englishing' as a creation of identity via exchanges, to tease out the links between merchant activity and the construction of new forms of national identity through exploration and trade.

Notes

1 Raymond Williams, *The Long Revolution* (Cardigan: Parthian, 2011), 12.
2 Thomas Elyot, *The Dictionary of Syr Thomas Eliot Knyght* (London: Thomae Bertheleti, 1538), 'Colybus'.
3 *The Dictionary of Syr Thomas Eliot Knyght*, 'Licitor, aris, ari'.

4 William Sclater, *The Quaestion of Tythes Revised* (London: John Legatt, 1623), 56.
5 Elizabeth Knowles, ed. *The Oxford Dictionary of Phrase and Fable* (Oxford: Oxford University Press, 2005), 'exchange is no robbery, a fair'. William Wyrley, *The True Use of Armorie Shewed by Historie, and Plainly Proved by Example* (London: Gabriel Carwood, 1592), 130.
6 William Stafford, *A Compendious or Briefe Examination of Certayne Ordinary Complaints, of Diuers of Our Country Men in These Our Dayes* (London: Thomas Marshe, 1581), fol. 29r.
7 John Mellis, *The Grounde of Artes [. . .] Further Endowed with a Thirde Part, of Rules of Practize, Abridged into a Briefer Methode Than Hitherto Hath Bene Published: With Diuerse Such Necessary Rules, as Are Incident to the Trade of Merchandize* (London: I. Harison and H. Bynneman, 1582), frontis.
8 *The Grounde of Artes*, unpag. Part 3, Chapter 13.
9 *The Grounde of Artes*, unpag. Part 3, Chapter 13.
10 *The Grounde of Artes*, unpag. Part 3, Chapter 14.
11 Carl Wennerlind, *Casualties of Credit : The English Financial Revolution, 1620–1720* (Cambridge; London: Harvard University Press, 2011), 19.
12 Michel Foucault, *The Order of Things : An Archaeology of the Human Sciences* (Abingdon: Routledge, 2002), 192.
13 Gerard Malynes, *The Maintenance of Free Trade, According to the Three Essential Parts of Traffique* (London: William Steffard, 1622), 26–8.
14 *Maintenance of Free Trade*, 81.
15 BL 708.g.2. Charters Granted to the EIC from 1601, Charter of 31 December 1601, fol. 5.
16 Andy Kesson, *John Lyly and Early Modern Authorship* (Manchester: Manchester University Press, 2014), 3.
17 John Lyly, *Euphues and His England* (London: Gabriel Cawood, 1580), 109v.
18 ODNB, John Stow, 1524/5–1605.
19 John Stow, *The Survey of London* (London: John Wolfe, 1598), 61.
20 Richard Hakluyt, *The Principal Navigations, Voyages, Traffiques and Discoveries of the English Nation Made by Sea or over-Land, to the Remote and Farthest Distant Quarters of the Earth, at Any Time within the Compasse of These 1600 Yeres* (London: George Bishop, Ralph Newberie, and Robert Barker, 1599–1600), 245.
21 Hugo Grotius, *Freedom of the Seas or the Right Which Belongs to the Dutch to Take Part in the East Indian Trade*, trans. Ralph Van Deman Magoffin (New York: Oxford University Press, 1916. 1608), 7.
22 Mónica Brito Vieira, "Mare Liberum Vs. Mare Clausum: Grotius, Freitas, and Selden's Debate on Dominion over the Seas," *Journal of the History of Ideas* 64, no. 3 (2003): 363.
23 Grotius, *Freedom of the Seas*, 7.
24 Hans Blom, "Hugo Grotius on Trust, Its Causes and Effects," in *Trust and Happiness in the History of European Political Thought*, ed. László Kontler and Mark Somos ((Leiden: Brill, 2018), 92.
25 Hugo Grotius, *The Illustrious Hugo Grotius of the Law of Warre and Peace with Annotations*, trans. C.B. (London: T. Warren, for William Lee, 1655), 215.
26 See Peter Borschberg, *Hugo Grotius, the Portuguese, and Free Trade in the East Indies* (Singapore: NUS Press, 2011), 100–1.
27 Joseph Hall, *Quo Vadis? A Just Censure of Travell* (London: Edward Griffin for Nathaniel Butter, 1617), 2.
28 Malynes, *Maintenance of Free Trade*, 58–9.

29 Margaret Trabue Hodgen, *Early Anthropology in the Sixteenth and Seventeenth Centuries* (Philadelphia: University of Pennsylvania Press, 1964), 241.
30 John Flavel, *Navigation Spiritualiz'd [Etc]* (London: J.C. for Thomas Fabian, 1677), 37.
31 Thomas Mun, *A Discourse of Trade, from England Unto the East-Indies Answering to Diuerse Objections Which Are Usually Made against the Same* (London: John Piper, 1621), 50.
32 See William A. Pettigrew, "The Failure of the Cloth Trade to Surat and the Internationalisation of English Mercantilist Thought, 1614–21," in *The East India Company, 1600–1857: Essays on Anglo-Indian Connection*, ed. William A. Pettigrew and Mahesh Gopalan (Abingdon: Routledge, 2017).
33 Istvan Hont, *Jealousy of Trade: International Competition and the Nation State in Historical Perspective* (London: Belknap, 2005), 3.
34 Gerrard Winstanley, *A Declaration from the Poor Oppressed People of England* (London?: s.n., 1649), sig. A2v-A3r.
35 Thomas L. Leng, " 'His Neighbours Land Mark': William Sykes and the Campaign for 'Free Trade' in Civil War England," *HR* 86, no. 232 (2013): 232.
36 William Walwyn, *The Compassionate Samaritane* (London?: s.n., 1644), 31.
37 Thomas Dekker, "The Shoemaker's Holiday," in David Bevington et al., eds., *English Renaissance Drama* (London: Norton, 2002), vii.2–3, 14–15.
38 "Shoemaker's Holiday," vii.17–20.
39 David Scott Kastan, "Workshop and/as Playhouse: Comedy and Commerce in 'the Shoemaker's Holiday'," *Studies in Philology* 84, no. 3 (1987): 328.
40 "Shoemaker's Holiday," vii.99, 148–50.
41 "Shoemaker's Holiday," vii.117–21.
42 Andrea C. Lawson, "Saying Farewell with Shoes: The Gift Cycle and Unresolved Class Tensions in 'the Shoemaker's Holiday'," *Early Theatre* 15, no. 2 (2012): 106.
43 Karen Newman, "Portia's Ring: Unruly Women and Structures of Exchange in the Merchant of Venice," *Shakespeare Quarterly* 38, no. 1 (1987): 19.
44 Stephen Greenblatt et al., eds., *The Norton Shakespeare* (London: Norton, 1997), MoV III.ii.153–9.
45 Bartholomew Fair in Ben Jonson, *The Alchemist and Other Plays*, ed. Gordon Campbell (Oxford: Oxford University Press, 1995), V.ii.55–62.
46 John Milton, Comus, in John Milton, *The Complete Shorter Poems*, ed. John Carey, rev. 2nd ed. (Harlow: Longman, 2007), 671. Further references are given in the text.
47 William Lawne, *An Abridgement of the Institution of Christian Religion Written by M. Ihon [Sic] Calvin*, trans. Christopher Fetherstone (Edinburgh: Thomas Vautrollier, 1585), 186 [III.x].
48 *An Abridgement of the Institution of Christian Religion Written by M. Ihon [Sic] Calvin*, 186.
49 Roger Fenton, *A Treatise of Usurie Diuided into Three Bookes* (London: William Aspley, 1611), 94.
50 There should be a reference to Gimelli Martin's work (Martin, Catherine Gimelli, "The Non-Puritan Ethics, Metaphysics, and Aesthetics of Milton's Spenserian Masque," *Milton Quarterly* 37, no. 4 (2003): 215–44), pages 231–2.
51 Blair Hoxby, *Mammon's Music: Literature and Economics in the Age of Milton* (New Haven, CT: Yale University Press, 2002), 23.
52 Lyly, *Euphues and His England*, f.109v.
53 Natasha Glaisyer, *The Culture of Commerce in England, 1660–1720* (Woodbridge: Boydell, 2006), 68.

54 S.R., *The Choice of Change: Containing the Triplicitie of Diuinitie, Philosophie & Poetrie* (London: Roger Ward, 1585), 2.25.
55 Laurence Fontaine, *The Moral Economy: Poverty, Credit, and Trust in Early Modern Europe*, First English edition. ed. (New York: Cambridge University Press, 2014), 248.
56 Hakluyt, *Principal Navigations*, fol. *6r.
57 *Principal Navigations*, fol. *6v.
58 Anthony Payne, "Hakluyt's London: Discovery and Overseas Trade," in *Richard Hakluyt and Travel Writing in Early Modern Europe*, ed. Daniel Carey and Claire Jowitt (Farnham: Ashgate, 2012), 23.
59 Robert K. Batchelor, *London: The Selden Map and the Making of a Global City, 1549–1689* (Chicago: University of Chicago Press, 2014), 106–7.
60 Graham Parry, *The Trophies of Time : English Antiquarians of the Seventeenth Century* (Oxford: Oxford University Press, 1995), 15.
61 Stow, *The Survey of London*, 468.
62 Stow, *The Survey of London*, 468.
63 Stow, *The Survey of London*, 4.
64 James Howell, *Londinopolis an Historicall Discourse or Perlustration of the City of London* (London: Henry Twiford, George Sawbridge, Thomas Dring, and John Place, 1657), iii.
65 William Camden, *Britain, or a Chorographicall Description of the Most Flourishing Kingdomes, England, Scotland, and Ireland [. . .] Translated Newly into English by Philémon Holland* (London: George Latham, 1637), 51.
66 Michael Drayton, *Poly-Olbion* (London: M. Lownes, J. Browne, J. Helme, and J. Busbie, 1612), 250.
67 John Denham, *Cooper's Hill* (London: s.n., 1643), 6.
68 William Smith, *Ingratitude Reveng'd: Or, a Poem Upon the Happy Victory of His Majesties Naval Forces against the Dutch* (London: Dixy Page, 1665), 8.
69 See J. D. Reed, *Virgil's Gaze: Nation and Poetry in the Aeneid* (Princeton, NJ: Princeton University Press, 2007), 144–5.
70 Matthew Prior, ed. *State-Poems* (London: s.n., 1697), 14.
71 Michael J. Braddick, *God's Fury, England's Fire: A New History of the English Civil Wars* (London: Penguin Books, 2008), 588.
72 Robert Hearne, *Loyalty's Severe Summons to the Bar of Conscience* (London: Thomas Milbourn, 1681), 32.
73 Francis Quarles, *Boanerges and Barnabas* (London: R Lowndes, 1646), 211.
74 John Praed, *An Essay on the Coin and Commerce of the Kingdom* (London: s.n., 1697), 57.
75 S.E., *The Toutch-Stone of Mony and Commerce* (London: Author, 1654), 1.
76 Nicholas Von Maltzahn, *Milton's History of Britain : Republican Historiography in the English Revolution* (Oxford: Clarendon Press, 1991), 96.
77 Jonson, *Bartholomew Fair*, V.iiii.121–6.
78 Jonson, *Bartholomew Fair*, Induction 10–11.
79 John Denham, *The Destruction of Troy, an Essay Upon the Second Book of Virgils Aeneis. Written in the Year, 1636* (London: Humphrey Moseley, 1656), Sig. A3r-v.
80 Phyllis Brooks Bartlett, ed. *The Poems of George Chapman* (New York: Russell & Russell, 1962), 175.
81 Both poems are cited from David Hopkins, *English Poetry: A Poetic Record, from Chaucer to Yeats* (London: Routledge, 1990), 96–7. Line references are taken from this edition, and given in the text.
82 A. E. B. Coldiron, "Public Sphere/Contact Zone: Habermas, Early Print, and Verse Translation," *Criticism* 46, no. 2 (2004): 214.

Works cited

Manuscript

BL 708.g.2

Print

Bartlett, Phyllis Brooks, ed. *The Poems of George Chapman*. New York: Russell & Russell, 1962.

Batchelor, Robert K. *London: The Selden Map and the Making of a Global City, 1549–1689*. Chicago: University of Chicago Press, 2014.

Bevington, David, Lars Engle, Katharine Eisaman Maus, and Eric Rasmussen, eds. *English Renaissance Drama*. London: Norton, 2002.

Blom, Hans. "Hugo Grotius on Trust, Its Causes and Effects." In *Trust and Happiness in the History of European Political Thought*, edited by László Kontler and Mark Somos, 76–99. Leiden: Brill, 2018.

Borschberg, Peter. *Hugo Grotius, the Portuguese, and Free Trade in the East Indies*. Singapore: NUS Press, 2011.

Braddick, Michael J. *God's Fury, England's Fire: A New History of the English Civil Wars*. London: Penguin Books, 2008.

Camden, William. *Britain, or a Chorographicall Description of the Most Flourishing Kingdomes, England, Scotland, and Ireland [. . .] Translated Newly into English by Philémon Holland*. London: George Latham, 1637.

Coldiron, A. E. B. "Public Sphere/Contact Zone: Habermas, Early Print, and Verse Translation." *Criticism* 46, no. 2 (2004): 207–22.

Denham, John. *Cooper's Hill*. London: s.n., 1643.

———. *The Destruction of Troy, an Essay Upon the Second Book of Virgils Aeneis: Written in the Year, 1636*. London: Humphrey Moseley, 1656.

Drayton, Michael. *Poly-Olbion*. London: M. Lownes, J. Browne, J. Helme, and J. Busbie, 1612.

Elyot, Thomas. *The Dictionary of Syr Thomas Eliot Knyght*. London: Thomae Bertheleti, 1538.

Fenton, Roger. *A Treatise of Usurie Diuided into Three Bookes*. London: William Aspley, 1611.

Flavel, John. *Navigation Spiritualiz'd [Etc]*. London: J.C. for Thomas Fabian, 1677.

Fontaine, Laurence. *The Moral Economy: Poverty, Credit, and Trust in Early Modern Europe*. First English edition. ed. New York: Cambridge University Press, 2014.

Foucault, Michel. *The Order of Things : An Archaeology of the Human Sciences*. Abingdon: Routledge Classics, 2002.

Glaisyer, Natasha. *The Culture of Commerce in England, 1660–1720*. Woodbridge: Boydell, 2006.

Greenblatt, Stephen, Walter Cohen, Jean E. Howard, and Katharine Eisaman Maus, eds. *The Norton Shakespeare*. London: Norton, 1997.

Grotius, Hugo. *The Illustrious Hugo Grotius of the Law of Warre and Peace with Annotations, Trans. C.B.* London: T. Warren, for William Lee, 1655.

———. *Freedom of the Seas or the Right Which Belongs to the Dutch to Take Part in the East Indian Trade*. Translated by Ralph Van Deman Magoffin. New York: Oxford University Press, 1916. 1608.

Hakluyt, Richard. *The Principal Navigations, Voyages, Traffiques and Discoveries of the English Nation Made by Sea or over-Land, to the Remote and Farthest Distant Quarters of the Earth, at Any Time within the Compasse of These 1600 Yeres*. London: George Bishop, Ralph Newberie, and Robert Barker, 1599–1600.

Hall, Joseph. *Quo Vadis? A Just Censure of Travell*. London: Edward Griffin for Nathaniel Butter, 1617.

Hearne, Robert. *Loyalty's Severe Summons to the Bar of Conscience*. London: Thomas Milbourn, 1681.

Hodgen, Margaret Trabue. *Early Anthropology in the Sixteenth and Seventeenth Centuries*. Philadelphia: University of Pennsylvania Press, 1964.

Hont, Istvan. *Jealousy of Trade: International Competition and the Nation State in Historical Perspective*. London: Belknap, 2005.

Hopkins, David. *English Poetry: A Poetic Record, from Chaucer to Yeats*. London: Routledge, 1990.

Howell, James. *Londinopolis an Historicall Discourse or Perlustration of the City of London*. London: Henry Twiford, George Sawbridge, Thomas Dring, and John Place, 1657.

Hoxby, Blair. *Mammon's Music: Literature and Economics in the Age of Milton*. New Haven, CT: Yale University Press, 2002.

Jonson, Ben. *The Alchemist and Other Plays*. Edited by Gordon Campbell. Oxford: Oxford University Press, 1995.

Kastan, David Scott. "Workshop and/as Playhouse: Comedy and Commerce in 'the Shoemaker's Holiday'." *Studies in Philology* 84, no. 3 (1987): 324–37.

Kesson, Andy. *John Lyly and Early Modern Authorship*. Manchester: Manchester University Press, 2014.

Knowles, Elizabeth, ed. *The Oxford Dictionary of Phrase and Fable*. Oxford: Oxford University Press, 2005.

Lawne, William. *An Abridgement of the Institution of Christian Religion Written by M. Ihon [Sic] Calvin*. Translated by Christopher Fetherstone. Edinburgh: Thomas Vautrollier, 1585.

Lawson, Andrea C. "Saying Farewell with Shoes: The Gift Cycle and Unresolved Class Tensions in 'the Shoemaker's Holiday'." *Early Theatre* 15, no. 2 (2012): 93–110.

Leng, Thomas L. "'His Neighbours Land Mark': William Sykes and the Campaign for 'Free Trade' in Civil War England." *HR* 86, no. 232 (2013): 230–52.

Lyly, John. *Euphues and His England*. London: Gabriel Cawood, 1580.

Malynes, Gerard. *The Maintenance of Free Trade, According to the Three Essential Parts of Traffique*. London: William Steffard, 1622.

Martin, Catherine Gimelli. "The Non-Puritan Ethics, Metaphysics, and Aesthetics of Milton's Spenserian Masque." *Milton Quarterly* 37, no. 4 (2003): 215–44.

Mellis, John. *The Grounde of Artes [. . .] Further Endowed with a Thirde Part, of Rules of Practize, Abridged into a Briefer Methode Than Hitherto Hath Bene Published: With Diuerse Such Necessary Rules, as Are Incident to the Trade of Merchandize*. London: I. Harison and H. Bynneman, 1582.

Milton, John. *The Complete Shorter Poems*. edited by John Carey. rev. 2nd ed. Harlow: Longman, 2007. 1667.

Mun, Thomas. *A Discourse of Trade, from England Unto the East-Indies Answering to Diuerse Objections Which Are Usually Made against the Same.* London: John Piper, 1621.

Newman, Karen. "Portia's Ring: Unruly Women and Structures of Exchange in the Merchant of Venice." *Shakespeare Quarterly* 38, no. 1 (1987): 19–33.

Parry, Graham. *The Trophies of Time : English Antiquarians of the Seventeenth Century.* Oxford: Oxford University Press, 1995.

Payne, Anthony. "Hakluyt's London: Discovery and Overseas Trade." In *Richard Hakluyt and Travel Writing in Early Modern Europe*, edited by Daniel Carey and Claire Jowitt, 13–23. Farnham: Ashgate, 2012.

Pettigrew, William A. "The Failure of the Cloth Trade to Surat and the Internationalisation of English Mercantilist Thought, 1614–21." In *The East India Company, 1600–1857: Essays on Anglo-Indian Connection*, edited by William A. Pettigrew and Mahesh Gopalan, 21–43. Abingdon: Routledge, 2017.

Praed, John. *An Essay on the Coin and Commerce of the Kingdom.* London: s.n., 1697.

Prior, Matthew, ed. *State-Poems.* London: s.n., 1697.

Quarles, Francis. *Boanerges and Barnabas.* London: R. Lowndes, 1646.

Reed, J. D. *Virgil's Gaze: Nation and Poetry in the Aeneid.* Princeton, NJ: Princeton University Press, 2007.

S.E. *The Toutch-Stone of Mony and Commerce.* London: Author, 1654.

Sclater, William. *The Quaestion of Tythes Revised.* London: John Legatt, 1623.

Smith, William. *Ingratitude Reveng'd: Or, a Poem Upon the Happy Victory of His Majesties Naval Forces against the Dutch.* London: Dixy Page, 1665.

S.R. *The Choice of Change: Containing the Triplicitie of Diuinitie, Philosophie & Poetrie.* London: Roger Ward, 1585.

Stafford, William. *A Compendious or Briefe Examination of Certayne Ordinary Complaints, of Diuers of Our Country Men in These Our Dayes.* London: Thomas Marshe, 1581.

Stow, John. *The Survey of London.* London: John Wolfe, 1598.

Vieira, Mónica Brito. "Mare Liberum Vs. Mare Clausum: Grotius, Freitas, and Selden's Debate on Dominion over the Seas." *Journal of the History of Ideas* 64, no. 3 (2003): 361–77.

Von Maltzahn, Nicholas. *Milton's History of Britain : Republican Historiography in the English Revolution.* Oxford: Clarendon Press, 1991.

Walwyn, William. *The Compassionate Samaritane.* London?: s.n., 1644.

Wennerlind, Carl. *Casualties of Credit : The English Financial Revolution, 1620–1720.* Cambridge; London: Harvard University Press, 2011.

Williams, Raymond. *The Long Revolution.* Cardigan: Parthian, 2011. 1961.

Winstanley, Gerrard. *A Declaration from the Poor Oppressed People of England.* London?: s.n., 1649.

Wyrley, William. *The True Use of Armorie Shewed by Historie, and Plainly Proved by Example.* London: Gabriel Carwood, 1592.

4 Epic, nationalism and the corporation

In 1622, Edward Waterhouse published an account of the recent massacre in Virginia which served, like so many contemporary texts on the subject, as a call for investment and adventure in the name of the company and the country alike:

> [I]t is to be wished, that euery good Patriot will take these things seriously into his thoughts, and consider how deeply the prosecution of this noble Enterprise concerneth the honor of his *Maiestie* and the whole Nation, the propagation of Christian Religion, the enlargement, strength, and safety of his Maiesties Dominions, the rich augmenting of his Reuennues, the imploiment of his Subiects idle at home, the increase of men, Mariners and shipping, and the raising of such necessary commoditie, for the importation of which from forren Countries so great and incredible summes are continually issued and expended.[1]

Waterhouse makes a fairly standard set of claims for the Virginia Company and, as I argued in Chapter 1, for companies more generally: They will increase shipping, augment the balance of trade and broadly benefit the nation in a variety of non-commercial ways, especially by spreading the Gospel. As Andrew Fitzmaurice has noted, the Virginia Company in particular engaged in print to encourage new investors, and as a way of 'adventuring' in and of itself, and Waterhouse is a classic example of the tradition.[2] But Waterhouse goes further, and imagines a sort of corporate nationalism, in which the chartered dominions of the Virginia Company become the patriotic concern of the 'whole nation'.

The claim that a corporation was acting in the national interest by securing trade or dominion became commonplace through the seventeenth century. Naturally, this applied particularly to the global trading companies who established claims for territories outside of Europe, albeit often in a piecemeal and uncertain way. Ideas of 'corporate nationhood' were established through the directions to explore and subsequent grants of land or territorial monopoly in charters. The idea moved beyond this legal basis once the question of trading as a natural right of Englishmen was raised and discussed through the lens of monopoly corporate activity. Chapters 1 and 2 focused on the political writings, like Waterhouse's *Declaration*, which supported or opposed the corporation in its claims to being a national good or a national trade. In this chapter, I consider another key genre for national identity, the epic poem, in order to demonstrate the ways in which corporate rhetoric became intertwined with literary representations of a nation's origins, ideals and imagined future.

Epic, exploration and national identity

Epic poetry is, ultimately, a myth of nationhood. It is a recounting of a familiar story: the great deeds of a member (often the founding member) of a nation, which synecdochically provide the archetype of that nation's self-conception. Achilles's valour, Odysseus's wisdom (or cunning), Aeneas's *pietas* and Dante's faith all stand as the epitome of a virtue highly prized by the culture that provided them, the ideal model to which contemporary society must aspire. Dante identified this trait in the *Aeneid*, arguing that Virgil "wish[ed] to praise the age which was seen to be arising in his time."[3] These epitomised qualities are, through the cultural capital of epic, re-valorised as constituting the origins of the national psyche; in this process, they are made to serve a purpose at the moment of writing by reinforcing or reinscribing the current society's self-presentation.

In the early modern period, epic was considered primarily as a moral or instructive guide for actions in the present. Milton argued that an epic should be "an interpreter of the best and sagest things"; Tasso defined a "heroic poem (that is, an epic)" as "an imitation of noble action, great and perfect."[4] It is, in fact, a typological relationship that provides the clearest link between the subject of epic (the national past) and the culture of its production (the national present). As Louise Cowan has noted, the epic provokes "conscious memories of the heroic past, sufficient for envisioning their people's role in the ongoing process of history."[5] Epic intervenes in the "process of history" precisely through its depiction of the absolute past, since it recreates that past in order to make it point forward, ineluctably, to a glorious future (which may either be the present in which the epic is written, or an even more distant future). Aeneas's shield and Michael's postlapsarian vision for Adam are the standard forms of this schema. Consequently, rather than existing in a valorised yet inaccessible past, epic poetry serves as an intervention into the continuous process of national self-fashioning.

Epic retells the construction of a national identity, and in doing so participates in that construction. The actions of the heroic past serve both as a key constitutive force of the present and a guide to sustaining national identity in the future. Epic, with its interest in the mythic origins of a nation, is a method by which a culture can reflect upon itself: the myth "is itself the model of which everyday reality is in some sense the symbol."[6] Yet epic can also betray an anxiety about those very symbols. As early modern Europe engaged with the new 'Others' beyond its boundaries, the divine mandate of traditional epic journeys to new homes or conquests was transmuted into anxious descriptions of exploration and proto-colonisation.

The 1650s saw the establishment of "the first English (later British) empire, and it contained the central contradiction of later imperial life – the forcible imposition of English liberties."[7] Even before formal considerations of empire, colonies abroad had struggled with the construction of a code of laws that addressed the difficulties of governing a new environment while retaining the rights and privileges that existed in England. The initial confluence between Englishman and Other occurred abroad, and consequently many of these apparent paradoxes were resolved on an individual basis, with governments in London (state and corporate) being unable or unwilling to introduce a standard legal or political form on colonies overseas – a state of affairs that occasionally led to protracted constitutional wrangling, such as the assembly of the Virginia Company's uncertain relationship with the English Parliament and laws, or the Parliamentary responses to the East India Company's use of martial law in St Helena in 1689.[8]

As a consequence, general contact with the foreign in England (indeed, Europe more generally) came initially through textual reconstruction. Just as the validity and value of exiting law was questioned by overseas adventure, this discursive contact called into question the very viability of existing language. Spenser's *The Faerie Queene* explicitly discusses the failings of descriptive potentiality when faced with what appears to be – or is presented as being – literally indescribable. Although the *topos* of inexpressibility was well established by the time Spenser was composing, it was usually contained to panegyric or love poetry, signifying something not indescribable as such, but which went beyond the boundaries of the traditional superlative (a notion ridiculed by Shakespeare in Sonnet 130). In panegyric, however, the object being described is always 'more than' (more beautiful, wiser, more like the sun and so forth), whereas in epic the object is fundamentally 'different' than, so that the epic metaphor is frequently constructed as a 'like-but-unlike'. Spenser and Dante return to this formulation of inexpressibility when faced with the divine that they have experienced; it is the nature of that experience that cannot be communicated.

Spenser's project, as Stephen Greenblatt has demonstrated, is informed by a cultural poetics that cannot adequately comprehend the contact with the alien, specifically in the form of the territories of the New World. Described in terms of lavish superabundance, these territories had to be positioned in relation to the very structures of representation and experience that they surpassed, just as the Bower of Bliss surpasses other mythological paradises:

> More sweet and holesome, then the pleasant hill
> Of *Rhodope*, on which the Nimphe, that bore
> A gyaunt babe, her selfe for griefe did kill:
> Or the Thessalian *Tempe*, where of yore
> Fayre *Daphne Phoebus* hart with loue did gore;
> Or *Ida*, where the Gods lou'd to repayre.
> (*FQ* II.xii.52)

The Bower cannot be accurately described, except in saying what it is not; it is simply more than what has gone before. Existing modes of description, then, are shown to be insufficient, as only the comparative is adequate to express the glory of the Bower. Even this, though, is ultimately shown to be inadequate: the final line of the stanza, as the Bower is "like *Eden* self, if ought with *Eden* mote compaire" (*FQ* II.xii.52). *The Faerie Queene* asks its readers to compare two incomparable and indescribable things, and in doing so reveals the limitations of its system of comparison and description. In this it is similar to *Paradise Lost*, where the reader "can know this landscape only by comparison, but it is by comparison to things that we have never seen."[9] *The Faerie Queene*, however, reveals its own fictive nature by invoking an incomparable Eden, and in doing so drawing attention to the very *system* of representation: All of these frames of reference are allowed to collapse when faced with that which truly defies description.

For the first explorers, that modulation of existing forms of description fails, at least in part, because the "American landscape has to European eyes the mysterious intimations of a hidden art."[10] That is, it is both strangely familiar and yet completely outside the European frame of reference, which must necessarily be expanded to encompass it. This alteration had the dangerously subversive potential for reciprocity; as Bartolomé de las Casas noted, the Spanish explorers were seized with a cruelty unrivalled in the Old World. According to de las Casas, the Spanish were prone to "tear [the natives] in pieces, kill them, martyr them, afflict them, torment them, & destroy them by strange sorts of cruelties never neither seen, nor read, nor heard of the like."[11] Paradoxically, this modulation of the European worldview was the prerequisite of its imposition; as Greenblatt puts it, "the radical undermining of Christian order is not the negative limit but the positive condition for the establishment of that order."[12] Although Greenblatt is referring to the Machiavellian posturing of divinity amongst the Virginia colonists, we can extend his argument across the New World: the Spanish cruelty (unnecessary, since de las Casas reports that the natives were "without malice, very obedient and very faithful" [9]) is a destructive test of the limits of Christian virtues that must take place for those very virtues to be imported into the

New World. As Karen Kupperman notes, "Christianity did not represent a package that [the natives] accepted entire; rather, they unpacked it and reassembled its parts."[13] The fear of this unpacking, evidence of an active alterity able to change a fundamental aspect of European-ness, necessitated the cruel imposition of Christian values.

The result of this liminality was the construction of a new system of inscription which depends upon constant reference to the failure, or at least inadequacy, of the old: it is no surprise, although he does not note it, that the sources Greenblatt cites actually precisely *fail* to "record their astonishment" (180) at the splendour of the Americas: "I beheld a thousand shapes, and a thousand forms, that I cannot express in writing."[14] Nor is this an uncommon theme, for English or Continental explorers; Bernal Díaz del Castillo reported that Tenochtitlan was too much for the *conquistadores* to take in:

> [A]lgunos de nuestros soldados decían que si aquello que vían, si era entre sueños, y no es de maravillar que lo escriba aquí desde manera, porque hay mucho que ponderar en ello que no sé como lo cuente: ver cosas nunca oídas, ni vistas, ni aun soñadas, como víamos.
>
> Some of our soldiers said that the things they saw were like a dream; and it is no marvel that I write them here in this manner, for there is so much to ponder that I do not know how to account for it all. The things we have seen on our travels, I cannot describe, for we have never heard of, or seen, or even dreamed of them before. [15]

For Bernal Díaz, the only way to account for these wonders is to place them specifically outside of the realm of description: The marvels of the new continent surpass "purely descriptive terminology, for there is nothing within the author's experience that can equal the diversity and perfection he sees in these new lands."[16] The New World is simply too rich, too abundant, too much like Eden, for the first travellers to completely comprehend.

So too *The Faerie Queene*, which draws on this tradition to ask, like the early explorers, that its audience trust the writer with no basis of shared experience:

> Who euer heard of th'Indian *Peru*?
> Or who in adventurous vessel measured
> The *Amazons* huge riuer now found trew
> Or fruitfullest *Virginia* who did euer view?
> Yet all these were when no man did them know,
> Yet haue from wisest ages hidden beene
> And later times thinges more vnknowne shall show.
> Why then should witlesse man so much misweene
> That nothing is but that which he hath seen?
>
> (*FQ* II.Proem.2–3)

The proem here asks for Faerie to be given the same status as these other marvellous, and hitherto unknown lands.[17] As Murrin puts it, in "contemptuous language Spenser flatly denies *any* imaginative status for his poem."[18] What is in doubt is not the *existence* of these strange lands, but the potential for understanding and imagining them. Ultimately, the poem, when faced with an experience beyond that easily appropriated to European systems of signification, simply refuses description entirely. Spenser refuses to explicitly outline the contours of the "goodly Citty,"

> Whose wals and towres were builded high and strong
> Of perle and precious stone, that earthly tong
> Cannot describe, nor wit of man can tell;
> Too high a ditty for my simple song.
>
> (*FQ* I.x.55)

That city signifies – at least in part – the New Jerusalem, which is actually described in considerable detail in Revelations 21, from which this brief quote suffices:

> And the building of the wall of it was of Jasper: and the city was pure Gold like unto clear glass. And the foundations of the wall of the city were garnished with all manner of precious stones: the first foundation was of Jasper, the second of Sapphire: the third of a Chalcedony, the fourth of an Emerald.[19]

Yet *The Faerie Queene* simply refuses any description: the walls may be of "perle and precious stone," suggesting the biblical New Jerusalem, but the poem describes them no further. The detail, and allegorical significance, of the description in Revelations is flattened into the unspeakable: By reducing the eleven verses of revelations to a single formulaic line, Spenser reiterates the failure of comparisons to express the archetypal city he seeks to portray. The marvellous places of Heaven, the New World and Faerie collapse into one another, and in doing so reveal a reliance on experiential education: these things, quite simply, must be seen to be believed.

The strangeness of these new-found lands offered an interpretative and political space in the English imagination into which corporations could insert themselves. From their inception, corporations were designed as mechanisms for exploration and expansion. The precursor to the Muscovy (Russia) Company, the Company of Merchant Adventurers to New Lands, was granted a charter in 1555 which specifically acknowledged the work they had already done "to discouer, descrie, and finde Iles, landes, territories, Dominions, and Seigniories vnknowen, and by our subiects before this not commonly by sea frequented."[20] The charter certified the work of exploration, and encouraged further "profitable adventure" by confirming the Company's monopoly privileges over whatever lands (if populated by infidels) and sea routes they discovered.

The charter also confirmed Sebastian Cabot as governor. Cabot, an itinerant navigational scholar who, after advising on English exploration in North America, had been named pilot-major of Spain before returning to England to advise on the sea route to Russia (and potentially beyond to China and the Spice Islands). Cabot had previously been named on a set of letters patent from Henry VIII addressed to his father, John, as well as his other brothers and their heirs and deputies (making the family a sort of corporation), giving them licence "to seeke out, discover, and finde whatsoever isles, countreys, regions or provinces of the heathen and infidels whatsoeuer they be, and in what part of the world soever they be which before this time have bene unknowen to all Christians."[21] The language of this, and similar, letters patent to individuals was brought into early corporate charters, confirming the status of the corporation as a vehicle for the expansion of geographical and economic boundaries.

For a long time after the discovery of these lands, corporations continued to stress their strangeness and difference. In large part, this was a rhetorical strategy aimed at the domestic public sphere, since one of the most effective defences of the corporate form was the argument that only a united group of merchants or settlers, able to share information and infrastructure, could hope to be successful in the face of such a difficult political and physical environment; we have already seen the ways in which the East India Company used such a strategy in Chapter 1. Charles II, in a proclamation in defence of the Royal African Company, gave prominent voice to that very argument in 1674:

> Whereas it is found by experience, that traffique with infidels and barbarous nations not in amity with us, and who are not holden by any league or treaty, cannot be carried on without the establishment of forts and factories in places convenient, the maintenance whereof requires so great and constant expence, that it cannot be otherwise defrayed, than by managing the whole trade in a joint stock.[22]

The perceived dangers of the African coasts, and the unwillingness of the natives to be held by treaty (marking them out as dangerous 'other' from Europeans, who at least in theory respected the international law of treaties) required a show of force and a permanent infrastructure, maintained at the Royal African Company's charge. Conversely, opponents of the company claimed that a better understanding of the topography and governance of these new lands would obviate the need for a company (or at least a joint stock) at all, as in this anonymous pamphlet from 1691:

> Our Fondness for *Fort St. George* and *Bombay* is very unaccountable, since the first is situated where is neither Port nor Harbour,

> only an open Road, where no Ships can ride upon breaking up of the Monsoons with any tolerable safety; nor is this Road well commanded by the Town or Fort, which for want of Water, besides its other defects, cannot hold out a Siege of ten dayes, and is the worst seated for Trade, or to make investments of Goods, of any place on the Coast of *Cormandell*. *Bombay* its true is more defensible, there is a Port, and it may be reliev'd by Sea, yet its altogether as useless as the other, except to make War again with the *Mogull*, which wou'd be a Folly so fatal, that it ought to be abandon'd purely to secure us from the being tempted into such a Misfortune; but its a place without Commerce, and the safety and conveniency of Ships Harbouring there wou'd be the same, were there no Fort.[23]

It is notable that the writer seeks to undermine corporate arguments by providing distinct geographical information about the placement of the forts: Fort St. George is not situated well because it does not take into account either the seasonal conditions in India (monsoons) or the local geography (it lacks water and does not overlook the road). Bombay, too, is a needless fort because the harbour is so naturally defensible that a fort is a European habit rather than a local necessity. The emphasis on these local features reveals a core element of the interlopers' rhetorical strategy: they present the company as secretive, in this case over local conditions, and promise that their version of the truth will correct this informational imbalance and demonstrate that there are better ways to manage the trade.

Regardless of the economic value of corporations, this debate, played out in the public sphere, demonstrates the ways in which overseas territories, possessions and treaties could be manipulated in the court of public opinion. In doing so, new conceptions and formations of 'national' were at stake – sovereignty over foreign lands, the extension of national power (and/or being an actor in international relations) and perhaps most importantly, the idea of a national trade (and who ought to take part in, and benefit from, that trade). These questions of how a nation should be constituted and imagined, found expression in literary as well as political writings, not least the epic poem.

Corporate epics

Over the course of the early modern period, the standard epic ideal of martial heroism seen in the *Iliad, Aeneid* or even the *Gerusalemme Liberata* was supplanted by the spirituality and commercialism which increasingly made up the early modern public sphere. This shift was most visible in epic when the question of exploration was raised. Was exploration the prerogative of the state and its noble servants, as a way of expanding honour and martial prowess? Or was it the function of traders, seeking to open new markets and provide luxury goods? This distinction between the motives for exploration affected domestic conceptions of class, questioning the sharp dividing line between the martial function of the aristocracy and the newly emergent and upwardly mobile bourgeois middle classes. David Quint has noted

> The divergent interpretations of the voyages that ran along class lines. The enterprise of discovery could alternately be understood as a heroic endeavor in the epic, aristocratic mold or as a business expedition undertaken by adventurous merchants.[24]

This distinction, however, between the 'martial' aristocracy and the 'businesslike' merchants was not always clear cut. The royalist translator Christopher Wase's praise poem upon the restoration of Charles II posits the king, not the merchant class, as the origin of trade:

> While you repair our wooden walls decays,
> Churches erect, and a fair city raise;
> While you in Peace unite divided Hearts,
> And with Free trade revive ingenuous Arts.[25]

Wase reconfigures the project of noble construction (military enclosures and churches) into that of "Free trade," co-opting the noblest figure in the land into the mercantile cause. Moreover, free trade has a restorative power, coupled with (and perhaps with an agency in) the new peace, as well as a clear cultural impact in those "ingenuous Arts." In fact, in Wase's imagined future, free trade becomes a crucial operative function of the nobility.

Yet Wase's poem, however hopeful it is of a remodulation of these categories at this moment of precarious triumph, is a reminder that the distinctions between nobility and trade were well established by the time he was writing. The failure of the Virginia Company a generation before offered a stark reminder for Wase and his contemporaries of the dangers of mixing aristocratic and mercantile interests.

Originally set up as a company for trade in New England, the Virginia Company raised capital by a lottery as well as the sale of land in the new territory it was granted by royal charter, each investor being rewarded with a plot of American soil to work. However, the company was plagued with problems of supply and survival in its overseas possessions, as well as faction and infighting within the company itself.[26] In both Virginia and the boardroom, a contrast was frequently made between practical contributors like sailors and merchants, and aristocratic investors who critics claimed had little to offer the company beyond capital.

By the time of the elections to the court (what we now might call the board of directors) of 1619, which effectively confirmed a hostile takeover from within, the company had descended into "violently opposed factions," each of which accused the other of "being self serving, of using their position for their own factional benefit and of pursuing personal profit."[27] Although these divisions were not generally as simple as gentry against merchants, there were certainly occasions when that was the case, as in one board meeting in 1622:

> The Court was diuided and Twenty of the Companie went on one side, and one and Twenty on the other, All the Lords Knights and gentlemen beinge on the one side.[28]

Virginia was an enterprise which, if not a colony (which is, as Alison Games and others point out, too anachronistic and simplistic a term), nevertheless had a certain amount of land management.[29] Consequently, it is no surprise to find that a significantly higher proportion of investors and participants in the Company came from an aristocratic background – Edmond Smith places the figure at around 44%, compared with 1.6% of the trade-oriented Levant Company.[30] That division in skills continued to create divisions in the boardroom; in 1623, when a motion was made for six gentlemen to be appointed assistants to the treasurer (that is, leader) of the company, an objection was raised because

> The mayne part and substance of the buissines consisted in matter of proffitt and tradinge: In which things Gentlemen beinge not expert, it was not conceaved, howe they by their Industrie and good carriage should so much advance the buissines.[31]

The phrase "gentlemen being not expert" is a telling one. The board dismissed the motion on the grounds that gentlemen were not properly experienced in the "industry" of trading. Although they were a useful link to the politics of the royal court, the economic functions of the company ought, the merchants believed, to be left in the hands of experts.

Likewise in Virginia itself, John Smith reported on the difficulties he had in establishing a colony with insufficient skilled labour: "nor had we a Mariner nor any had skill to trim the sayles but two saylers and my selfe, the rest being Gentlemen, or them were as ignorant in such toyle and labour [. . .] What I did with this small meanes I leave to the Reader to judge"[32] Smith's report may have been slightly exaggerated, allowing him to claim credit for the colony's survival despite having to work with these "effete aristocrats."[33] Nonetheless, there is a clear divide between the land-seeking gentlemen and the sailors, farmers and merchants who aimed to build a prosperous trading outpost.

This distinction between nobles and merchants played out in contemporary epic poetry. Camões's Portuguese epic on the voyage of Da Gama, *Os Lusíadas*, takes its title not from a single individual but from the entire nation (the sons of Lusus); the focus of the epic is Portuguese trade with the East Indies, and the virtues of their policy of maritime supremacy. Richard Fanshawe, a member of the gentry, translated Camões's epic in 1655. His translation collapses the distinction between military and mercantile classes, emphasising the conflation of these roles in the noble captain:

> (For *Trade* brings *Opulence* and *Rarieties*,
> For which the *Poor* doe *sweat*, the *Rich* doe *Pine*)
> Of two *great* fruits, which will from thence redound,
> *His* shall the *glory; thine*, the *Gain* be found.[34]

Da Gama is here speaking to the Emperor of India, and appears to cast himself simply as a noble emissary: he offers all the economic reward of any alliance to the natives, so long as he (as substitute for the King of Portugal) receives the glory. Similarly, he seems to disdain the practice of trade, suggesting that only the poor should "sweat" for it, while the rich simply "pine" for the "rarities" it can deliver to them. Yet the locals are more aware of Da Gama's mission, as the Emperor's closing offer reveals:

> Added to this, his avaritious Eye
> Upon the gainful Trade of PORTUGALL
> Makes him obey; and rather to comply
> With the brave *Captain*, then the *Moorish* gall.
> In short, he bids DE GAMA presently
> Get him aboard his *Fleet;* and, without all
> Suspect of harm, whatever *Merchandice*
> To send ashore to sell, or truck for Spice.
> (VIII.77)

Trade, in fact, is as much the goal of Da Gama as any glory – he wishes to return to Portugal with spice as well as fame. The offer reveals the real value to the Europeans of Oriental trade, since "trucking" their merchandise for spice (and with it, undermining the Spanish/Dutch trading empires) allows the realisation of surplus value from that merchandise, and was (as we have seen) by far the most profitable interaction with the foreign available in the seventeenth century. Moreover, the Emperor's offer reveals the inherent balance in cultural value; not only is he able to understand the true purpose of these negotiations (a notable contrast to the European accounts of Native Americans), but also the offer of trade places the two cultures into a mutually beneficial relationship.

Fanshawe's dedicatory epistle gestures towards the effect that foreign trade can have on domestic culture:

> How much more obliged am I to bring unto your Lordship this TREASURE-TROVE, which (as to the second life, or rather Being, it

> hath from me in the English-Tongue) is so truly a Native of YORK-SHIRE, and holding of your Lordship.
>
> (Sig. A2v)

It is difficult, in a preface to a poem about the discovery of the East, not to read "treasure-trove" as either the spices themselves, or the profit to be made from them. In any case, Fanshawe's image assigns a local identity to the exotic, and this is achieved by the translator's agency. It is, like the focus on trade, the intermediary process which is assigned the most importance. The 'value' of translation, here, is that it allows an appropriation of a foreign text to a political context – less explicit, here, than in other prefaces, but nonetheless the emphasis on the 'political' ramifications of a text so closely concerned with (nobly figured) expansion and foreign trade cannot be overlooked. By placing the text as a "holding" of his dedicatee, the Second Earl of Strafford, Fanshawe recasts his role of translator as a type of Vasco da Gama, travelling to foreign lands and appropriating their produce.

Other translated epics, too, dealt with the questions of expansion and trade raised by corporations. Josuah (sometimes Joshuah) Sylvester translated Du Bartas's *Divine Weeks and Works* (originally published in two parts in France in 1578 and 1584), and his work went through at least nine editions between 1592 and the third, and final, folio edition in 1641. Now largely overlooked, Sylvester's translation was extremely popular and well regarded by his contemporaries, as was the case with Du Bartas's French original a generation before. The poem divides creation into two weeks: the first week broadly follows the Genesis account of creation, compendiously detailing the things created on each day and speculating on theological questions. The second week offers a history of mankind from Eden to the Last Judgement, although Du Bartas died before days five to seven were completed, meaning the poem lacks its intended Messianic and Eschatological dénouement. It is in this second week that Sylvester found most of his opportunities to bring the translation closer to the English experience, particularly by the interpolation of London and its merchants.

Sylvester was personally familiar with the workings of trading corporations; he was probably the son of a clothier, and served in the Merchant Adventurers before returning to London in the early 1590s to take up translation.[35] Although Sylvester left the Merchant Adventurers, he returned to their employ at the end of his life, taking a position as their secretary in Middelburg in 1613. He had actually been recommended as a secretary for the company at Stade by Robert Devereaux, second Earl of Essex, in a letter he wrote in 1597. The Earl reported that he had

> Received a very good report of his [Sylvester's] sufficiency and fitness for the same, being both well qualified with language and many other good parts as also reputed honest & of good conversation.[36]

In the same letter Sylvester is referred to as still being a member of the company, although he is obviously seeking to utilise his linguistic, rather than financial, skills. Although the Merchant Adventurer records are patchy, there is no evidence that Sylvester was actually involved directly in the wool trade (which was tightly controlled by a few merchant families). There is, though, some evidence that he may well have been involved in the import trade from Germany: The Draper's Company record that Joshua Sylvester, "a m[erchant] adv[enturer] . . . over to Middleburrough," took Edward Irby as an apprentice on 16th July 1617, just over a year before his death.[37] Clearly, whether or not he was trading directly, Sylvester had an intimate knowledge of the activities of the Merchant Adventurers, and links to livery companies back in London.

On a number of occasions throughout the translation Sylvester makes explicit changes, marked through italicisation and in some cases glossed. In one of these, Sylvester's experience abroad is figured in much the same way as Fanshawe's translating practice when his biography impinges upon the translation, in a description of the planetary motions:

> Both up and down and with contrarie paces
> At once they poste to two contrary places:
> *Like as myself, in my lost Marchant-yeares*
> (*A losse alas that in these lynes appears*)
> *Wafting to* Brabant, *Englands golden Fleece*
> (*A richer prize than Jason brought to Greece*).[38]

Like Fanshawe, Sylvester is concerned with the bringing back of rarities to England, although his involvement in the wool trade gives the "golden fleece" a more practical signification than simply classical allusion given the wealth and importance of the Merchant Adventurer's trade in cloth. Likewise, the "loss" of time that appears "in these lines" might be a standard comment on his own lack of skill, a version of the trope of false modesty, but also suggests that it is his trading experience, not a classical education, on which Sylvester must draw to make a worthy translation.

A further, crucial imposition of Sylvester into Du Bartas's text is the substitution of London for Paris which comes in the description of Eden: Anyone who views Eden will "despise" the "remnant world" just as those who have travelled to these great cities will see that they are far beyond even comparison with the "homely hamlets" of previous experience:

> When afterwards he happens to behold
> Our wealthy London's wonders manifold
> [. . . . .]
> Then at the signes the shops, the waights, the measures,
> The handy-crafts, the rumors, trades, and treasures.
> But of all sights, none seems him yet more strange
> Then the rare, beautious, stately, rich Exchange.

Another while he marvails at the Thames,
Which seems to bear huge mountains on her streams:
Then at the faire-built Bridge; which he doth judge
More like a tradefull City then a Bridge;
And glancing thence a-long the Northren shoare,
That princely prospect doth amaze him more.[39]

Sylvester describes London primarily through the prism of economic activity, and particularly, although this is not made explicit, corporate-economic activity. London's status as a "wealthy" city is a product of commerce, made visible in the shops, the Exchange, and especially the "tradeful city" within a city on London Bridge, all of which are corporate in nature. Even the weights and measures relate to corporate activity, since it was the livery companies which were responsible for the regulating of trading standards. As well as the domestic corporations for buying and selling, Sylvester's inclusion of the 'huge mountains' floating on the Thames does suggest what the East India Company called its 'great' ships for the voyages to the East. At the time of the translation, the EIC were rapidly expanding their high-tonnage fleet from the docks at Blackwall and Deptford, and their carracks were "some of the largest in the English merchant navy."[40]

Sylvester makes another insertion of London as an extension of Du Bartas's general comment on international trade in the description of mankind's settlement of the globe:

And that the treasures which strange Soyls produce,
Might not seem worth-les, for the want of use;
But that the In-land Lands might truck and barter
And vent their Wares about to every Quarter.[41]

Here the *Divine Works* (in both the original and translation) endorses the model of God's ordering of trade across Earth based on want and supply which was discussed in Chapter 3: an overabundance of a particular material or manufacture in one part of the globe becomes a spur for "truck and barter," and subsequently a balancing of resources which allows all to thrive and waste (the "want of use") to be minimised. The phrase "truck and barter," as well as pointing forward to Fanshawe's translation of da Gama's trucking for spice, also recalls an earlier passage in the *Divine Weeks*, discussing the confusion of languages after Babel, in which the beneficial effects of trade have been set out:

Each language alters, either by occasion
Of trade, which (causing mutuall commutation
Of th' Earths and Oceans wares) with hardy luck
Doth words for words barter, exchange and truck.[42]

Here, too, the poem prioritises the idea of the mutuality of the world's "wares," but extends the material trade of those wares into the abstract realm of languages. Consequently, linguistic importation or substitution is also part of the divine order, leading mankind back towards perfect understanding.

In this context, then, Sylvester's addition of an extended description of London as a prominent centre of trade takes on an additional religious-historic significance. Sylvester lays out the geographical and mercantile diversity of the trading community of London in order to place the city within the grander scheme of divinely ordained exchange and community:

> *For, as in LONDON (stuft with every sort)*
> *Heer's the Kings Palace, there the Innes of Court:*
> *Heer (to the Thames-ward, all a-long the STRAND)*
> *The stately Houses of the Nobles stand:*
> *Heer dwell rich Merchants; there Artificers;*
> *Heer Silk-men, Mercers, Gold-Smiths, Jewellers:*
> *There's a Church-yard furnisht with choice of Books;*
> *Heer stand the Shambles, there the Rowe of Cookes:*
> *Heer wonne Up-Holsters, Haberdashers, Horners;*
> *There Pothecaries, Grocers, Taylours, Tourners:*
> *Heer Shoo-makers; there Ioyners, Coopers, Curriers;*
> *Here Browers, Bakers, Cutlers, Felters, Furriers:*
> *This Street is full of DRAPERS, that of Diars:*
> *This Shop with Tapers, that with Womens Tyars:*
> *For costly Toyes, Silk Stockings, Cambrick, Lawne,*
> *Heer's choice-full Plenty in the curious PAWN:*
> *And All's but an Exchange, where (brieflie) no-man*
> *Keeps ought, as private. Trade makes all things common.*[43]

Here the links to livery companies are made explicit, and once more Sylvester associates the wealth of London with the material commodities interchanged between "rich merchants." The Exchange features once more, but now as a microcosm of the city as a whole, so that Sylvester's London is entirely preoccupied with the trade in goods and luxuries which prompts the circulation of "all things," and increases the general wealth. The dazzling choice of consumer goods and plenty that Sylvester catalogues is filtered through the activities of the livery companies, by shifting the focus from the goods themselves to the shops that supply them. In doing so, Sylvester creates a corporate identity for London that goes beyond the Corporation of the City: in Sylvester's London, physical space itself is 'incorproated', both as direct places of business but also with the imposition of corporate activity into non-traditional spaces such as fine houses and churchyards.

Sylvester had, in fact, presented this section of the poem (entitled 'The Colonies') to James I in manuscript in 1603, with only minor differences in spelling between that presentation copy and the passage on London quoted previously. In his dedicatory epistle, Sylvester apologises for only being able to present a part of the poem, because of "the grievous visitacion of God's heavie hand upon your Highness' poor cittie of London."[44] By being away from the city, Sylvester notes he has been denied vital assistance in his work: "But wanting both leasure in myself; & (here in the country) such helps, as I could have wished, to copie the entire worke." It is unclear whether Sylvester means that he was unable to secure a full copy to translate from, or whether he needed help from others in London. We may, I think, assume the latter: one obvious advantage of London over the countryside would be access to French speakers, perhaps even at the Royal Exchange he praises within the poem, well known as a place "Of Nations, and of languages."[45]

Unlike others who translated parts of epic, Sylvester does not offer any specific reasons why this section of the *Divine Weeks* is particularly apposite. He does suggest that this section is somehow microcosmic of the poem as a whole, telling James that "by a part, I might (as it wear) give Your Highness possession of the whole."[46] The poetic encomium to James included in the manuscript stresses neither colonial ambition nor population increase, but rather the need for a spiritual monarchy: "Make Christ thy guide (in whom was never guile)/To rule thy subjects in his gospels union."[47] Yet if the ambition of the translation was James's spiritual well-being, then a section from the first week, with its interpellation of broad theological questions into the Genesis story, would make more sense. The choice of the 'Colonies' from the second week suggests, rather, a focus on sound religious government; many passages engage with questions of good government, as well as the need for colonisation if the full spiritual destiny of an Elect Nation (England rather than France, of course, as the interpolations changing Paris for London make clear) is to be fulfilled.

Other epics, too, had moments at which they considered trading or other overseas activity. William Davenant's *Gondibert* (1651–52), despite the ostensible subject matter of a Lombard Duke, has lengthy digressions on government and trade. Most striking of these is the lengthy discursion on the lodestone, a quasi-mystical stone with inherent magnetism, which in his tale can serve as a compass. The stone allows travel to the Americas, figured as a mystical land:

> Heav'ns reserv'd world they in the West shall see;
> To which this stone's hid virtue will direct.
> Religion then (whose Age this world upbraids,
> As scorn'd deformitie) will thither steer;
> Serv'd at fit distance by the Arts, her Maids,
> Which grow too bold, when they attend too neer.

> And some, whom Traffick thither tempts, shall thence
> In her exchange (though they did grudge her shrines,
> And poorly banish'd her to save expence)
> Bring home the Idol, Gold, from new-found Mines.
> (II.6.32–4)

Despite persistent rumours and optimism, English explorers never found any gold mines – the bullion brought from the Americas was obtained by trade or piracy (itself often a joint-stock enterprise) with the Spanish. The dreamlike reference to gold mines recalls Davenant's earlier poem of proto-imperialist ambition, 'Madagascar', in which the vision of the island is sublimated into an ambition for its metallic resources: "I wish'd my Soule had brought my body here, / Not as a Poet, but a Pioner."[48] In both texts the desire for gold, or commerce, is intertwined with other nationalist-corporate impulses, whether exploration and colony, or the spread of religion.

In *Paradise Lost*, conversely, trade is antithetical to the main plot. The role of trader is taken by the anti-hero, Satan. His mission to seduce Adam and Eve is framed by metaphors that, through their relationship to the seventeenth-century context of the spice trade, highlight the ambiguity and uncertainty of Satan's intentions. J Martin Evans has demonstrated that Satan

> Rehearses virtually all the major roles in the repertoire of English colonial discourse. By turns buccaneer, pilgrim, empire-builder, lover, missionary, and merchant, he embodies not only the destructive potential of imperial conquest but something of its glamor and energy as well.[49]

Evans, however, is primarily concerned with the "colonial discourse" concentrated on the Americas, and so it is the roles of "empire-builder, lover [and] missionary" that he explores. His reading of Satan as a "merchant" is (perhaps necessarily) brief, and suggests an equivalence between Satan's description of his "purchase" of Eden with an apple (X.466–504), and the "settlers who bought Manhattan Island" for a few beads.[50] However, as I have shown elsewhere, Milton's use of Satan as a trader allows for a meditation on the role of trade, and the corporation, in good governance and questions of morality in both Heaven and Earth.[51] In his use of economic positioning and metaphor, Satan reveals his own ignorance both of proper theological gratitude, and what it means to serve as part of a collective.

The ship of state

Davenant's *Gondibert*, as we have seen, occasionally exhibits some of this corporate-economic thinking, particularly in the way in which corporate activity, particularly overseas trade, is combined with the kind of questions of morality and religion which were explored in the previous chapter. The Noah myth, for example, is recounted in terms reminiscent of economic activity rather than biblical exegesis:

> The Worlds one Ship, from the old to a new World bound,
> Fraighted with Life (chief of uncertain Trades!)
>
> [II.vi.67]

Here, the story of Noah is transmuted into terms of exploration and commerce. By including the direction of travel from old to new World, Noah's journey becomes part of a typological schema which includes the voyages of Columbus, Magellan and perhaps even da Gama. "Freighting" and "trades" both point to an expansion of economic activity as a consequence of the voyage; the term "fraighted with life" points more to the Colombian exchange than the luxury goods promoted by corporate trade, although given the trade in animals and, sadly, people, undertaken by the corporations, this is not a clear distinction. Equally, the description of "life" as the chief of the "uncertain trades" allows a play between the two meanings of "trade" as "skill" and "exchanges." It thus places physical and spiritual development within the realms of corporations in their role as managers of trades, either as guilds or the organising agents for long-distance oceanic trade. This second reading invites greater focus on economic activity in the sense that "trade" means "exchanges" or commerce.

The connection between ships and morality is strengthened later in the poem. In a digression on Verona, the narrator imagines merchants using churches to think about their ships at sea:

> Th' advent'rous Merchant, whom a Storm did wake,
> (His Ships on *Adriatick* Billows tost)
> Does hope of Eastern winds from Steeples take,
> And hastens there a Currier to the Coast.
>
> [II.i.17]

Later in the poem the narrator links churches and ships once more, this time from a mountaintop perspective:

> Whose heighth Two rising Forrests over-looks;
> And on *Pine*-tops the Eye-sight downward cast;
> Where distant Rivers seem bestrided Brooks,
> Churches but Anchor'd Ships, their Steeples, Masts.
>
> [III.2.13]

The ship/church simile operates on a slightly different level from the river/brook. The comparison is one of scale, whereas the transformation of a church to a ship is one of kind. Although there is a visual resemblance between the spire and the mast, the comparison is particularly apt because of the communities which inhabit each space. As the next chapter demonstrates in more detail, congregations were increasingly thought of as small corporations or commonwealths and, as Robert Boyle pointed out, "Statesmen and Philosophers are wont to compare a Commonwealth to a Ship."[52] Lancelot Andrewes began one of his regular sermons preached before James I, on Jonah and the whale, by noting "It is no new thing to resemble the *Church*, the *Common-wealth*, yea the *World*, to a *Ship*," and continued to gloss the story of the storm which tossed Jonah overboard as a type of God's wrath against mankind for their sins by an analogy to "a Great *Arke*, or *Argosy*, wherein were imbarqued all Mankind."[53] Both of these authors (and many others who use the ship/commonwealth comparison) compare the ruler of a state to the pilot of the ship, with the sailors as the populace more generally. This was, of course, original to Plato, although neither text makes the allusion explicit.

Consequently, the image was particularly used at moments of perceived crisis. Samuel Fawcet, for example, in a sermon preached before the haberdashers in 1641, drew the parallel between Jonah in the storm and the ship of state:

> But how many among us even in these stormie and tumultuous times, when the whole ship of Church and State, is in danger to be drowned, how many of us like *Jonah*, are asleepe still? and minde nothing, lay nothing to heart, put to no hand to helpe the common cause? Alas, (ye will say) we stand low, what can we doe? I tell you, every one of you, may and ought to doe something for the common cause, as the Master of the ship said to *Jonah*, what meanest thou, O sleeper? arise, call upon thy God that we perish not.[54]

Fawcet, like the many writers who turned to the story of Jonah in the 1640s, calls for an increased sense of commonality by focusing on the calls from the sailors for Jonah to join them in prayer for the salvation of the ship. The maritime commonwealth is subsequently used as a model for the commonwealth of England "by what meanes soever, nationall stormes doe rise in a Kingdom, we should looke above instrumentall causes, and say with the Mariners in *Jonah, Thou Lord hast done as it pleased thee.*"[55] The Jonah story is perhaps particularly apposite; he does, however unwillingly, ultimately act for the good of the commonwealth on board through his act of self-sacrifice in leaving it according to divine mandate, after the casting of lots: "He said unto them, Take me up, and cast me forth into the sea; so shall the sea be calm unto you: for I know that for my sake this great tempest is upon you."[56] The Jonah story also allows Fawcet to reconfigure Plato's hierarchical image into one of equality, most obviously in the repeated use of the phrase "common cause." But Fawcet's text also stresses personal reason and choice over following instructions: there is no one giving orders in the "stormie and tumultuous times," but rather a need for the soldiers to act as a collective without instruction.

The image of the ship adrift in a great tempest returned at the restoration; one anonymous author, bemoaning the failings and corruptions of Parliament, called for the public to "take hold of those means, which may save the Ship of this Commonwealth before it utterly sinks."[57] Conversely, Milton (alert as usual to the prevailing images of political discourse) employed the metaphor in a plea for the republicans to keep to their course: "But let our governors beware in time· least thir hard measure to libertie of conscience be found the rock wheron they ship wrack themselves as others have now don before them in the cours wherin God was directing thir stearage to a free Commonwealth."[58]

For early modern trading companies, of course, the imagery of a ship was particularly apposite. Already small commonwealths in their corporate communities, they relied on ships, and careful management of shipping, to function. With the use of the ship came benefits such as advances in scientific, cultural and geographical knowledge, which companies "bound together through intricate physical and conceptual transformation."[59] Ships also meant the creation of mixed communities which nonetheless had to function as effective commonwealths. These were most often hybrid cultures of English and non-English (European and extra-European) sailors and traders, or by functioning effectively across rank, as Mark Knights (and the Early Modern Research Group) points out in the opening lines of *The Tempest*, where "Aristocratic birthright" must give way to "professional expertise" in the face of the storm.[60]

As this example suggests, naval communities, and the hierarchies and specialisms within those communities, were already distinct from those on land by the time global trading companies began their operations. Over the course of the early modern period, navigational vernacular "thickened to produce a private language . . . a system of shared meanings from which landsmen were excluded, creating solidarity within the sub-culture." In effect, sailors were forming their own commonwealths, in language, hierarchy and community distinct from those they at least nominally belonged to on land.

The church/ship comparison is apposite not just in terms of the nature of those two groups whose rituals, language, dress and behaviour helped them form sub-commonwealths. Moreover, as Withington has shown, the connections between London and the incorporated port towns encouraged the increasing commercialisation and incorporation of the British economy and state during the seventeenth century.[61] The navy itself was "a floating community that could be as large as many a town or county community."[62] At the same time, there was a "clear trend" away from "reliance on private shipping" over the seventeenth century, begun during the Interregnum, and intensified after the Restoration.[63] Corporate charters often stressed that part of the rationale for the Company was that they were "very beneficial both for the increase of our navy and mariners," and, as we have seen, an increase in shipping was generally accepted as a benefit of the corporations by their supporters and detractors alike.[64]

Clergymen preached to the sailors by drawing on maritime themes from the gospels (most obviously Jonah) to appeal to the experience of the sailors. Other preachers sought to adopt maritime language, as in the case of John Flavel (or Flavell), a Presbyterian minister primarily concerned with the spiritual well-being of the maritime community in Dartmouth (and beyond). His *Navigation Spiritualiz'd* followed the lead of other preachers who put the spiritual in terms of their audience's skills and experience, in this case borrowing the image of a compass to create a series of catechisms based on directional points, so East-South-East became "Ever Strive Earnestly to live under, and to improve the means of Grace."[65] Throughout the text, though, Flavel compares spiritual and economic activity, naturally turning to those voyages undertaken by monopoly trading companies, especially to the East Indies:

> Shouldst thou by skill in Natural Navigation carry safe all the treasures of the *Indies* into thine own Port, yea, gain the whole world, and for want of skill in spiritual Navigation lose thy soul, thou wouldst be the greatest loser in the world. So far wilt thou be from profiting by any of thy Sea-voyages.[66]

Travel to the Indies is a recurring theme of the introductory notes to the volume, as the pinnacle of "humane wisdom"[67] which is positioned against the spiritual wisdom which sea voyages ought to inculcate by virtue of their proximity to God's works and the high risk of death.

The book continues with a series of chapters, each addressing different aspects of mercantile life, made up of an observation, an application of scripture, a reflection (usually a prayer or self-reflection for the reader to make) and finally, a short poem. A number of the chapters deal explicitly with trade, and in particular trade which, although not explicitly discussed as such, is corporate, including a quotation from Du Bartas on the range of goods available from around the globe (mostly covered by corporate monopolies, such as currants, spices, furs and cordage) and a comparison of equinoctial trade winds, "blowing for the most part one way" with those saints who are "never out of a Trade-winds way to Heaven"; that is, their whole lives are bent in one spiritual direction.[68] He is in particular concerned with an apparent decline in trade, despite favourable conditions:

> There are many sad Complaints abroad (and I think not without cause) that Trade fails, nothing turns to account. And though all

> Countries be open, and free for Traffick, a general Peace with all Nations, yet there seems to be a Dearth, a secret Curse upon Trading. You run from Country to Country, and come losers home.[69]

The cause of these losses, unsurprisingly, is a lack of faith – not only do individuals set out for voyages without sufficient prayer and spiritual thought, but those running companies are too distracted by business to be concerned with prayer:

> Men make this their business, they will be rich: And hence it is, they are not onely unmerciful to themselves, in wearing and wasting their own spirits with carking cares, but to such also as they employ; neither regarding the Souls or Bodies of Men: Scarce affording them the liberty of the Lord's Day (as hath been too common in our *New-found-Land* Employments;) or if they have it, yet they are so worn out with incessant Labours, that that precious time is spent either in sleep or idleness.[70]

Flavel returns to the theme of corporate policing of behaviour in his dedicatory epistle attached to the 'Disswasive" against sins of drunkenness which is appended to the *Navigation Spiritualiz'd*. The epistle was written to Sir John Frederick, an MP in the Convention and Cavalier Parliaments, director of the East India Company and master of the Grocer's Company. Flavel once more takes the opportunity to correlate the conduct of the community on board ship and the success of the merchant (or merchant-company) which supports the ship:

> Those sins of theirs, against which I have here engaged, are the *Jonahs* in your Ships: 'tis sin that sinks them, and drives them against the Rocks. *One sinner destroys much good*, Eccles. 8. 11. How much more a lewd Crew of them conspiring to provoke God! The *death* of their Lusts, is the most probable means to give *life* to your Trade. And as these Counsels prosper in their hearts, so will your Business thrive in you[r] hands.[71]

Flavel even goes on to imagine himself as a shareholder in the voyage:

> Well then, I will make bould to send this small *Adventure* in your Ships; and if the Return of it be but the Conversion of one Soul to God, I shall reckon that I have made a better Voyage than you, let your Returns be never so rich.[72]

The link between religious rhetoric, adventuring and corporations has been teased out by Andrew Fitzmaurice for John Donne and the Virginia Company, and although not as humanist in its character, Flavel's connection of spiritual and commercial success would have been familiar for those aware of Donne's sermons to the other company.[73] Flavel's insertion of himself as a spiritual adventurer, with the presumed return not just of souls for God, but a general increase in trade with the "secret curse" of sin lifted, shows us something of the ways in which aspects of corporate life – trade, governance and religion – overlapped and integrated with one another. The Corporation provided a model not just for organising long voyages, but also for a version of the ship of state, a vehicle for national identity and a path to salvation. It is this matter of faith expressed in and through the corporation that I consider in the next chapter.

Notes

1 Edward Waterhouse, *A Declaration of the State of the Colony and Affaires in Virginia with a Relation of the Barbarous Massacre in the Time of Peace and League, Treacherously Executed by the Natiue Infidels Vpon the English* (London: G. Eld for Robert Mylbourne, 1622), 34.
2 Andrew Fitzmaurice, "'Every Man, That Prints, Adventures': The Rhetoric of the Virginia Company Sermons," in *The English Sermon Revised: Religion, Literature and History 1600–1750*, ed. Lori Anne Ferrell and Peter McCullough (Manchester: Manchester University Press, 2000).
3 Anthony K. Cassell, *The Monarchia Controversy: An Historical Study with Accompanying Translations of Dante Alighieri's Monarchia, Guido Vernani's Refutation of the Monarchia Composed by Dante and Pope John Xxii's Bull, Si Fratrum* (Washington, DC: The Catholic University of America Press, 2004), 119.
4 Don M. Wolfe, ed. *Complete Prose Works of John Milton* (New Haven, CT: Yale University Press, 1953–82), I:811; Wesley F. Craven, *Dissolution of the Virginia Company: The Failure of a Colonial Experiment* (Oxford: Oxford University Press, 1932); Torquato Tasso, *Discourses on the Heroic Poem*, ed. Mariella Cavalchini and Irene Samuel (Oxford: Clarendon Press, 1973), 14.
5 Louise S. Cowan, "Introduction: Epic as Cosmopoesis," in *The Epic Cosmos*, ed. Larry Allums (Dallas: The Dallas Institute Publications, 1992), 4.
6 Isabel Gamble MacCaffrey, *Paradise Lost as "Myth"* (Cambridge: Harvard University Press, 1967), 16.
7 M. J. Braddick, *God's Fury, England's Fire: A New History of the English Civil Wars* (London: Penguin Books, 2008), 588.
8 See Warren M. Billings, *A Little Parliament: The Virginia General Assembly in the Seventeenth Century* (Richmond, VA: Library of Virginia, 2004), 210–11; Philip J. Stern, "Politics and Ideology in the Early East India Company-State: The Case of St Helena, 1673–1709," *The Journal of Imperial and Commonwealth History* 35, no. 1 (2007); John M. Collins, *Martial Law and English Laws, C.1500–C.1700* (Cambridge: Cambridge University Press, 2016), 225–7.
9 Sharon Achinstein, *Milton and the Revolutionary Reader* (Princeton, NJ: Princeton University Press, 1994), 217.
10 Stephen Greenblatt, *Renaissance Self-Fashioning* (Chicago: University of Chicago Press, 1980), 180.
11 Bartolomé de las Casas, *The Spanish Colony* (London: Thomas Dawson for William Brome, 1583), 10–11.

12 Stephen Greenblatt, "Invisible Bullets," in *Shakespearean Negotiations: The Circulation of Social Energy in Renaissance England* (Oxford: Clarendon Press, 1988), 30.
13 Karen Ordahl Kupperman, *Indians and English: Facing Off in Early America* (Ithaca, NY: Cornell University Press, 2000), 141.
14 Peter Martyr, *The Decades of the New World* (1511), op. cit. Greenblatt, *Renaissance Self-Fashioning*, 181.
15 Bernal Díaz del Castillo, *Historia Verdadera De La Conquista De La Nueva España* (Madrid: Emprenta del Reyno, 1632), A chap. 87. My translation.
16 David A. Boruchoff, "Beyond Utopia and Paradise: Cortes, Bernal Diaz and the Rhetoric of Consecration," *MLN* 106, no. 2 (1991): 331.
17 On the links between FQ II.Proem and contemporary accounts of New World discovery, see Shannon Miller, *Invested with Meaning: The Raleigh Circle in the New World* (Philadelphia: University of Pennsylvania Press, 1998), 36–7.
18 Michael Murrin, *The Allegorical Epic: Essays in Its Rise and Decline* (Chicago: University of Chicago Press, 1980), 134.
19 Rev. 21:18–19; the description continues to comprise 12 foundations, each keyed to a precious stone.
20 Richard Hakluyt, *The Principal Navigations, Voyages, Traffiques and Discoveries of the English Nation Made by Sea or over-Land, to the Remote and Farthest Distant Quarters of the Earth, at Any Time within the Compasse of These 1600 Yeres* (London: George Bishop, Ralph Newberie, and Robert Barker, 1599–1600), I.268.
21 *Principal Navigations*, II.ii.5.
22 Charles II, *Whereas It Is Found by Experience, That Traffique with Infidels and Barbarous Nations Not in Amity with Us . . . Cannot Be Carried on without the Establishment of Forts and Factories in Places Convenient* (London: John Bill and Christopher Barker, 1674), 1.
23 Anon, *Free Regulated Trade, Particularly to India the Interest of England* (London?: s.n., 1691), 2–3.
24 David Quint, *Epic and Empire : Politics and Generic Form from Virgil to Milton* (Princeton, NJ: Princeton University Press, 1992), 261.
25 Christopher Wase, "On the Restoration of Charles II," Bod. MS Eng. Poet e4.
26 The best account of the failure of the company remains Craven, *Dissolution of the Virginia Company: The Failure of a Colonial Experiment.*
27 Andrew Fitzmaurice, "American Corruption," in *The Monarchical Republic of Early Modern England : Essays in Response to Patrick Collinson*, ed. John F. McDiarmid (Aldershot: Ashgate, 2007), 228.
28 Court of Virginia, December 4th, 1622 in Susan M. Kingsbury, ed. *The Records of the the Virginia Company of London: The Court Book*, 4 vols. (Washington, DC: Government Printing Office, 1906), 170.
29 Alison Games, *The Web of Empire: English Cosmopolitans in an Age of Expansion 1560–1660* (Oxford: Oxford University Press, 2008), 124.
30 Edmond J. Smith, *Networks of the East India Company, C.1600–1625* (Cambridge, 2016), 197.
31 Court of Virginia February 4, 1623 in Kingsbury, *The Records of the the Virginia Company of London: The Court Book*, 235.
32 John Smith, *The Generall Historie of Virginia* (London: I.D. and I.H. for Michael Sparkes, 1624), 24.
33 Susan Castillo Street, "Forging a Transatlantic Persona: Panegyric Verse and John Smith's Generall Historie of Virginia, New-England and the Summer Isles," *The Yearbook of English Studies* 46(2016): 76.
34 Richard Fanshawe, *The Lusiad, or, Portugals Historicall Poem Written in the Portingall Language by Luis De Camoens; and Now Newly Put into English*

by Richard Fanshaw (London: Humphrey Moseley, 1655), VII.62. Further references are given in the text.
35 ODNB 'Joshuah Sylvester 1562/3–1618'.
36 Lambeth Palace Library MS 661, fol. 187: letter from Robert Devereux second earl of Essex to Company of Merchant Adventurers in Stade, 1597. My thanks to Thomas Leng for providing this reference.
37 ROLLCO 'Joshuah Sylvester'.
38 Susan Snyder, ed. *The Divine Weeks and Works of Guillaume De Saluste, Sieur Du Bartas*, Translated by Josuah Sylvester, 2 vols. (Oxford: Clarendon Press, 1979), I.iv.347–51.
39 *Divine Weeks and Works*,. i.1.338–64.
40 K. N. Chaudhuri, "The East India Company and the Organization of Its Shipping in the Early Seventeenth Century," *The Mariner's Mirror* 49, no. 1 (1963): 29.
41 Snyder, *Divine Weeks and Works*, II.ii.3.651–4.
42 *Divine Weeks and Works*, II.ii.2.471–4.
43 *Divine Weeks and Works*, II.ii.3.655–72.
44 BL Royal MSS 17.a.XLI, fol.5r.
45 T[homas] D['Urfey], Collin's Walk through London and Westminster, 1690, 63 [in Glaiyser, 47]
46 BL Royal MSS 17.a.XLI, fol.5r.
47 BL Royal MSS 17.a.XLI, fol.2v.
48 William Davenant, *Madagascar with Other Poems* (London: John Haviland for Thomas Walkly, 1638), 18. For an overview of Madagascar in the English corporate colonial imagination, see Edmond J. Smith, " 'Canaanising Madagascar': Africa in English Imperial Imagination, 1635–1650," *Itinerario* 39, no. 2 (2015).
49 J. Martin Evans, *Milton's Imperial Epic: Paradise Lost and the Discourse of Colonialism* (Ithaca, NY: Cornell University Press, 1996), 70–1.
50 Milton's *Imperial Epic: Paradise Lost and the Discourse of Colonialism*, 70.
51 Liam D. Haydon, "Paradise Lost and the Politics of the Corporation," *SEL Studies in English Literature 1500–1900* 57, no. 1 (2017): 135–55.
52 Robert Boyle, *Occasional Reflections Upon Several Subiects* (London: W. Wilson for Henry Herringman, 1665), 70.
53 Lancelot Andrewes, Xcvi. Sermons by the Right Honorable and Reverend Father in God, Lancelot Andrevves, *Late Lord Bishop of Winchester* (London: George Miller, for Richard Badger, 1629), 511.
54 Samuel Fawcet, *A Seasonable Sermon for These Troublesome Times* (London: R. Cotes, for John Sweeting, 1641), 10.
55 *A Seasonable Sermon for These Troublesome Times*, 15.
56 Jonah 1:12.
57 Anon, *Castigio Temporum, or, a Short View and Reprehension of the Errours and Enormities of the Times, Both in Church and State and What Is the Most Probable Means to Cure the Distempers in Either* (London: s.n., 1660), 14.
58 John Milton, *The Readie & Easie Way to Establish a Free Commonwealth* (London: s.n., 1660), 92–3.
59 Henry S. Turner, *The Corporate Commonwealth: Pluralism and Political Fictions in England 1516–1651* (Chicago: University of Chicago Press, 2016), 84.
60 Mark Knights and Early Modern Research Group, "Commonwealth: The Social, Cultural, and Conceptual Contexts of an Early Modern Keyword," *The Historical Journal* 54, no. 3 (2011): 674.
61 Phil Withington, *The Politics of Commonwealth: Citizens and Freemen in Early Modern England* (Cambridge: Cambridge University Press, 2005), 14.

62 J. D. Davies, *Gentlemen and Tarpaulins: The Officers and Men of the Restoration Navy* (Oxford: Clarendon Press, 1991), 15.
63 M. J. Braddick, *State Formation in Early Modern England, C. 1550–1700* (Cambridge: Cambridge University Press, 2000), 220.
64 Charter of the Fellowship of English Merchants for New Trades (19 Eliz. [1577]), in Cecil Thomas Carr, ed. *Select Charters of Trading Companies, 1530–1707* (London: Selden Society, 1913), 29.
65 John Flavel, *Navigation Spiritualiz'd [Etc]* (London: J.C. for Thomas Fabian, 1677), A7r.
66 *Navigation Spiritualiz'd [Etc]*, A8v.
67 *Navigation Spiritualiz'd [Etc]*, A6r.
68 Snyder, *Divine Weeks and Works*, II.ii.3.673–86; Flavel, *Navigation Spiritualiz'd [Etc]*, 96–7.
69 *Navigation Spiritualiz'd [Etc]*, 83.
70 *Navigation Spiritualiz'd [Etc]*, 85.
71 *Navigation Spiritualiz'd [Etc]*, K1v.
72 *Navigation Spiritualiz'd [Etc]*, K2r.
73 See Fitzmaurice, "'Every Man, That Prints, Adventures': The Rhetoric of the Virginia Company Sermons."

Works cited

Manuscript

BL Royal MSS 17.a.XLI
Bod. MS Eng. Poet e4
Lambeth Palace Library MS 661

Print

Achinstein, Sharon. *Milton and the Revolutionary Reader*. Princeton, NJ: Princeton University Press, 1994.

Andrewes, Lancelot. *Xcvi. Sermons by the Right Honorable and Reverend Father in God, Lancelot Andrevves, Late Lord Bishop of Winchester*. London: George Miller, for Richard Badger, 1629.

Anon. *Castigio Temporum, or, a Short View and Reprehension of the Errours and Enormities of the Times, Both in Church and State and What Is the Most Probable Means to Cure the Distempers in Either*. London: s.n., 1660.

———. *Free Regulated Trade, Particularly to India the Interest of England*. London?: s.n., 1691.

Billings, Warren M. *A Little Parliament: The Virginia General Assembly in the Seventeenth Century*. Richmond, VA: Library of Virginia, 2004.

Boruchoff, David A. "Beyond Utopia and Paradise: Cortes, Bernal Diaz and the Rhetoric of Consecration." *MLN* 106, no. 2 (1991): 330–69.

Boyle, Robert. *Occasional Reflections Upon Several Subiects*. London: W. Wilson for Henry Herringman, 1665.

Braddick, Michael J. *State Formation in Early Modern England, C. 1550–1700*. Cambridge: Cambridge University Press, 2000.

———. *God's Fury, England's Fire: A New History of the English Civil Wars*. London: Penguin Books, 2008.

Carr, Cecil Thomas, ed. *Select Charters of Trading Companies, 1530–1707*. London: Selden Society, 1913.

Casas, Bartolomé de las. *The Spanish Colony*. London: Thomas Dawson for William Brome, 1583.

Cassell, Anthony K. *The Monarchia Controversy: An Historical Study with Accompanying Translations of Dante Alighieri's Monarchia, Guido Vernani's Refutation of the Monarchia Composed by Dante and Pope John Xxii's Bull, Si Fratrum*. Washington, DC: The Catholic University of America Press, 2004.

Castillo, Bernal Díaz del. *Historia Verdadera De La Conquista De La Nueva España*. Madrid: Emprenta del Reyno, 1632.

Castillo Street, Susan. "Forging a Transatlantic Persona: Panegyric Verse and John Smith's *Generall Historie of Virginia, New-England and the Summer Isles*." *The Yearbook of English Studies* 46 (2016): 75–89.

Charles II. *Whereas It Is Found by Experience, That Traffique with Infidels and Barbarous Nations Not in Amity with Us . . . Cannot Be Carried on without the Establishment of Forts and Factories in Places Convenient*. London: John Bill and Christopher Barker, 1674.

Chaudhuri, K. N. "The East India Company and the Organization of Its Shipping in the Early Seventeenth Century." *The Mariner's Mirror* 49, no. 1 (1963): 27–41.

Collins, John M. *Martial Law and English Laws, C.1500–C.1700*. Cambridge: Cambridge University Press, 2016.

Cowan, Louise S. "Introduction: Epic as Cosmopoesis." In *The Epic Cosmos*, edited by Larry Allums, 3–26. Dallas: The Dallas Institute Publications, 1992.

Craven, Wesley F. *Dissolution of the Virginia Company: The Failure of a Colonial Experiment*. Oxford: Oxford University Press, 1932.

Davenant, William. *Madagascar with Other Poems*. London: John Haviland for Thomas Walkly, 1638.

Davies, J. D. *Gentlemen and Tarpaulins: The Officers and Men of the Restoration Navy*. Oxford: Clarendon Press, 1991.

Evans, J. Martin. *Milton's Imperial Epic: Paradise Lost and the Discourse of Colonialism*. Ithaca, NY: Cornell University Press, 1996.

Fanshawe, Richard. *The Lusiad, or, Portugals Historicall Poem Written in the Portingall Language by Luis De Camoens; and Now Newly Put into English by Richard Fanshaw*. London: Humphrey Moseley, 1655.

Fawcet, Samuel. *A Seasonable Sermon for These Troublesome Times*. London: R. Cotes, for John Sweeting, 1641.

Fitzmaurice, Andrew. " 'Every Man, That Prints, Adventures': The Rhetoric of the Virginia Company Sermons." In *The English Sermon Revised: Religion, Literature and History 1600–1750*, edited by Lori Anne Ferrell and Peter McCullough, 24–42. Manchester: Manchester University Press, 2000.

———. "American Corruption." In *The Monarchical Republic of Early Modern England: Essays in Response to Patrick Collinson*, edited by John F. McDiarmid. Aldershot: Ashgate, 2007.

Flavel, John. *Navigation Spiritualiz'd [Etc]*. London: J.C. for Thomas Fabian, 1677.

Games, Alison. *The Web of Empire: English Cosmopolitans in an Age of Expansion 1560–1660*. Oxford: Oxford University Press, 2008.

Greenblatt, Stephen. *Renaissance Self-Fashioning*. Chicago: University of Chicago Press, 1980.

———. "Invisible Bullets." In *Shakespearean Negotiations: The Circulation of Social Energy in Renaissance England*, 21–65. Oxford: Clarendon Press, 1988.

Hakluyt, Richard. *The Principal Navigations, Voyages, Traffiques and Discoveries of the English Nation Made by Sea or over-Land, to the Remote and*

Farthest Distant Quarters of the Earth, at Any Time within the Compasse of These 1600 Yeres. London: George Bishop, Ralph Newberie, and Robert Barker, 1599–1600.

Haydon, Liam D. "*Paradise Lost* and the Politics of the Corporation." *SEL Studies in English Literature 1500–1900* 57, no. 1 (2017): 135–55.

Kingsbury, Susan M., ed. *The Records of the the Virginia Company of London: The Court Book*. 4 vols. Washington, DC: Government Printing Office, 1906.

Knights, Mark, and Early Modern Research Group. "Commonwealth: The Social, Cultural, and Conceptual Contexts of an Early Modern Keyword." *The Historical Journal* 54, no. 3 (2011): 659–87.

Kupperman, Karen Ordahl. *Indians and English: Facing Off in Early America*. Ithaca, NY: Cornell University Press, 2000.

MacCaffrey, Isabel Gamble. *Paradise Lost as "Myth"*. Cambridge: Harvard University Press, 1967.

Miller, Shannon. *Invested with Meaning: The Raleigh Circle in the New World*. Philadelphia: University of Pennsylvania Press, 1998.

Milton, John. *The Readie & Easie Way to Establish a Free Commonwealth*. London: s.n., 1660.

Murrin, Michael. *The Allegorical Epic: Essays in Its Rise and Decline*. Chicago: University of Chicago Press, 1980.

Quint, David. *Epic and Empire : Politics and Generic Form from Virgil to Milton*. Princeton, NJ: Princeton University Press, 1992.

Smith, Edmond J. " 'Canaanising Madagascar': Africa in English Imperial Imagination, 1635–1650." *Itinerario* 39, no. 2 (2015): 277–98.

———. *Networks of the East India Company, C.1600–1625*. Cambridge, 2016.

Smith, John. *The Generall Historie of Virginia*. London: I.D. and I.H. for Michael Sparkes, 1624.

Snyder, Susan, ed. *The Divine Weeks and Works of Guillaume De Saluste, Sieur Du Bartas, Translated by Josuah Sylvester*. 2 vols. Oxford: Clarendon Press, 1979.

Stern, Philip J. "Politics and Ideology in the Early East India Company-State: The Case of St Helena, 1673–1709." *The Journal of Imperial and Commonwealth History* 35, no. 1 (2007): 1–23.

Tasso, Torquato. *Discourses on the Heroic Poem*. Edited by Mariella Cavalchini and Irene Samuel. Oxford: Clarendon Press, 1973.

Turner, Henry S. *The Corporate Commonwealth: Pluralism and Political Fictions in England 1516–1651*. Chicago: University of Chicago Press, 2016.

Waterhouse, Edward. *A Declaration of the State of the Colony and Affaires in Virginia with a Relation of the Barbarous Massacre in the Time of Peace and League, Treacherously Executed by the Natiue Infidels Vpon the English*. London: G. Eld for Robert Mylbourne, 1622.

Withington, Phil. *The Politics of Commonwealth: Citizens and Freemen in Early Modern England*. Cambridge: Cambridge University Press, 2005.

Wolfe, Don M., ed. *Complete Prose Works of John Milton*. New Haven, CT: Yale University Press, 1953–82.

5 The corporation of heaven

The previous chapters have demonstrated the ways in which the associational forms of the corporation were used to address contemporary political problems. These included practical issues, such as facilitating long-distance trade or the organisation of communities and local government; they also provided answers to more abstract questions of the common good, the nation state and a society newly aware of issues of trust and risk. In this chapter I want to combine these socio-political elements of the corporate form with the practice and practitioners of early modern religion. In particular, how did turmoil and the refashioning of the body politic engage with the interplay between associations, commonwealths and heaven which developed within religious writing? How and why, in other words, did the idea of the corporation as the visible and invisible church take on political and mercantile elements?

I begin by outlining the ways in which the idea of the corporation was used during the Civil Wars to reinforce both religious and political ideas of unity and collectivity. I then explore the ways in which the corporation, as a form of political organisation, was used as a counter to the idea of divinely ordained kingship, with preachers and writers coming instead to the image of a corporate heaven, composed of a collective of angels and saints. Finally, I look at how that rhetoric shifted once more at the end of the Civil Wars, when, with Restoration approaching, the idea of the corporate commonwealth, on earth and in heaven, became contested once more.

One of John's apocalyptic visions in the Book of Revelation concerns the destruction of the city of Babylon, and details the particular effect that this will have on the merchants of that city:

> And the merchants of the earth shall weep and mourn over her; for no man buyeth their merchandise any more [. . .] And the fruits that thy soul lusted after are departed from thee, and all things which were dainty and goodly are departed from thee, and thou shalt find them no more at all. The merchants of these things, which were made rich by her, shall stand afar off for the fear of her torment, weeping

> and wailing, and saying, Alas, alas that great city, that was clothed in fine linen, and purple, and scarlet, and decked with gold, and precious stones, and pearls! For in one hour so great riches is come to nought. And every shipmaster, and all the company in ships, and sailors, and as many as trade by sea, stood afar off.[1]

This narrative is the culmination of a trope running through scripture, of those too obsessed with worldly things – often epitomised by the merchant – to consider the state of their immortal soul. The trope is also observed in a more positive way, with instances such as Jesus's commands to give up worldly things (Luke 14:33) or the pearl of great price in Matthew 13:45–6 acting as a reassurance that worldly things need be no bar to salvation, so long as they are not the prime focus of the spiritually minded individual.

For the English translators of the Bible, it was no doubt especially fitting that the finery described was not just extravagant in itself, but particularly associated with Eastern luxury and indolence in the early modern imagination. That merchants might bring in these sorts of goods to corrupt honest men with "luxurious lust" was a common fear among early modern writers.[2] We saw in Chapter 2 the moral quandaries provoked by the corporation – whether it was trustworthy, how it might demonstrate that trustworthiness (or credit) and the role it had in regulating the creditworthiness of its members. In effect, these were questions of faith: Speculations over corporate behaviour essentially came down to competing visions of human actions, and thus belief systems for economic and moral performance.

In the book of Hosea, lamenting the degradation of the seed of Jacob, the prophet laments that Judah has lost its faith by using the trope of the cheating merchant: "He is a merchant, the balances of deceit are in his hand: he loveth to oppress."[3] Early modern writers, too, linked the issue of faith with proper behaviour in commercial matters:

> First, it is manifest that cōtractes are for the moste parte voluntarie, and that bargaines are made with the mutuall consent of the buyer and seller, so that each one maye take deliberation and make choice of that, which he woulde haue, to see whether it be best for his purpose or no. Of this sorte are the exchaunge of thinges, suretiship, letting, hiring, morgaging, borrowing, lending, couenanting, buying, selling, and other mo like vnto these. These things, as experience doth proue, euen the holiest men cannot be without, so long as they lyue in this fraile world. Neither doth the Lorde of the lawe in any place forbidde these kinde of contractes, but planteth them rather in his common weale of Israell, that the people might knowe & acknowledge them to be the ordinaunces of God: the abuse, deceipt, guyle, & confidence in them is flatly forbidden by the worde of the Lorde.[4]

The Lord does not forbid contracts; indeed, He encourages them, as a model of good behaviour, and his own contract, through His ordinances, with the people of Israel. In fact, it is only the bad contracts – those designed to abuse or deceive – which are forbidden, since good contracts are not just necessary for even the holiest of men, but also serve as an exemplar of honest behaviour. David Zaret has shown the ways in which contracts would later be used by Puritan preachers, drawing on the "broadest principles and most general practices" to enable their congregations to understand the mutual, informed consent that lay behind the covenant with God.[5]

As well as general references to merchants, there are occasions, too, in which merchant companies are described in scripture, particularly in the story of Joseph. After Joseph's brothers kidnap him and steal his coat, they throw him in a pit and are deciding what to do with him when

> A company of Ishmaelites came from Gilead with their camels bearing spicery and balm and myrrh, going to carry it down to Egypt.[6]

The brothers decide to hand over Joseph, but before they can, another group, this time "Midianites merchantmen," lift Joseph out of the pit and sell him on as a slave.[7] 'Company' recurs throughout the Bible as a term for an unnumbered multitude, rather than a financial organisation.[8] This group of Ishmaelites is probably not a 'company' in the sense of a chartered corporation, but it does perhaps draw on that meaning in this usage of 'a group of traders', and that sense would have been available to the translators of the Authorised Version to link earthly and spiritual traffic.

The image of the merchant too busy with trade to consider his soul was picked up by Milton in *Areopagitica*:

> A wealthy man addicted to his pleasure and to his profits, finds Religion to be a traffick so entangl'd, and of so many piddling accounts, that of all mysteries he cannot skill to keep a stock going upon that trade. What should he doe? fain he would have the name to be religious, fain he would bear up with his neighbours in that. What does he therefore, but resolvs to give over toyling, and to find himself out som factor, to whose care and credit he may commit the whole managing of his religious affairs; som Divine of note and estimation that must be. To him he adheres, resigns the whole ware-house of his religion, with all the locks and keyes into his custody; and indeed makes the very person of that man his religion; esteems his associating with him a sufficient evidence and commendatory of his own piety.[9]

Milton's parable may be of a 'wealthy man', but his language makes it clear that this is a trader, and quite probably a corporate trader, through words such as 'traffic', 'stock', 'factor' and 'warehouse'. Although

Milton's tract is designed to remind us to think for ourselves (rather than letting any priest or censor give us information accepted with criticism), his image of the merchant 'entangled' in his trade would have been a familiar one to early modern readers.

This link between trade, wealth and salvation was explicated at length by John Wing, a minister who preached before the Merchant Adventurers at Middelburg, in Zeeland; the printed version of the sermon is dedicated to the deputy of that company, Edward Bennet. In a lengthy exegesis of Psalms 3:14 ("For the merchandise therof, is better then the merchandise of silver, and the gayne therof, it better then fine golde."), Wing explained the way in which earthly trade was a poor shadow of the trade in truth, with just enough of a resemblance to instruct those traders in the higher pursuit of faith. To do so, he established a series of weak resemblances between earthly and heavenly traffic, dividing trade into its good (good sales, best barters, excellent exchange) and bad (misadventure, bad debts, dishonest servants) forms, and cataloguing the ways in which heavenly traffic had all the good and none of the bad:

> To be *free* of the heavenly corporation of these happy merchants, (whereof Christ is the only head, & governour) is to be *free indeede*: every thing is *reall*, the earth cannot yeelde *any one* commodity soe universally *currant*, and *staple*, as *every one* is, that we trade for here. [. . .] who would not be willing, and *free*, to buy and sell, where he knowe's he cannot be deceived, but shalbe sure of the best?[10]

Wing here paints a picture of a perfect marketplace, in which the spiritual trade is carried on in the real versions of symbolic parts of the Christian faith, such as bread and wine: because they are the perfect versions of these things, they are manifestly 'real' and 'staple', and so no deceit can be practiced, so long as the merchants recognise the truth of these objects. In fact, to those familiar with the idea of the universal balance of trade, ordained by God (as discussed in Chapter 3), the idea that heaven was also a perfect marketplace would have made sense through that very system of resemblances.

Wing was naturally concerned about the danger to merchants from concentrating too much on their trade, but unlike the image of merchants presented in Revelation, or *Areopagitica*, he argued that earthly and heavenly traffic could co-exist:

> When we shall not neede *wholy* to cast aside our civill callings, but *abate* something of our too *quick*, & *eager edge* after them, & take this imployment vp into the *best* and *soveraigne* place, setting all other in the *second* and *subordinate*, vnder it. We neede not *let fall* our civill merchandise, to fall *to this* spirituall, it is enough to

> keepe it downe that it be not *predominant* in vs aboue the coelestiall, or *equall* to it, in our *estimation, affections*, and *actions*, all earthly things must be *much inferiour* to heavenly, if they have their *owne places;* yet may they sit with these *best things*, though not neere the *best place*, the merchandise of *wisdome*, & *wealth*are not two contraryes *expelling* one another, they are not *incompatible* with one another, but may dwell together.[11]

Here again we see Wing's concept of weak resemblance, this time between wisdom and wealth – they can dwell together so long as the accumulation of wealth is not a means in itself, but a sort of mercantile typology, in which civil merchandising is used by the merchant to consider the trade in wisdom, truth or faith.

Wing may have exhorted the Merchant Adventurers to be part of the 'heavenly corporation', but the church was itself, of course, a corporation on Earth, or, more precisely, an aggregate of corporations. The medieval (Catholic) church, once it became nominally independent from the states in which it operated after the Concordat of Worms (1122), increasingly organised itself as a multinational corporation. Ekelund et al. have argued that the medieval church was an "m-form firm," a corporation composed of a centralised office for long-term planning (the papacy) and autonomous, regional divisions (monasteries, chapter houses, dioceses and so on) who "acted quite independently in representing the One True Church."[12]

In England, the corporate form of the church was developed in a slightly idiosyncratic way with the idea of the 'corporation sole': a corporation made up of a single person, an office holder of the church. This person – Maitland, who identified the development of the legal fiction, took the country parson, but the concept held for any church office up to the archbishop – took the place of the church corporations for the management of church possessions.[13] This was a corporation established by the concept of Dignity, which Kantorowicz defines as a "corporation by succession" – that is, composed solely of the office holder, whether bishop or king, and "encompassing the present bearer of the Crown the whole *genus*, the past and present bearers of Royal Dignity."[14] This had, in practice, the effect of removing *escheatment* rights (the reversion of property to the Crown on the death of an office holder), but it also meant that those who headed corporate groups, like abbots or Bishops, were members of a corporation (the church), leaders of a corporation (monastery, bishopric), and a corporation sole by Dignity. Like the incipient nation state, the early modern church was actually a series of overlapping corporate polities.

In England, the post-Reformation church clung to the model of the corporation, although with a natural move away from an emphasis on centralised corporate government, and a weakening of the power of the corporation sole. Instead, they turned to a different idea of the corporation to position themselves as self-governing groups of the faithful, as the 'visible church' of a particular parish or congregation. Thomas Jackson, for example, in a sermon printed in 1625 on John 5:39 ("search the scriptures"), reminded his auditors to gather together as a spiritual corporation even as he exhorted them to rely on their own interpretation of the bible:

> Euery visible Church is a Society or Corporation Ecclesiastique: And no assembly or multitude of men, how great soeuer, albeit they priuately professe the same faith, can truely be said to make one visible Society or Corporation Ecclesiastique, vnlesse they haue their publique meetings to heare the Word of GOD preached or read vnto them.[15]

Jackson actually develops a comparison between competing visions of the church and competing corporations in public life, asking what "if the question were, Which is the best or ancientest Corporation in this Kingdome?," and noting that such a question could only be answered first by comparing their charters and then asking which of them did "rightliest vse, practice, or enioy the benefits or priuiledges" of that charter. The order of precedence, of course, was the way in which the London livery companies organised themselves, so Jackson's question combines an ecclesiastical appeal to tradition with the corporate practices of early modern London.[16]

Just as the visible church was a corporation in both community and organisation, so too was the 'invisible church', the collective of the faithful (or elect), who may not have been in the same location, but were nonetheless a community in faith. This was an idea particularly prevalent in biblical exegesis, which borrowed the idea of the immortal corporation to explain a continuum of the faithful from generation to generation:

> I have before shewed, that the prophets speak to Israel, as a corporation or body, which after a sort continueth one and the same through many generations; when yet, as touching their particular persons or generations, they are different & contrary; as godly fathers in the state of grace and life, may beget wicked children without grace, and in state of death.[17]

As with the idea of the corporation, here we have a sense of one eternal collective, which is nonetheless composed of many different, changing parts. 'Israel' becomes something of an imaginary group or nation composed of the elect, which may be occasionally 'contrary' (as it often was in scripture), but is ultimately one long genus of faith in a manner similar to the corporation sole.

However, as Ainsworth's closing sentences demonstrates, such a description was not just reserved for the faithful:

> In which places in truth, this Antichrist is described, not as any one person or particular man, & (as the Logitians speake) an *Individuum:* but as a corporation of men, and as it were, a certaine kingdome: wherein yet, there is alwaie some one, who excelleth and ruleth ouer the rest, who *setteth his owne marke vpon them*, Reuel. 13. 17. For first Paul mencioneth *an Apostacie*, that is, a generall departure, & reuolting from the faith, which indeed maketh one bodie or corporation, and one kingdome: this is a matter which can not be effected suddenlie, but requireth many yeeres thereunto.[18]

Here is the opposite effect that the corporation can have, drawing together not the faithful, but those who 'revolt from the faith'. As Jackson suggested, it was not simply the coming together which made an association faithful, because it required the active participation and moral decisions of the members of that company. Antichrist is thus reconfigured to be both the individual who 'excelleth and ruleth' over the rest, and the corporation of apostates who have slowly turned away from the church, or even rotted from inside. One might see parallels here with Milton's Satan, who, as I discuss below, is both the chief rebel and one of a rebellious crew which travesties the form of the corporation of angels.

A free trade to heaven

By the middle of the seventeenth century the rhetoric on heavenly corporations shifted slightly, as it was becoming more common for preachers to use the rhetoric and organising principles of the corporation to help their parishioners imagine heaven. In 1648, Edward Barber, the General Baptist and advocate of universal religious freedom, debated Edmund Calamy. Although the crowd turned against him at the debate, he nonetheless published the speech he intended to give, in which he argued that any spiritual assembly 'where ever gathered together under Heaven, in the name of Christ, according to his order' took on something of the nature of a corporation, able to set its own laws and exclude any members they wished, since they were 'under Christ their King, the freest Independant Corporation or state under Heaven'.[19] For Barber, the aptness of the corporate image was in the idea of the self-governing unit. Barber was a Merchant Taylor before being called to preach, so the language of corporation was undoubtedly familiar to him. Nonetheless, the imagery takes on a particular force when transmuted into the heavenly or spiritual corporation: that trope combines the positive collectivism and self-determination of the corporation with the sense that this form of government has been divinely ordained, or is even necessary for salvation.

The Civil Wars, in particular, seem to have encouraged this link. As traditional forms of social organisation were challenged, and eventually overturned, new languages of political experimentation and change were developed. Commonwealth-men, Independents and radicals alike looked for new models of collective organisation, and found the corporate model an excellent channel by which to claim divine inspiration for their attempts to re-shape society:

> The Lambs twelve Apostles [. . .] teacheth and convinceth that all must be builded on their most holy doctrine, that will be within the corporation of the Holy City.[20]

By re-reading heaven as a corporate body, instead of a kingdom, these groups were able to turn a key piece of royalist propaganda to their own ends. It ought to be no surprise that corporate and spiritual language interacted in this way. Phil Withington has noted the crossover between urban corporate activity and the spiritual politics of the nation more generally:

> Across the corporate system there existed a degree of reciprocity between city commonwealth and the 'commonwealth of England' that was expressed in tangible material and political gains for citizens, and articulated through the language of spiritual and social reform.[21]

This same link was evident between the secular and spiritual corporation. The 'corporation of heaven', an ideal and idealised system of organization, was a natural bridge for the 'spiritual and social' reformist tendencies of radical preachers, particularly those who advocated independent congregations or the kinds of radical reforms proposed by groups such as the Levellers or Diggers.

The biblical rationale for the heavenly corporation came from Philippians 3.20, 'For our conversation is in heaven, from whence also we look for the Saviour'. Interpretations of the verse often stressed the communal nature of the 'conversation'. The Independent minister and religious reformist Jeremiah Burroughs printed a tract called *Gospel-Conversation*, using John 18:36 ("My kingdom is not of this world") to link together conversation, trade and heaven:

> And then from hence follows in the third place: *All that are in Christ's Kingdom, have the priviledg of a free-trade to Heaven, they have free traffick to Heaven:* there is now a blessed intercourse between Heaven and them, that they have by being subjects of this Kingdom: As we know the subjects of this Kingdom have many freedoms that forreigners have not, that those that belong to another Kingdom

> have nothing to do with. So the subjects of Christs Kingdom have a freedom of coming into Gods presence, of trading to the promised Land that others have not; others are cast out of Gods sight and cannot trade to Heaven so as beleevers do that are brought under the Kingdom of Christ.[22]

Here, the play on 'intercourse' as both conversation and trade opens up the biblical verse to contemporary ideas on international trade and the movement of people: entering the Kingdom of heaven is compared to the exercise of natural mercantile rights, enjoyed by Englishmen/the faithful but denied to strangers/unbelievers. Burroughs thus transmutes the biblical model of salvation as entry into a new space into a corporate ideal of a like-minded, even national, group trading together across nation states.

In a treatise published two years later, entitled 'On Conversing in Heaven', Burroughs returned to the theme and spent considerable time glossing the verse as an example of model behaviour:

> For our Conversation is in Heaven; so they are to be joyn'd together: from whence (first) before we come to speak of this Heavenly Conversation that the Apostle mentions, we have this point, That the Examples of men whose Conversations are heavenly, are to be followed.[23]

For Burroughs, the fact of conversation is an inclusive one, it is itself a sign of joining together under God; so, too, will following the example of those in the conversation lead to a spiritual fellowship.

Moreover, the meaning of 'conversation' to the early modern mind was broader than current usage. In 1611, Randle Cotgrave's *Dictionary of the English and French Tongues* gave 'commerce' and 'association' as definitions of 'conversation', and Wilkins' *Essay towards a Real Character* similarly listed 'deal' and 'live' as cognate terms for 'conversation'.[24] Perhaps inspired by these alternate meanings, preachers adapted the biblical verse to mean 'citizenship'. John Kettlewell, whose glosses on scripture were recommended enthusiastically by Thomas Bray, founder of the Society for the Propagation of the Gospel, provided perhaps the clearest interpretation of the verse late in the century:

> And of the Unity of this Church, or Collection of all Believers, do those Scriptures speak, which represent all that are in Heaven and all that are in Earth, as one whole Family. Eph. 3. 15. As one Household. 1 Tim. 3. 15. and Gal. 6. 10. or, as one City, Heb. 12. 22. Whence accordingly all, who are at any time in this world, are said to have their Citizenship or Corporation in Heaven, Phil. 3. 20. And all who are admitted into Christs Church here, to be Fellow-Citizens with the Saints, and Domesticks with Prophets, and Apostles, and with all others, who are gone to God before. Eph. 2. 19. What is the

> one Body, saith St Chrysostom on the words of St. Paul, there is one Body? 'Tis all believers, of every place, saith he, both those who now are, and who formerly have been, and who hereafter shall be.[25]

Kettlewell's analysis of scripture deliberately collapses a whole set of social groupings: citizenship, aligned with corporation (presumably the urban corporation), is mentioned twice, alongside family and household ('domestick'). In doing so, Kettlewell suggests an equivalence between these ways of forming, and belonging to, social groups, in order to emphasise the idea of unity.

It was no great leap to discuss the values of such communality and citizenship in the language of the corporation. As early as 1614, separatist preachers were making the connection between the 'spiritual body politicke'[26] of the true church (of whatever theological inclination) which was self-selected by its members and the corporation: "By Gods ordinance, this one ordinary congregation of Christians is a spirituall bodie politike; and so it is a free congregation independent."[27] Such imagery, though, took on renewed force with the outbreak of civil war. Daniel Featley was a preacher and the chaplain to archbishop George Abbott (who was himself involved with the East India Company, including the potential suppression of Kayll's *Trade's Increase* as discussed in Chapter 1). Featley made the connection between heavenly and social organisation while stressing the corporate nature of the city:

> As in Cities and societies on earth, men have communion and society one with another, the less have interest in the greater, and the greater in the less, and all have interest one in another: the inferiours receive from the superiours, protection and provision, and the superiours, receive from the inferiours, subjection and submission. So it is in this heavenly Corporation, in this spiritual Jerusalem: *Jerusalem is a City at unitie in it self;*[28]

The language of a 'heavenly Corporation' is telling – Featley clearly means by it a hierarchical system, as he qualifies the 'subjection and submission' of inferiors as a return for 'protection and provision'. However, this is a mutually beneficial system, with both greater and lesser sharing 'interest' in the system.

Other preachers were explicit in the linking of a corporate structure on earth with the collective of heaven. John Priaulx, in a text arguing for the ceremony of Confirmation, argued that the practice

> Would set a Crown upon the Churches head; it would be lookt upon, as an Assembly of the first-born, whose Names are enrolled

> in heaven, as a Corporation of Saints, and Men would flow in to the glory of it.[29]

Priaulx plays on the duality inherent in the word 'corporation', allowing both the meanings 'one body' and 'a collective' to circulate in his text at once. The use of the word 'assembly' reinforces the idea of a collection of the virtuous, while the idea of 'flowing in' suggests that the assembly is not just a gathering of individual souls but a co-mingling.

Such imagery was not unusual. The godly were frequently reminded that 'after *Christ* [the Church] was Corporationall, of a Company of Christians, Covenanted to be a Church Body'.[30] A clear parallel is drawn by this author (L.F.) between the biblical practice of creating churches and the contemporary need for the Elect to gather together. In fact, L.F. goes further, suggesting that the corporation of the elect on Earth completes the corporational desires of Heaven:

> They are Compleat, or Celestiall, *viz.* the Gospel and its Institutions, are called the *Kingdome* of *heaven* oft, which are Corporationall: 1. An incorporate Church, with its Ministry, and Members, and their Functions: and all their Sabbath-meetings, exerciseings and observations.[31]

The parallel is designed to be instructive; the church-as-corporation draws together members on Earth into one complete corporation with God, so that each action on Earth was a part of the divine whole.

Yet the corporation went beyond the drawing together of the Elect. John Maynard, the representative of Sussex at the Westminster assembly of divines, gave a sermon before Parliament in 1644. Just as John Wing had, he reflected upon Psalm 23 ('Buy the truth and sell it not'); in doing so, he developed the mercantile imagery of 'buying' to a lengthy discussion on the relative value of goods and truth. Goods, he claimed, were interchangeable, whereas truth was a singular commodity:

> In trading for things of the world there is a latitude, Merchants have their liberty: they are not limited to one Port, nor restrained to one Mart, or to deal in one commodity: so they make a good return, it mattereth not much what kinde of wares they bring home. But they who approve themselves free of [. . .] that glorious Corporation in heaven, & trade to purpose for the things above, and not prove bankrupts in the great day of account, a necessity lieth upon them, and woe unto them if they buy not *Truth*. Let their Ships seeme never so well fraighted, their Shops and Ware-house never so richly furnished, yet if they want this pearl of great price, they are broken and undone for ever.[32]

Maynard gives one of the few examples where, unlike the play in texts such as Priaulx and L.F., the reference to the corporation is unequivocally a contemporary trading company. The sermon goes on to point out truth is not traded as such, but rather:

> This buying is not of the nature of common contracts, in which there is a just proportion between the price and the purchase, but rather such as hath some remote Analogy or resemblance to it: such as that, where the Lord by solemn Proclamation offereth a free and open market.[33]

The analogy is taken from Isaiah, 'Ye that have no silver, come, buy and eat'.[34] By suggesting that the equivalence between trade and fulfilment is 'analagous', Maynard presents the tantalising possibility of truth-by-exchange; that is, the ways in which corporate activity – presumably overseas – might generate truth. As Blair Hoxby has observed, for early modern writers, economic language offered a way of "thinking systematically about the conditions of intellectual exchange that were likeliest to generate truth without bound."[35] It is not surprising, then, that the same comparison between truth and trade is made in John Milton's *Areopagitica*, a call for liberty in speech and printing:

> Truth and understanding are not such wares as to be monopolized and traded in by tickets and statutes [. . .] like our broad cloth and our wool packs.[36]

As we saw previously, *Areopagitica* is generally sceptical of the corrupting influence of trade on the individual soul and intellect, and this image of customs and monopoly serves the same purpose as the wealthy man 'addicted to his pleasure and to his profits' who gives over his care in religion to 'som factor'. In both cases, trade leads to a closing down of opinions and beliefs, meaning that individuals cease to take responsibility for their own salvation. However, Milton, like Maynard, does seem at least to acknowledge the possibility that trade can be advantageous. In *Areopagitica* it is the restraint of trade (the monopolisers) that causes a spiritual defect. Likewise, in *The Reason of Church-Government* Milton accepts at least the potential that, by the practice of international trading, merchants can also partake in 'heavenly traffic', becoming 'dispensers of treasure inestimable, without price'.[37]

Other patterns of behaviour were advocated as beneficial imitations of divine action. The liberty-through-service of both corporate citizens and the inhabitants of the City of God was a recurring theme of early modern sermons. Preachers reminded their listeners and readers that to be part of a spiritual collective required service, and drew out the nuances involved in terms such as 'freedom' and 'freemen':

> To do what we would is not Freedom, but servitude; to do what God would, is the Freedom that belongs to the Citizens of the Heavenly corporation, the City of God, the Church of God; [38]

Two years later, James Duport, a poet, translator, Cambridge Professor of Greek and an ejected prebend, was invited to preach at St Paul's to mark the Restoration. He too took the opportunity of the sermon to draw comparisons between the rights and duties of citizens on earth and in heaven:

> Ye are (as S. *Paul* said of himself) *citizens of no mean citie* [. . .] remember withall that ye are citizens too of a far nobler and better citie, *viz*. the Church of God, the heavenly Jerusalem, the citie which is from above. Members ye are and freemen, at least ye profess your selves to be free of this corporation, of this company [. . .] for the Gospel of Christ that is your *grand Charter*, by which you hold all your spiritual priviledges, rights, and immunities.[39]

Duport's understanding of the heavenly city comes through contemporary terminology of corporate governance; the faithful take their place as freemen, with rights guaranteed and enumerated by a charter, so long as they obey the terms of that charter (as the ominous 'at least ye profess your selves to be free' subtly reminds us). Terms such as 'members' and 'freemen' emphasise the equality inherent in the image, which suggests a collective citizenship sharing the same privileges.

Duport was not the first preacher at St Paul's to suggest equivalence between corporate and spiritual activity. While dean of St Paul's John Donne gave a sermon delivered to members of the Virginia Company. In it, he warned the company against acquisitiveness: 'Let not the riches and commodities of this world, be in your contemplation in your adventures.'[40] Instead, he exhorted them to be an open and inclusive society whose actions imitated biblical examples:

> Preach in your just actions, as to the *Citie*, to the *Countrey* too. Not to seale up the secrets, and the mysteries of your businesse within the bosome of *Merchants*, and exclude all others: to nourish an incompatibilitie betweene *Merchants* & *Gentlemen;* that *Merchants* shall say to them in reproach, You have playd the *Gentlemen;* and they in equall reproach, You have playd the *Merchant:* but as *Merchants* grow up into worshipfull Families, and worshipfull Families let fall Branches amongst *Merchants* againe; so for this particular Plantation, you may consider *Citie* and *Countrey* to be one Body; and as you give example of a just Government to other Companies in the *Citie*, (that's your bearing witnesse in *Ierusalem;*) so you may be content to giue Reasons of your Proceedings, and Account of

> Moneyes leuied ouer the *Countrey*, for that's your bearing witnesse in *Iudaea*.[41]

Just as Kettlewell would at the end of the century, Donne collapses the distinctions between family, urban corporation (city) and state. Indeed, it is only by having these social units in harmony that God's work in Virginia can be carried out.

Donne, given the Virginian context, naturally has the additional category of the trading and territorial company, and it is in this context that his concern over families ought to be read, reflecting a tension within the government of the company between merchants and nobles. Donne finds a neat way to circumvent the divide by suggesting that new merchants will become noble (or 'worshipfull', a word freighted by its involvement in corporate language), and that these noble families will produce merchants. Although Donne's metaphor is not entirely neutral (merchants go 'up' into the noble families, who 'fall' to become merchants), it does offer a positive, communal vision of a society in which self-improvement, or at least personal change, in Virginia is to everyone's benefit.

These questions of social composition, and particularly corporate society, were refracted into contemporary literature; indeed, literary texts provided an ideal forum for imaginative constructions of society along corporate lines. As Mary Poovey has noted, in the seventeenth century 'one of the functions of performed by imaginative writing in general was to mediate value – that is, to help people understand the new credit economy and the market model of value that it promoted.'[42] As I have argued already, it is impossible to understand that credit economy without an understanding of the corporation's role within it. It was within the context of 'value' that a mediation on corporate society could take place within the literary text – just as Donne relocates 'value' away from earthly commodities to preaching through action, so too did other writers use the New World to reflect on social hierarchies and integration.

As has long been recognised by scholars, Shakespeare used *The Tempest* to reflect on forms of government and colonisation. The fantastical setting, mirroring travellers' tales and Utopian fiction, allowed for the same sorts of reflections as those genres could make on ideal forms of government and society. The play presents an island governed in a kind of bastardised meritocracy: Prospero rules by virtue of his magic, Caliban serves because of his servile nature and Ariel serves as a sort of indentured servant (denied liberty 'before thy time be out'[43]), having been freed by Prospero before the play opens.

However, the play unsettles these categories as it progresses. First, we learn that Prospero's command of magic is an art acquired when he ought to have been governing Milan: 'my library/Was dukedom large enough' (I.ii.109–110). Caliban is certainly prone to animalistic impulses, and becomes the servant of drink; nevertheless, he reveals that, rather than being the 'freckled whelp' (I.ii.285) of Prospero's description, only fit for service, he had actually been in charge of the island before Prospero's arrival, so sees him as 'a tyrant, a sorcerer, that by his cunning hath cheated me of the island' (III.ii.40–1).

These issues are largely a backdrop to the overarching plot of Prospero's triumphant return to power via the marriage of his daughter. However, the atmosphere of political instability and the possibility of experimentation that they create enable a fuller engagement with political economy in the sub-plot. This comes in the form of sailors and fellow travellers, largely left to their own devices by their superiors, who speculate on the ideal form of a commonwealth:

GONZALO: Had I plantation of this isle, my lord, –
ANTONIO: He'ld sow't with nettle-seed.
SEBASTIAN: Or docks, or mallows.
GONZALO: And were the king on't, what would I do?
SEBASTIAN: 'Scape being drunk for want of wine.
GONZALO: I' the commonwealth I would by contraries
Execute all things; for no kind of traffic
Would I admit; no name of magistrate;
Letters should not be known; riches, poverty,
And use of service, none; contract, succession,
Bourn, bound of land, tilth, vineyard, none;
No use of metal, corn, or wine, or oil;
No occupation; all men idle, all;
And women too, but innocent and pure;
No sovereignty; –
SEBASTIAN: Yet he would be king on't.
ANTONIO: The latter end of his commonwealth forgets the beginning.

(II.i.143–59)

Although Gonzalo's speech has something of the tradition of misrule about it, we might also see in it a considered response to the questions of overseas exploration and trade – it is no accident that Gonzalo considers the island a plantation, and makes the question of 'traffic' (that is, trade) his first priority. Unlike the aristocratic concerns of Prospero and Antonio, Gonzalo's commonwealth is libertarian; despite Antonio and Sebastian's suggestions, Gonzalo makes no claim to sovereignty beyond the initial design of the new colony. It is they, not Gonzalo, who are attempting to cling to the political economy of the old world, while Gonzalo uses the space of the island to imagine a radical new social order.

However, by the time of the Civil Wars the Utopian (or imaginary travel) genre had largely fallen out of fashion, and it was through angels that early modern writers were able to reflect on (imaginary, or at least invisible) social models. While the bible seemed to advocate Kingship – although plenty of republican-oriented commentators found counter-examples – the matter and organisation of angels remained the subject of theological speculation. After the Reformation, of course, belief in the power of angels (and intercessionary saints) was theoretically limited, although not eradicated entirely. As Marshall and Walsham note, early modern belief in angels was transmuted away from direct intervention, limiting their power to perform miracles; instead, 'Angels represented a celestial model for human society rather than unpredictable supernatural forces.'[44] They make this claim specifically in relation to prayer and the mass, with human worship believed to follow and conjoin with angelic patterns, but it was also true in the matter of social organisation. As Donne reminded the celebrants of a marriage, striving for goodness and grace was the will of God, and 'the nearer we come to that state in this life, the liker we are to those angels here.'[45]

George Herbert, for example, deployed the rhetoric of an inclusive monarchy in his poem 'To all Angels and Saints':

> Oh glorious spirits, who after all your bands
> See the smooth face of God without a frown
> Or strict commands;
> Where ev'ry one is king, and hath his crown,
> If not upon his head, yet in his hands.[46]

Although Herbert's main intention in the poem is to encourage an active sense of personal salvation (hence every individual has Grace 'in his hands'), there is nonetheless some speculation on angelic society. The phrase 'ev'ry one is king' gestures towards a uniformity at least among the saints and angels, with all being equal before God.

As well as the questions of national identity discussed in the previous chapter, *Paradise Lost* engages with questions of politics and community through its depictions of the angelic collective. Published in 1666, it was probably being composed (albeit as a drama) from the early 1650s onwards, and resonates with many of the social and political questions of the Commonwealth, for whom Milton was a crucial spokesman.

As Joad Raymond's work has shown, the Civil Wars "created an intellectual and soteriological environment in which angels had a powerful valence, as metaphors and a means of analysing and redescribing society."[47] The angels of *Paradise Lost* reflect with relative frequency on the way their own society is ordered, prompted both by Satan's critique and their own activities, and restate the principle of being a collective in the manner of a corporation, governed (as is proper) by God.

This model of organisation is praised and celebrated by Abdiel in his refutation of Satan's arguments on the political system of Heaven. He argues that, rather than lowering the status of the angels, Messiah makes them 'Under one head more near/United' (V.830–1). This is true in warfare, too, when the heavenly army is 'Under their Head imbodied all in one' (VI.779). Although this conception of a united body politic under a single head cannot but bring to mind the Hobbesian understanding of the state, famously displayed in the frontispiece to *Leviathan*, it is also the way in which the early modern corporation was defined:

> *Corporation (corporatio)* is a permanent thing, that may have succession; it is an Assembly and joyning together of many into one fellowship, brotherhood and minde, whereof one is Head and cheif, the rest are the body.[48]

This interpretation is given greater strength by Abdiel's use of the word 'imbodied', suggestive of 'incorporation' in the sense of 'one body' or 'bodies joined together'. A similar rhetorical move occurs in the joyful chorus of Heaven, in which the angels sing "So oft in festivals of joy and love/Unanimous, as sons of one great Sire" (VI.94–5). The unanimity (one of Milton's favourite puns on the sharing of a soul) of the angelic body politic is both its strength and its organisational principle.[49]

The idea of the angels as a body corporate was not unique to Milton. Robert Dingley, for example, dismissed the idea that Heaven was merely a state of mind (Satan's argument in *Paradise Lost*, of course) by arguing that 'Heaven is a place, we need not doubt, for the body of Christ is there; And that the main host and corporation of Angels [is] in that place.'[50] Dingley's use of 'corporation' has the sense here (and elsewhere in the text) of a collective, organised body, akin to Milton's depiction of the angels. Dingley's text was not simply a discourse on the state and location of angels, but an active model to be followed, advertising itself as offering 'consolation in our adversities; and reformation of our lives'.[51]

Similarly, Stephen Charnock twice referred to angelic bodies as a 'corporation' in his *Discourse Upon the Wisdom of God*. He began by exhorting his readers to 'cleave to the Truth of the Gospel, that we may not be counted by God as part of the Corporation of Fallen Angels.'[52] However, lest the reader believe that the corporate form was reserved for devils, Charnock goes on to remind his readers that the loyal angels also acted like a corporation: 'Whilst the Devil endeavoured to spoil the Corporation of Angels, and make them a Body contrary to God, God makes Angels and Men one Body under one Head, for his Service.'[53] Gabriel's echo of these words is probably accidental, but it does indicate something of the shared intellectual traditions created by the idea of the heavenly corporation.

The ideal corporate community envisaged by preachers and *Paradise Lost* alike speaks to an attempt to rethink the body politic, and, in Milton's case, a response to the failure of majority republicanism. D. Alan Orr has shown the ways in which English political thought moved from the concept of a state based on the monarch's body (two bodies) to a 'fully impersonal conception of the state';[54] this model allowed, even demanded, the sense of the state itself as a perpetual corporation. As long ago as 1982, T. C. Barnard had observed that radicals in London 'eschewed futile demonstrations and infiltrated the city government until they dominated the Common Council of the corporation.'[55]

Corporations were a key practical and intellectual battleground of the Civil Wars. Yet the question remains, why choose corporate imagery instead of that of classical Europe, a more obvious – and easily available – model for a commonwealth? As Sean Kelsey notes, the imagery of the Commowealth generally 'bore little discernible relation to the republican ideology of either Greece or Rome.' Instead, it 'celebrated principles such as patriotic nationalism, corporate decision-making and representative government.' That is, the Commonwealth preferred the veneration of ideas, rather than specific models, and included in that the ideal of corporate government.[56]

The appeal of the corporation to the Commonwealth-men lay, at least in part, in the very flexibility of the corporate form; if the Civil War was primarily a contest over ideas, the corporation as a form and concept was theoretically suitable for both sides in the way that the classical or biblical models (whether of republic or kingship) were not. The corporation, of course, encouraged this suppleness, in its legal form and behaviour: As Philip Stern points out, the artificial man of the corporate body politic could be 'neither loyal nor treasonous, pious or apostate'.[57] They could, though, easily be accused of being either, or both, at any given time.

Historians have demonstrated the extent to which urban corporations became politicised during the Civil Wars. Paul Halliday's *Dismembering the body Politic* illustrates the fact that 'from 1642, borough corporations were dismembered by forces within and far beyond them.' As well as suffering when their boroughs were captured by Parliamentary or Royalist forces, the corporations themselves, 'long inhibited by their consensual ideas from dismissing their own, overcame their reluctance, and for the first time, undertook their own dismemberment.'[58] The dismembering of these corporate bodies continued throughout and beyond the Civil Wars. Reprisals against urban corporations after the Restoration, especially in the form of the 1661 Corporation Act, demonstrated, in Phil Withington's words, 'that powerful groups now restored to power regarded the corporate system itself as culpable for the upheavals of the last eighteen years.'[59]

This was certainly the case for one of the key figures in the Restoration, George Monck, who would be rewarded with the Duchy of Albemarle. During his time in Scotland, he wrote back to Whitehall, accusing them of vesting power in the army at the expense of the civil polity:

> You should endeavour by a new way to wrest the Power out of their own hands, and to prosecute the same Designe; This making the

> Army a Corporation in a manner Independent from the Civil Power, and creating to it an Interest, distinct from that of the Peoples.[60]

Here, Monck discusses the balance of power in terms which seem to echo Hobbes's famous description of urban corporations as 'many lesser commonwealths in the bowels of a greater, like worms in the entrails of a natural man.'[61] Monck's charge against Parliament is not simply that an 'Independent' army (with all the socio-political baggage that charge carries) has been established, but that it has been done by way of a corporation. By the end of the Civil Wars, the corporate form was capable of being read as something which was, at least potentially, dangerously separate from the state.

Samuel Hudson, arguing for unity in faith, gave a dire warning of what would happen to the spiritual life if the congregation were given priority over the Church as a whole. In terms which echoed the arguments of Henry Jacob, and his contemporary L.F., Hudson parallels individual churches and the 'Church Catholic' with the state and corporations:

> It would make the Churches of Christ stand divided one from another in respect of government, and thereby bring ruine upon one another. Even as in a civil State, if particular Corporations should be independent from the whole in point of government, it would quickly bring destruction upon the whole.[62]

Herbert Thorndike, a theological scholar who had spent much of the Civil Wars attempting to justify a Presbyterian church form and privileges, published a pamphlet in 1659 which attempted to provide a broadly acceptable basis for a post-Restoration Church of England. In it, he considered whether describing the church as a corporation might not have unintended consequences in placing it under state power:

> Upon this ground, hee may dissolve the Church into the Commonwealth, and make the power of it an eschere to the Civil Power that is Christian, with lesse violence than the *Leviathan* doth: Because, whatsoever Corporations or Fraternities are bodied by sufferance of the State, dissolve of themselves at the will of it, and resolve the powers which they have created into the disposition of it.[63]

He therefore concludes that the church is above the decrees of the state, having been founded by 'Gods Charter, upon which the Corporation of the Church subsisteth.'[64] Thorndike seems to accord with other writers who see earthly forms imitating heavenly, in God's use of a 'charter' to establish a corporation; however, he differs from these writers by obliquely expressing what was clearly a current concern over the proper relationship between state, corporation and faith.

The corporation thus becomes, over the course of the seventeenth century, a touchstone for discussions of faith; its ideologies of collectivity, service and responsibility were models for preachers. Moreover, thinking about religion in these terms also allowed for a reflection on contemporary life – how was the society of heaven organised, and what did that mean for communities on Earth? Merchant companies, religious communities and the state thus overlapped in early modern writing, and the corporation, becoming politicised across the ideological divides of the century, offered a utopian vision of a unified and cohesive society.

Notes

1 Revelations 18:11–17.
2 William Lithgow, "Slave Market," in *Early Modern Tales of Orient: A Critical Anthology*, ed. Kenneth Parker (London: Routledge, 1999), 151.
3 Hosea 12:7.
4 H.I., *Fiftie Godlie and Learned Sermons, Diuided into Fiue Decades, Conteyning the Chiefe and Principall Pointes of Christian Religion, Written in Three Seuerall Tomes or Sections, by Henrie Bullinger Minister of the Churche of Tigure in Swicerlande* (London: Ralph Newberrie, 1577), 267.
5 David Zaret, *The Heavenly Contract: Ideology and Organization in Pre-Revolutionary Puritanism* (Chicago: University of Chicago Press, 1985), 169.
6 Genesis 37:25.
7 Genesis 37:28.
8 For example, the "company of prophets" in 1 Samuel 10:5, or the miracle of the loaves and fishes, given to the "great company" who gathered to see Jesus (John 6:5).
9 Milton, *Areopagitica in Don M. Wolfe*, ed. Complete Prose Works of John Milton (New Haven, CT: Yale University Press, 1953–82), II.544.
10 John Wing, *The Best Merchandise* (Flushing: Martin Abraham van der Nolck, 1622), 56.
11 *The Best Merchandise*, 128.
12 Robert B. Ekelund et al., *Sacred Trust: The Medieval Church as an Economic Firm* (Oxford: Oxford University Press, 1996), 21–2.
13 F. W. Maitland, "The Corporation Sole (1900)," in *Maitland: State, Trust and Corporation*, ed. D. Runciman and M. Ryan (Cambridge: Cambridge University Press, 2003). For a study of this concept within a larger associational framework, see Edward Cavanagh, "Corporations and Business Associations from the Commercial Revolution to the Age of Discovery: Trade, Jurisdiction and the State, 1200–1600," *History Compass* 14, no. 10 (2016).
14 Ernst Kantorowicz, *The King's Two Bodies: A Study in Medieval Political Theology* (Princeton, NJ: Princeton University Press, 2016), 449.
15 Thomas Jackson, *Christs Answer Unto Johns Question* (London: G. P. for Iohn Clarke, 1625), 68.
16 *Christs Answer Unto Johns Question*, 68.
17 Henry Ainsworth, *A Reply to a Pretended Christian Plea for the Anti-Chistian [Sic] Church of Rome* (London: s.n., 1620), 180.
18 George Sohn, *A Briefe and Learned Treatise, Conteining a True Description of the Antichrist* (Cambridge: John Legate, 1592), sig. 3r.
19 Edward Barber, *An Answer to the Eight Quæries Propounded by the House of Commons, to the Assembly Called Divines, Sitting at Westminster, April. 22. 1646: Never to This Day by Them Answered, nor They Called to an Accompt by the Parliament, for Their Ignorance or Negligence Therein* (London?: s.n., 1648), 9.

20 Edward Holyoke, *The Doctrine of Life, or, of Mans Redemption* (London: T. R. for Nath. Ekins, 1658), 194.
21 Phil Withington, *The Politics of Commonwealth: Citizens and Freemen in Early Modern England* (Cambridge: Cambridge University Press, 2005), 243.
22 Jeremiah Burroughs, *Gospel-Conversation* (London: Peter Cole, 1650), 153.
23 *Two Treatises of Mr. Jeremiah Burroughs* (London: Thomas Goodwyn et al., 1652), 92.
24 Randle Cotgrave, *A Dictionarie of the French and English Tongues* (London: A. Islip); John Wilkins, *An Essay Towards a Real Character, and a Philosophical Language* (London: Samuel Gellibrand and John Martyn, 1668).
25 John Kettlewell, *Of Christian Communion to Be Kept on in the Unity of Christs Church and among the Professors of Truth and Holiness* (London: s.n., 1693), 3.
26 William Bradshaw, *The Vnreasonablenesse of the Separation Made Apparant* (Dort [Dordrecht]: George Waters, 1614), Sig. M2v.
27 Henry Jacob, *A Confession and Protestation of the Faith of Certaine Christians in England* (Unknown: s.n., 1616), Sig. B1v.
28 Daniel Featley, *Threnoikos the House of Mourning Furnished with Directions for the Hour of Death* (London: G. Dawson, 1660), 197.
29 John Priaulx, *Confirmation Confirmed and Recommended from Scripture, Antiquity, and Reason in a Sermon Preached in the Cathedrall Church of St. Mary in Sarum* (London: I.R. for Iohn Courtney), 31.
30 L.F., *A Speedy Remedie against Spirituall Incontinencie* (Unknown: s.n., 1641), Sig. A3r.
31 *A Speedy Remedie against Spirituall Incontinencie*, Sig. A4r.
32 John Maynard, *A Sermon Preached to the Honorable House of Commons, at Their Late Solemne Fast*, Wednesday, Feb. 26. 1644. (London: George Bishop, for Samuel Gellibrand, 1645), 3.
33 *A Sermon Preached to the Honorable House of Commons, at Their Late Solemne Fast*, Wednesday, Feb. 26. 1644., 7.
34 Geneva Bible, Isaiah 55:1.
35 Blair Hoxby, *Mammon's Music: Literature and Economics in the Age of Milton* (New Haven, CT: Yale University Press, 2002), 26.
36 Wolfe, *Complete Prose Works of John Milton*, II.535–6.
37 *Complete Prose Works of John Milton*, I.806.
38 J. Votier, Vox Dei and Hominis, *God's Call from Heaven Ecchoed by Mans Answer from Earth* (London: T. C. for Nathanael Webb, and William Grantham, 1658), 37.
39 James Duport, *Evangelical Politie* (Cambridge: John Field, 1660), 13.
40 John Donne, "To the Honorable the Virginia Company," in *Five Sermons Upon Speciall Occasions* (London: Thomas Jones, 1626), 5.
41 "To the Honorable the Virginia Company," 34–5.
42 Mary Poovey, *Genres of the Credit Economy: Mediating Value in Eighteenth- and Nineteenth-Century Britain* (Chicago, IL: University of Chicago Press, 2008), 1–2.
43 The Tempest in Stephen Greenblatt et al., eds., *The Norton Shakespeare* (London: Norton, 1997), I.ii.247. Further references are given in the text.
44 Alexandra Walsham and Peter October Marshall, "Migrations of Angels in the Early Modern World," in *Angels in the Early Modern World*, ed. Alexandra Walsham and Peter October Marshall (Cambridge: Cambridge University Press, 2006), 8.
45 John Donne, *Fifty Sermons* (London: Ja. Flesher for M.F., J. Marriot, and R. Royston, 1649), 8.

46 George Herbert, "To all Angels and Saints," in *The Temple*, ed. George Herbert (Cambridge: T. Buck and R. Daniel, 1633), ll. 1–4.
47 Joad Raymond, *Milton's Angels: The Early-Modern Imagination* (Oxford: Oxford University Press, 2010), 89–90.
48 Thomas Blount, *Glossographia* (London: Tho. Newcombe for George Sawbridge, 1661).'Corporation'.
49 For a fuller examination of Milton's use of the corporation as part of the politics of heaven, see Liam D. Haydon, "Paradise Lost and the Politics of the Corporation," *SEL Studies in English Literature 1500–1900* 57, no. 1 (2017).
50 Robert Dingley, *The Deputation of Angels, or, the Angell-Guardian* (London: T.R. for Edw. Dod, 1653), 93–4.
51 *The Deputation of Angels, or, the Angell-Guardian*, frontis.
52 Stephen Charnock, *Several Discourses Upon the Existence and Attributes of God* (London: D. Newman, T. Cockerill, Benj. Griffin, T. Simmons, and Benj. Alsop, 1682), 341.
53 *Several Discourses Upon the Existence and Attributes of God*, 360.
54 D. Alan Orr, *Treason and the State : Law, Politics and Ideology in the English Civil War* (Cambridge: Cambridge University Press, 2002), 4.
55 T. C. Barnard, *The English Republic 1649–1660* (Harlow: Longman, 1982), 13.
56 Sean Kelsey, *Inventing a Republic : The Political Culture of the English Commonwealth, 1649–1653* (Manchester: Manchester University Press, 1997), 106.
57 Philip J. Stern, *The Company-State: Corporate Sovereignty & the Early Modern Foundations of the British Empire in India* (Oxford: Oxford University Press, 2011), 7.
58 Paul D. Halliday, *Dismembering the Body Politic : Partisan Politics in England's Towns, 1650–1730* (Cambridge: Cambridge University Press, 1998), 59–60.
59 Phil Withington, "Urban Citizens and England's Civil Wars," in *The Oxford Handbook of the English Revolution*, ed. Michael J. Braddick (Oxford: Oxford University Press, 2015), 325.
60 George Monck, *A Collection of Several Letters and Declarations, Sent by General Monck* (London: s.n., 1660), 19.
61 Thomas Hobbes, *Leviathan* (London: Andrew Crooke, 1651), II.29.
62 Samuel Hudson, *A Vindication of the Essence and Unity of the Church Catholike Visible* (London: A. M. for Christopher Meredith, 1650), Sig. B1r.
63 Herbert Thorndike, *An Epilogue to the Tragedy of the Church of England* (London: J. M. and T. R. for J. Martin, J. Allestry, and T. Dicas, 1659), 6–7.
64 *An Epilogue to the Tragedy of the Church of England*, 35.

Works cited

Print

Ainsworth, Henry. *A Reply to a Pretended Christian Plea for the Anti-Chistian [Sic] Church of Rome*. London: s.n., 1620.

Barber, Edward. *An Answer to the Eight Quæries Propounded by the House of Commons, to the Assembly Called Divines, Sitting at Westminster, April. 22. 1646: Never to This Day by Them Answered, nor They Called to an Accompt by the Parliament, for Their Ignorance or Negligence Therein*. London?: s.n., 1648.

Barnard, T. C. *The English Republic 1649–1660*. Harlow: Longman, 1982.

Blount, Thomas. *Glossographia*. London: Tho. Newcombe for George Sawbridge, 1661.

Bradshaw, William. *The Vnreasonablenesse of the Separation Made Apparant*. Dort [Dordrecht]: George Waters, 1614.

Burroughs, Jeremiah. *Gospel-Conversation*. London: Peter Cole, 1650.

———. *Two Treatises of Mr. Jeremiah Burroughs*. London: Thomas Goodwyn et al., 1652.

Cavanagh, Edward. "Corporations and Business Associations from the Commercial Revolution to the Age of Discovery: Trade, Jurisdiction and the State, 1200–1600." *History Compass* 14, no. 10 (2016): 493–510.

Charnock, Stephen. *Several Discourses Upon the Existence and Attributes of God*. London: D. Newman, T. Cockerill, Benj. Griffin, T. Simmons, and Benj. Alsop, 1682.

Cotgrave, Randle. *A Dictionarie of the French and English Tongues*. London: A. Islip, 1611.

Dingley, Robert. *The Deputation of Angels, or, the Angell-Guardian*. London: T.R. for Edw. Dod, 1653.

Donne, John. *Fifty Sermons*. London: Ja. Flesher for M.F., J. Marriot, and R. Royston, 1649.

———. "To the Honorable the Virginia Company." In *Five Sermons Upon Speciall Occasions*. London: Thomas Jones, 1626.

Duport, James. *Evangelical Politie* Cambridge: John Field, 1660.

Ekelund, Robert B., Robert D. Tollison, Gary M. Anderson, Robert F. Hébert, and Audrey B. Davidson. *Sacred Trust: The Medieval Church as an Economic Firm*. Oxford: Oxford University Press, 1996.

Featley, Daniel. *Threnoikos the House of Mourning Furnished with Directions for the Hour of Death*. London: G. Dawson, 1660.

Greenblatt, Stephen, Walter Cohen, Jean E. Howard, and Katharine Eisaman Maus, eds. *The Norton Shakespeare*. London: Norton, 1997.

Halliday, Paul D. *Dismembering the Body Politic : Partisan Politics in England's Towns, 1650–1730*. Cambridge: Cambridge University Press, 1998.

Haydon, Liam D. "Paradise Lost and the Politics of the Corporation." *SEL Studies in English Literature 1500–1900* 57, no. 1 (2017): 135–55.

Herbert, George. *The Temple*. Cambridge: T. Buck and R. Daniel, 1633.

H.I. *Fiftie Godlie and Learned Sermons, Diuided into Fiue Decades, Conteyning the Chiefe and Principall Pointes of Christian Religion, Written in Three Seuerall Tomes or Sections, by Henrie Bullinger Minister of the Churche of Tigure in Swicerlande*. London: Ralph Newberrie, 1577.

Hobbes, Thomas. *Leviathan*. London: Andrew Crooke, 1651.

Holyoke, Edward. *The Doctrine of Life, or, of Mans Redemption*. London: T. R. for Nath. Ekins, 1658.

Hoxby, Blair. *Mammon's Music: Literature and Economics in the Age of Milton*. New Haven, CT: Yale University Press, 2002.

Hudson, Samuel. *A Vindication of the Essence and Unity of the Church Catholike Visible*. London: A. M. for Christopher Meredith, 1650.

Jackson, Thomas. *Christs Answer Unto Johns Question*. London: G. P. for Iohn Clarke, 1625.

Jacob, Henry. *A Confession and Protestation of the Faith of Certaine Christians in England*. Unknown: s.n., 1616.

Kantorowicz, Ernst. *The King's Two Bodies: A Study in Medieval Political Theology*. Princeton, NJ: Princeton University Press, 2016. 1957.

Kelsey, Sean. *Inventing a Republic : The Political Culture of the English Commonwealth, 1649–1653*. Manchester: Manchester University Press, 1997.

Kettlewell, John. *Of Christian Communion to Be Kept on in the Unity of Christs Church and among the Professors of Truth and Holiness*. London: s.n., 1693.

L.F. *A Speedy Remedie against Spirituall Incontinencie*. Unknown: s.n., 1641.

Lithgow, William. "Slave Market." In *Early Modern Tales of Orient: A Critical Anthology*, edited by Kenneth Parker. London: Routledge, 1999.

Maitland, F. W. "The Corporation Sole (1900)." In *Maitland: State, Trust and Corporation*, edited by D. Runciman and M. Ryan, 9–31. Cambridge: Cambridge University Press, 2003.

Maynard, John. *A Sermon Preached to the Honorable House of Commons, at Their Late Solemne Fast, Wednesday, Feb. 26. 1644*. London: George Bishop, for Samuel Gellibrand, 1645.

Monck, George. *A Collection of Several Letters and Declarations, Sent by General Monck*. London: s.n., 1660.

Orr, D. Alan. *Treason and the State : Law, Politics and Ideology in the English Civil War*. Cambridge: Cambridge University Press, 2002.

Poovey, Mary. *Genres of the Credit Economy: Mediating Value in Eighteenth- and Nineteenth-Century Britain*. Chicago: University of Chicago Press, 2008.

Priaulx, John. *Confirmation Confirmed and Recommended from Scripture, Antiquity, and Reason in a Sermon Preached in the Cathedrall Church of St. Mary in Sarum*. London: I.R. for Iohn Courtney, 1662.

Raymond, Joad. *Milton's Angels : The Early-Modern Imagination*. Oxford: Oxford University Press, 2010.

Sohn, George. *A Briefe and Learned Treatise, Conteining a True Description of the Antichrist*. Cambridge: John Legate, 1592.

Stern, Philip J. *The Company-State: Corporate Sovereignty & the Early Modern Foundations of the British Empire in India*. Oxford: Oxford University Press, 2011.

Thorndike, Herbert. *An Epilogue to the Tragedy of the Church of England*. London: J. M. and T. R. for J. Martin, J. Allestry, and T. Dicas, 1659.

Votier, J. *Vox Dei & Hominis. God's Call from Heaven Ecchoed by Mans Answer from Earth*. London: T. C. for Nathanael Webb, and William Grantham, 1658.

Walsham, Alexandra, and Peter October Marshall. "Migrations of Angels in the Early Modern World." In *Angels in the Early Modern World*, edited by Alexandra Walsham and Peter October Marshall, 1–40. Cambridge: Cambridge University Press, 2006.

Wilkins, John. *An Essay Towards a Real Character, and a Philosophical Language*. London: Samuel Gellibrand and John Martyn, 1668.

Wing, John. *The Best Merchandise*. Flushing: Martin Abraham van der Nolck, 1622.

Withington, Phil. *The Politics of Commonwealth: Citizens and Freemen in Early Modern England*. Cambridge: Cambridge University Press, 2005.

———. "Urban Citizens and England's Civil Wars." In *The Oxford Handbook of the English Revolution*, edited by Michael J. Braddick, 312–29. Oxford: Oxford University Press, 2015.

Wolfe, Don M., ed. *Complete Prose Works of John Milton*. New Haven, CT: Yale University Press, 1953–82.

Zaret, David. *The Heavenly Contract: Ideology and Organization in Pre-Revolutionary Puritanism*. Chicago: University of Chicago Press, 1985.

Coda

The seventeenth century can be called the most corporate of centuries (until our own, perhaps). It was the moment at which the corporate form was fully worked out. It was a period of experimentation, when a whole range of governmental, financial and associational models were discussed in theory and tried in practice. Corporations were the driving force behind spectacular economic growth (especially in the 1660s and 1690s), and the expansion of English territory in Ireland, the Americas, Africa and East Asia. They were also sites of cultural expression, as the corporate form was used in writing to experiment with conceptualisations of national identity, religion and trade.

Corporations had power and influence to rival their modern incarnations, even if it was not quite so legally and culturally consolidated. By the turn of the eighteenth century, though, as the state increasingly centralised governmental functions to itself, and the faith in the great multinational corporations was eroded by their actions abroad, the first phase of corporate imagination was drawing to a close.

By 1700, that is, ideas around the behaviour and forms of corporations were increasingly ossified. As we saw in Chapter 1, although there was a significant increase in the number of documents dealing with corporations, the debates in the late seventeenth century corporate public sphere ran along increasingly narrow lines: restrictions on trade, enforcement of rights and the good-faith management of corporate behaviour. Economic anxiety, at least in fiction, was created at one remove from the corporations, and focused on the social consequences of individual behaviour rather than the collective actions of the body corporate; rather than the fears of corporate mismanagement, for example, cultural attention turned to the problems of the stock market and fears of stock-jobbing, however inflated.[1]

The establishment of permanent joint stocks, and a growing cultural familiarity with this manifestation of the corporate form, helped to reassure investors and the general public alike of the stability and value of corporate activity. Not only did pamphlet writers defend corporate activity, but also ancillary publications such as stock-lists and price currents began to offer additional, public, information for merchants and investors alike.[2] Moreover, as the corporation, especially in the form of the City of London and Bank of England, became formally integrated into state finance and government, the risks associated with the joint stock began to dissipate. The rise of the Whig faction, their determination to protect trade and investment, and the institutional changes to state finance and the public debt which took place after 1688 meant that default was highly unlikely.[3] Different risks were created by this apparent stability, of course; the collapse of the South Sea Company in 1720 would be a stark demonstration of the danger of speculation in a seemingly stable marketplace, but in the late seventeenth and early eighteenth centuries investments in corporations were generally perceived to be institutionally safe.

With the growing confidence in commercial activity came an increased desire to establish a national identity and history based on trade. The history of London was rewritten to emphasise its place as a mart or entrepot for global trade, and so a site of a multiplicity of exchanges. Camden, Stow, Howell and others wrote seventeenth-century London into a continuum of ever-expanding trade. This cultural move attempted to establish a classical precedence for London, as well as expressing a confidence in an economic system which appeared (or could be made to appear) to offer almost infinite growth. It was London's status as a home for transnational corporate activity which underpinned these narratives, with the city becoming the 'world's exchange', and the Thames the driving current of global maritime trade.

The early modern integration of corporate trade into national identity can be seen, too, in the production of commercially aware epic poetry. *Os Lusiados*, in the original and English translation, valorised the mercantile exploits of its explorer-hero (even as it appeared to disavow them, in a complex code of aristocratic honour). Translation, or 'Englishing', was in itself conceived of as a form of trade, a bringing back of foreign treasure to England to be spread around the country. Sylvester's translation of Du Bartas's *Divine Weeks and Works* also employs this strategy, with an insertion which emphasises that his years spent as a trader contributed to the development of his poetic craft. Consequently, Sylvester interpolated the trading society of London into the poem as part of a broader strategy to essentialise the corporate economy at the heart of the city. The London that Sylvester depicts is organised around livery companies and multinational trading corporations, and these are the links that allow global commerce, as well as the development of "in-land lands," so that his London, too, is a crucial node in the global and domestic economy – or rather, the global and domestic economies are not considered as separate systems, since the common point of London's corporations erases such a difference.[4]

As well as these questions of national ideology, Milton's *Paradise Lost* frequently depicts angels stressing their status as parts of a collective.

Abdiel repeatedly tells Satan that to be "joined in one" (V.834) with God is not to lose oneself, but to be raised up, since God does not desire "To make us less, bent rather to exalt/Our happy state" (V.829–30). Upon his return to the loyal collective, Abdiel is pleased to find his news already known and he resumes his place in the collective without reward or distinction. He is praised for his actions – 'Servant of God, well done' – but even this apparent individualism is in reality a sublimation to the collective; it removes the name of Abdiel in favour of a definition which is inherently general, since all angels are (or ought to be) servants of God.

So too in other moments of conflict or didacticism within the poem. Gabriel affects surprise that Satan has left his "deserted host" (IV.922) behind him, and reminds Satan that despite the individualism of his rebellion, he remains inescapably part of a collective ("fit body to fit head" [IV.953]). Raphael tells Adam and Eve that their destiny is to join in this unanimity of spirit and "winged, ascend/Ethereal, as we" (V.498–9). This ascension is possible because all things are of the same kind, if not the same form, of divinely imbued "first matter" (V.472). Even the creation story emphasises unanimity, such as the storks who:

> In common, ranged in figure wedge their way,
> Intelligent of seasons, and set forth
> Their airy caravan high over seas.
>
> (VII.426–8)

Here, as with the angels, *Paradise Lost* emphasises collective action, and in the metaphor of the caravan which ranges 'over seas' introduces something of the multinational corporation, travelling bounded together with a common purpose.

The link between the corporation and the spiritual was well established by the time Milton was composing his epic. The idea that heaven was organised as a corporation, open to those who would seek to become "freemen [. . .] of this corporation, this company" of saints, had the effect of creating a tradition of the responsible collective.[5] For these preachers, individuals were accountable to God for their actions, and in return they had the rights of freemen, re-imagining heaven as a participatory community in which individualism took the form of choosing actions designed to advance the collective, that is, a corporation.

Preachers and writers, particularly those inclined to the Parliamentary cause, deployed the idea of this heavenly corporation as a rhetorical turn away from monarchical government towards a privileging of the collective. The image of the 'corporation of heaven' was one which privileged equality and unanimity for a godly purpose. Naturally, it was advantageous to the republican state to circulate such an understanding of both heavenly and earthly organisation; it also endowed the corporate form with a political and moral purpose beyond its economic remit. The corporation, that is, became a way of thinking about social organisation and moral value.

It would, then, be no exaggeration to say that the corporation has been one of the most important social, political and economic ideas of the last half-millennium. It is, at its heart, a way of structuring relations; the corporation is a form in and through which individual or groups of merchants can work, but also one which allows a sort of arms-length international relations between the state which charters the corporation and the state in which it conducts its business. The corporation is a social model of collective activity (and responsibility), and in the early modern period the corporation functioned in several overlapping spheres of trade, governance (of people and places), religion and charity, among others – few corporations operated in all of these spheres (although some did), but all corporations engaged with more than one of them.

Consequently, as Henry Turner has cogently argued, the corporation is partly a "problem of scale," which "invites us to analyse the forces of translations whereby wholes become parts and parts become new wholes again."[6] But it is also a problem of interpolation: Establishing what a corporation believes, or how the corporate form is best structured, and who that might benefit, is difficult precisely because of the instability and hybridity of corporate identity which Turner has shown politically, and this work has shown culturally. That very instability, though, as the writers of the seventeenth century realised, is also an opportunity. The corporation can stand for a whole range of cultural, political and economic positions, and can be used in fiction and political writing alike to imagine ways of organising society, of assessing trustworthiness, of establishing identity for other groups or even of generating and maintaining faith.

Consequently, this book is not an attempt to provide an overarching structure of corporate ideology as it was manifested in the seventeenth century. It is doubtful whether any such project could succeed, so integrated was the corporation in early modern thought albeit in such a paradoxically insubstantial and porous way. Rather, it is a thematic view of corporate discourse, which aims to represent some of the range of meanings that the corporate might create or enable, many of which have gradually become lost since the seventeenth century.

It is too, I hope, an upsetting of 'the archive', at least to some degree. The corporations I discuss here have left behind dazzlingly voluminous archives, full of fascinating and worthwhile stories, but that vastness is also a limit; corporate archives will rarely help us understand the circulation of their ideas, and generally steer historians towards a rather functional vision of their activities – *homo economicus* is alive and well in studies of corporate history, which tend to overlook the cultural biases of their protagonists in favour of more or less rational explanations of action centred on economics or other self-interest.

Finally, although with some trepidation, it is worth asking what the seventeenth century might teach us in our own particular historical moment. Capitalism, as it is now embodied in and by the modern corporation, seems to work outside of the traditional constraints of the nation state. Thus, calls on Google or Vodafone to pay their 'fair share' of tax, and plans to 'bring back jobs' taken out of the nation by profit-driven corporations are a mark of the state's weakness in the face of corporate activity. Indeed, they are perhaps even a reaction to a new form of transnationalism, which not only crosses borders but moves between the 'real' and the 'abstract': Global companies such as Amazon or Apple work by integrated electronic and physical materials, while others, such as Facebook, Twitter and Snap, have as their core business something which does not exist in a physical sense, and which their consumers do not in fact pay for, and so cannot be regulated, taxed or integrated effectively into society.

These are clearly radically different challenges to those of the seventeenth century. However, in some ways they arise from the same fundamental questions about how we organise society and commerce: What is a corporation *for*? Who does it serve? Should it be regulated? If so, how? These were key questions for early modern commentators on political economy, just as they are today. Holding territory overseas, involvement in state finance and the protection of rights from, or within, corporations, were sites of conflict in the early modern public sphere. These questions were manifested in literature, too, and the cultural production of the early modern period went some way to settling these questions, even if that was only ever a precarious balance rather than a permanent settlement (just as, indeed, it is in our own society).

There is one crucial exception to this cross-temporal comparison: there has been, over the twentieth century, a shift in the way in which the corporate form is used, with a slow dying out of the charitable or public works corporation. In part, this is a consequence of the increasing involvement of for-profit corporations (or the state approximating the same) in areas such as infrastructure where these forms might previously have been used. The corporation now exists almost exclusively as an economic body, with concomitant emphasis on profit maximisation for its shareholders. In March 2017, 3.8 million corporations were registered at Companies House in the UK, but just 6620 incorporated charities.[7] Not only would such an imbalance have been unlikely in the seventeenth century, but also the clear divide between those types of companies (in purpose, membership and regulation) would make no sense. Although there were multinational profit-making corporations in the early modern world, there were also a plethora of corporations, permanent or otherwise, established not to make money but to improve, govern or benefit the common weal.[8]

In losing this range of corporations, and the associational practices that go with them, we have perhaps also lost the vibrant intellectual discourse that they once stimulated. In allowing the closing down of possibilities vis-à-vis the forms of corporations, we have normalised the profit-seeking joint stock, and so overlook the radical potential that a corporation once instilled in writers and thinkers. As scholars of the early modern period, we owe it to ourselves and our subjects to rediscover the sense of wondrous possibilities that the corporation once offered.

Notes

1 On the low numbers of stock-jobbers compared with the outsize fear of the practice, see Anne L. Murphy, *The Origins of English Financial Markets: Investment and Speculation before the South Sea Bubble* (Cambridge: Cambridge University Press, 2009), 178–91.

2 See John J. McCusker and Cora Gravesteijn, *The Beginnings of Commercial and Financial Journalism: The Commodity Price Currents, Exchange Rate Currents and Money Currents of Early Modern Europe* (Amsterdam: NEHA, 1991).

3 Douglass C. North and Barry R. Weingast, "Constitutions and Commitment: The Evolution of Institutions Governing Public Choice in Seventeenth-Century England," *The Journal of Economic History* 49, no. 4 (1989).

4 Susan Snyder, ed. *The Divine Weeks and Works of Guillaume De Saluste, Sieur Du Bartas*, Translated by Josuah Sylvester, 2 vols. (Oxford: Clarendon Press, 1979), II.ii.3.653.

5 James Duport, *Evangelical Politie* (Cambridge: John Field, 1660), 13.

6 Henry S. Turner, *The Corporate Commonwealth: Pluralism and Political Fictions in England 1516–1651* (Chicago: University of Chicago Press, 2016), 228.

7 Companies House, "Incorporated Companies in the United Kingdom, October to December 2016," (2016). The Charity Commission does not provide a breakdown of the types of charity (corporation, trust, association and so forth), so the data were personally collated from the searchable register on 7th March 2017: http://apps.charitycommission.gov.uk/ShowCharity/RegisterOfCharities/AdvancedSearch.aspx

8 See, for example, Paul Slack, *The Invention of Improvement: Information and Material Progress in Seventeenth-Century England* (Oxford: Oxford University Press, 2015); Koji Yamamoto, *Taming Capitalism before its Triumph: Public Service, Distrust, and 'Projecting' in Early Modern England.* (Oxford: Oxford University Press, 2018).

Works cited

Companies House. "Incorporated Companies in the United Kingdom, October to December 2016." 2016.

Duport, James. *Evangelical Politie* Cambridge: John Field, 1660.

McCusker, John J., and Cora Gravesteijn. *The Beginnings of Commercial and Financial Journalism: The Commodity Price Currents, Exchange Rate Currents and Money Currents of Early Modern Europe*. Amsterdam: NEHA, 1991.

Murphy, Anne L. *The Origins of English Financial Markets: Investment and Speculation before the South Sea Bubble*. Cambridge: Cambridge University Press, 2009.

North, Douglass C., and Barry R. Weingast. "Constitutions and Commitment: The Evolution of Institutions Governing Public Choice in Seventeenth-Century England." *The Journal of Economic History* 49, no. 4 (1989): 803–32.

Slack, Paul. *The Invention of Improvement: Information and Material Progress in Seventeenth-Century England*. Oxford: Oxford University Press, 2015.

Snyder, Susan, ed. *The Divine Weeks and Works of Guillaume De Saluste, Sieur Du Bartas, Translated by Josuah Sylvester*. 2 vols. Oxford: Clarendon Press, 1979.

Turner, Henry S. *The Corporate Commonwealth: Pluralism and Political Fictions in England 1516–1651*. Chicago: University of Chicago Press, 2016.

Yamamoto, Koji. *Taming Capitalism before its Triumph: Public Service, Distrust, and 'Projecting' in Early Modern England*. Oxford: Oxford University Press, 2018.

Index

For Product Safety Concerns and Information please contact our EU
representative GPSR@taylorandfrancis.com
Taylor & Francis Verlag GmbH, Kaufingerstraße 24, 80331 München, Germany

www.ingramcontent.com/pod-product-compliance
Ingram Content Group UK Ltd.
Pitfield, Milton Keynes, MK11 3LW, UK
UKHW021959180926
475701UK00003B/100

* 9 7 8 1 0 3 2 0 9 4 9 9 1 *